NOT AN EASY TALE TO TELL: JACKIE ROBINSON ON THE PAGE, STAGE, AND SCREEN

Edited by Ralph Carhart
Associate editors Bill Nowlin,
Carl Riechers, and Kate Nachman

Society for American Baseball Research, Inc.
Phoenix, AZ

Not an Easy Tale to Tell: Jackie Robinson on the Page, Stage, and Screen
Edited by Ralph Carhart
Associate editors Bill Nowlin, Carl Riechers, and Kate Nachman

ISBN: 978-1-970159-72-1
E-book ISBN: 978-1-970159-71-4
Library of Congress Control Number: 2022903594
Book design: Jennifer Bahl Hron
Cover fonts: Tomarik & Trade Gothic | Chapter fonts: Trade Gothic & Chaparral Pro

Society for American Baseball Research
Cronkite School at ASU
555 N. Central Ave. #416
Phoenix, AZ 85004
Phone: (602) 496-1460
Web: www.sabr.org
Facebook: Society for American Baseball Research
Twitter: @SABR

Table of Contents

Acknowledgements

The creators of this book wish to extend their thanks to Matthew J. Richards, vice president and general manager of sales, and Andy Krause, sport product manager at Getty Images, for their invaluable assistance. Thanks to Kay Kron at the Chicago Children's Theatre. We would also like to thank Gregory Wolf and Todd Lebowitz from SABR, for their advice and assistance. The deepest gratitude to Cecilia Tan, whose steerage of this volume, and the entire SABR library, is unparalleled. Finally, warmest thanks to Jennifer Bahl Hron, for going far above and beyond.

Introduction
Not An Easy Tale To Tell

By Ralph Carhart

When Jack Roosevelt Robinson set foot on the green grass of Ebbets Field on April 15, 1947, he understood the enormity of the moment and his role in it. He was breaking through a barrier that had been in place for 60 years, and by doing so was elevating his entire race. He knew the importance of his every action on and off the field, both in how they were perceived by White America, as well as his fellow Black citizens who had longed for this pivotal moment for decades. For certain by the end of his short life, a life spent in activism where he was often the central character, he had some understanding of the impact he would have on history.

What is less certain is if Jackie Robinson was aware of the profound influence he would have on fiction. The passage of time has elevated him beyond mere trailblazer and placed him closer to the rarified stratosphere of myth. Perhaps the biggest reason for that evolution from man to legend has been the seemingly endless fictional representations that have appeared on movie and television screens, theatrical stages, and pages of novels since he signed his first contract with Branch Rickey on Montague Street in Brooklyn, in 1945.

Almost as soon as he got his first hit with the Dodgers, Robinson became an important character in the American story. He quickly became the exact kind of symbol that Black Americans, and a significant percentage of their White counterparts, longed to elevate. For the latter, the very singularity of his elevation, which should have signified just how far we had to go, instead became "proof" that we were already there. As with the election of Barack Obama as President of the United States 60 years later, Jackie Robinson's promotion to the Dodgers was, for many, evidence that racism was defeated. He became St. George, slayer of the dragon of hatred and a figure that fiction has, in many ways, completely divorced from reality.

It began with the low-budget 1950 film, *The Jackie Robinson Story*, which starred the man himself and laid the foundation for many of the simplified myths that have come to be taken as truths of the story of White baseball's integration. The line between fiction and reality was blurred by the fact that it was really Robinson reciting the lines written for him by Arthur Mann, Branch Rickey's personal secretary. In the space where altered memories become accepted as hard facts, the truth was garbled by the sound of Robinson's own voice saying, "Mr. Rickey, I have two cheeks."

The creators of these fictions are not entirely to blame for their inability to properly represent Robinson in their works. His story, from his birth in Cairo, Georgia to his death 53 years later in Stamford, Connecticut, is one that defies many of the conventional structures of traditional storytelling. He was a socially progressive activist who was a lifelong Republican. He was a proud Black man whose own personal mentors included a roster of important White men, from Branch Rickey, to William Black (the president of Chock Full o' Nuts Coffee), to New York Governor Nelson Rockefeller. He was a staunchly patriotic American who, later in life, struggled to salute the flag because the country he loved did not love him back.

Beyond all the seeming contradictions, it is difficult to tell the Robinson story because of just how much he accomplished in his short life. His illustrious college athletic career, his brief but important military history, his role as a husband and father, his time in baseball, and his post-playing career that included efforts in business, politics, activism, and philanthropy—to encapsulate all of that into a two-hour Hollywood film is a near impossible task. Perhaps that is the reason few have tried. The only artist who ever attempted to do so in a standard biopic, Spike Lee, found financial backing for his multi-faceted project impossible to come by.

Nearly all the representations of Robinson in fiction instead choose to focus on a particular moment, or the echoes of a specific event. His court-martial for his refusal to sit at the back of a military bus, his brief tenure in the Negro Leagues, his historic 1947 season—each of these account for important individual moments in Robinson's life, but none of them succeed in encapsulating the full measure of the man.

It is more than just the limits of time that are prescribed to a conventional film script that stand in the way of fiction properly presenting Robinson's story. It is also because he has become more than just a man. Major-league baseball bears some responsibility for this canonization. Ever since the universal retirement of his number 42 in 1997, there has been an annual tradition of honoring Robinson, his accomplishments, and his sacrifice. As others have pointed out, the festivities have become weighed down with a tragic irony, as the number of Black athletes playing in the majors continues to shrink. As baseball struggles with racial issues it has not properly addressed in the present, it chooses to elevate the moment in its history where it overcame its prejudices and finally became the American Pastime. Robinson, of course, is the central figure in that tale, a tale that has come to represent much more than the drama that unfolded on a baseball diamond 75 years ago.

The elevation of Robinson from man to legend was not assured. After the release of *Story*, it took 30 years before another high-profile attempt at telling Robinson's tale. The hesitation was an old refrain. Wealthy, largely-White producers balked at making a financially risky investment in a project with a Black man as the central character, especially if it did not involve explosions or chase scenes. It took almost a decade after Robinson's death, after both the family and society had a chance to assess his legacy, that the proliferation of the fictional character of Jackie Robinson started to flood the public consciousness.

This volume takes a look at the evolution of Robinson the man into Robinson the symbol, and how artists of various stripes have helped to create that character. He has been the central figure in two big screen adaptations, a Broadway musical, countless children's theatre productions, a pair of thriller novels, several television films, a comic book series, a jazz suite, and even in the written works of his own daughter, Sharon Robinson. Some of these works have the approval and cooperation of the family. Others do not. Robinson has also appeared as an off-screen or minor character in countless other creations. He has become a symbol so embedded in the national psyche that his presence in any tale automatically harkens to the idea of possibility, of perseverance, of right defeating wrong, of all that is good in the American mythology.

The tragic cost of that fictionalization is that for all but historians and the most ardent of baseball fans, the complexity of the man that was Jackie Robinson has been simplified. We do stray from the fictional Robinson in this book. We explore the multiple appearances he made on television as a guest on game and talk shows, as well as his time as the host of his own radio program. We also look at Ken Burns's epic documentary entitled, simply, *Jackie Robinson*. It is in this lone case, where the filmmaker had the luxury of a four-hour running time and the stringent rules of relating history, that we get anything close to a whole-picture view of Robinson.

For all that is lacking when a work of fiction attempts to portray Robinson, there are reasons why artists keep trying—why, in fact, we saw fit to combine to write this very book. Simply put, every now and then, one of them succeeds. Perhaps it is only for a moment, like Chadwick Boseman's explosive anguish as he smashes a bat to kindling in *42*, or in Andre Braugher's untapped rage as he is arrested by military police in *The Court-Martial of Jackie Robinson*. Or maybe it's found in an awkward, tender exchange between Robinson himself and Hollywood and Broadway legend, Ruby Dee, which reminds us that Robinson's story is not only one of anger, but love. It can even be found in taking the creative leap to feature a Robinson who, like St. George anew, slays the Lovecraftian monster Cthulhu, using only his Louisville Slugger.

The other reason that artists keep returning to Robinson is because he is one of the most inspirational figures of the twentieth century not in spite of, but because of his complexities. He did more than change the game of baseball. He changed America, and by doing so inspired multiple generations of artists to look to him to help tell their stories. That truth is just another contradiction. For, in utilizing Robinson as a symbol, they invariably highlight, time and again, how his actual story is not an easy tale to tell.

Robinson prepares for his shot on the set of *The Jackie Robinson Story*. photo courtesy of Getty Images

Interview with Sharon Robinson

By Ralph Carhart

In September 2020, I had the good fortune of speaking with Sharon Robinson, Jackie's daughter, over the course of two interviews in which we discussed representations of her father. The conversation is frank, detailed, and gives a keen insight into just how involved the Robinson family has been in telling their patriarch's tale. Sharon also discussed her father's artistic legacy, the role of context in telling history, and what it was like for a little girl to see her father portray himself in a movie for the first time, surrounded by a group of her White friends.

Ralph Carhart: Thanks so much for speaking with me. How are you doing today?

Sharon Robinson: I'm good, I'm good.

RC: I'm going to ask you some questions about the long arc of your father in film and other fictional adaptations of him, and I'm going to start way back at the beginning. I know that you were only one month old when *The Jackie Robinson Story* started filming, but were there any family stories that were floating around about the making of this picture? Did he ever talk about his experience and what that was like for him?

SR: The stories I heard were from Ruby Dee and my mother. My mother and brother and I came out to the set when I was a month old. And Ruby Dee tells me, because she was playing my mom, that she held me when I was a month old on the set. It's interesting that my dad didn't talk about the making of the film, but he didn't go back, so he didn't talk about his baseball years.

I didn't know anything about the making of the film, really, or even about the film, until I saw it at day camp. It was a rainy day and rainy days meant that we all gathered in the big gym/everything room, sat on the floor, and watched movies.

RC: Did the counselors ask you if you were OK with that?

SR: There was no warning or preparation, and it was shocking to me, uncomfortably shocking. I was the only Black kid there. I didn't know about or understand race or racism at the time. I was 7 or 8. I felt very uncomfortable watching this film surrounded by campers who I knew. I was watching this part of my father's story that I didn't know, and I didn't know what it meant. It made me uncomfortable because I also lived in an all-White neighborhood and went to school with all White kids and I'm like, well, what does this mean?

That was my first real experience with that film. Silly enough, I didn't go home and say, "You know what they showed today in the camp?" I was a quiet kid at that point in my life and very shy – so I didn't make a big deal out of it when I got home. I sat with these uncomfortable feelings for a number of years.

RC: Did you ever talk to your father about those feelings, or to your mother about it?

SR: I did not. I didn't really deal with it until I became an adult and I had to see that film again and had to hear people say they thought it was a great film.

RC: What do you think of it?

SR: Now as an adult? I realize why I was so uncomfortable. I didn't even recognize my father playing himself. I mean, I saw him there. But he was more passive than I knew him to be. I didn't like the voice. He had a high voice but when you combine that with the directing and the writing, you know...

RC: You talked a little bit about Ruby Dee. She was pregnant herself during the making of the film, and I know she became very attached to you as a baby. I know she and your mom got closer later in life with their advocacy and their philanthropy. Did you have a close relationship with her as well?

SR: I had a very loving relationship with her. I didn't see her often, but when I did, there was a bond. I adored her. There were two people in our family that were actresses. I'm saying family; I'm saying close friends. So it was Ruby Dee and Billie Allen. We called her Aunt Billie and she wasn't as acclaimed by any means, and she was more of a Broadway stage actress, but the two of them – and they were friends too. When either one of them was around, I was in heaven.

RC: It's interesting that you talk about how the film lacks your father's fire and passion because Ruby was later interviewed as regretting the way she portrayed your mom as rather passive. The director said to her, "This is a film about Jackie, you're just there to support him and play it as such." She realized after she met your mother that she made all the wrong choices. That wasn't who your mother was at all.

SR: Yeah, no. [laughs]

RC: Between your father's passing and when the Broadway musical, *The First*, came out in 1981, there were no fictionalizations of Jackie. Was that a choice on the family's part or did New York and Los Angeles just take a while to call you?

SR: That is absolutely correct. My dad died in '72. I was just coming out of college. We were focused on getting the Foundation up and running and my mother had taken over my father's construction company that they founded before he died.

RC: The one that provided housing for the underserved.

SR: Yeah, and they were focused on that. And he was not recognized by baseball yet, so it was a quiet period, absolutely.

RC: I know your mother was a consultant on the musical. Were you a part of that process at all?

SR: Yes, I was definitely around, but I was a single parent with a toddler in '81. So I would come to the set, we met all the cast, we saw the pre-production stuff, but I was not involved. I didn't read scripts or anything like that. They definitely involved us and wanted us to be there, but I think, unlike *42*, my mother was less involved in the creation of it. They pulled her in more around the marketing.

RC: The newspapers mentioned that she was present for first rehearsal and gave that inspirational speech that actors always need at a first rehearsal.

SR: I think that was her role. I don't know that she read scripts. I have been going through papers and I still haven't seen any notes on *The First*, where I saw notes on other things.

RC: Other fictionalizations? Other times she was a creative consultant?

SR: Right, like where Spike [Lee] was working on his version of *The Jackie Robinson Story*.

RC: It was so kind of him to share the script with the world for our quarantine entertainment.

SR: It sure was.

RC: It's a shame that it didn't get made. So many of the fictionalizations focus on 1946 and 1947 and that's about it. Lee's took a more holistic view of his life, beyond baseball into his activism and what came next. It's a shame it never happened.

SR: He feels the same way! That's why he finally released it and that's exactly what he said to me. I did not see it when he released it publicly, but he sent me a copy. He called and he said, "Did you ever read this" and "I want you to read this" and "This is why I'm disappointed."

RC: The other part of it that I really loved was the way, because so many of the stories tend to isolate Jackie, as though he was alone on his journey, Lee's script made Don Newcombe a character; he made Roy Campanella a character; he made Joe Black a character. Lee's story recognizes that Jackie opened the door, but then there was so much more to the story that came after.

SR: Exactly. Yeah, well that's the problem when you only do '46 and '47, you don't get to see the aftermath.

RC: After *The First*, there was this cottage industry that was created where plays were written about Jackie intended for school age audiences.

SR: Lots of them, yeah.

RC: I was wondering if your family was ever involved in any of those or did they happen on their own?

SR: They all happened on their own. Various groups would invite us, it may have been in a different city or wherever, but I don't know that we really went.

RC: You have made your father a character in your own writing, and you've written books that are largely focused on that same age group. I'm curious, what is it about your father's story that you think is particularly relevant to kids?

SR: It's his character that, to me, makes it most relevant. It was his strength of character that made him successful. Along with that comes the supports that he had: my mother, his mother, those kinds of supports. I always felt that his story was very translatable for children as long as we can contemporize it. By making it about his character, it helps support kids in their own development. In my research with Major League Baseball, we realized that we had kids playing baseball up to the age of 12 and then we started losing them. So, I was trying to get the kids younger than that *and* older than that; to keep them engaged in baseball in an interesting way. But also, I felt that this movement from elementary school into middle school was so critical to a child's development that I wanted to work with them during a period when they listened, and you can have some direct influence on them; help them so they are more prepared as they go from middle school into high school and then consequently into life. So that was kind of my thinking around age group in my writing and with the program I created along with Scholastic and Major League Baseball.

RC: I guess they are more open vessels, right? To be willing to hear new things and learn new ways. Very few 5- or 6-year-olds are racist. They're willing to hear stories about all people. It's not until we get older that those prejudices set themselves in.

SR: Correct, yeah.

RC: There were a couple of TV projects: *The Court Martial of Jackie Robinson* and *Soul of the Game*. I know your mother is on record stating that she didn't like *Soul of the Game* because it portrayed a much less authentic version of your father and the dynamic that he had with Satchel Paige, but what did she, and you, think of *Court Martial*?

SR: Loved it.

RC: Yeah? Why?

SR: It was well done. It was part of his life that people didn't know about; part of his early activism people didn't know about. We were very impressed. As far as I know, we didn't have a lot of involvement in that process. I can't say for sure that my mother didn't read scripts. I haven't finished going through all her papers. Our general goal, not so much with major motion pictures, but on books and some of the other creative processes, was to get as much factual stuff out there and allow people to do their own creative process. So, rarely will I agree to consult on a book about my dad. I don't even think I could be objective about it.

RC: It's great that you have that personal insight to see that.

SR: I respect people and I respect their work as artists, but I don't get involved in it. We get very involved if someone is doing a sculpture because that's likeness. Or an art piece when we are asked to be involved, we will comment on art. So right now, for example, well it all got stymied because of COVID, but there is a hologram piece. We've been very involved with the kinds of things where you are trying to make him look like himself.

RC: Is there one of those happening right now?

SR: Yeah, Major League Baseball has been working on it for a long time, but like I said, everything stopped. They were very close to finishing up. It was supposed to be for the Smithsonian Museum. I did a lot of work with them, and I've seen the hologram and commented. They've been trying to get the facial stuff right. I also have a young, female artist right now that is doing a gigantic mural for a youth sports facility. She just sent me the work and I thought it looked really promising.

Sharon Robinson and I had to end our initial conversation at this point, but a few days later we resumed our chat.

SR: I did get to one of my mom's files, and she answered your question. This was a file where she worked with Leslie Moonves. I guess he was president of Lorimar back then? 1990. He did *The Court Martial*. She definitely was a consultant on it. And she opens up by saying, after her conversation with the producer, "and I mentioned the resurgence of interest in Jack that had been evidenced since 1987, the 40th anniversary of his entering into baseball. It manifested in proposals to me, books in progress, even the enhanced value of his memorabilia. Enclosed are a few clippings to give you some idea of projects underway. I have great faith that a quality production with fresh material in depth would be well received."

RC: What were the specific parts of the film that you and your mom thought were well-executed?

SR: First of all, it was a story that most people didn't know about. That alone, we were happy about. I'm just looking over her notes on [pause]. Interesting... "I have just completed my work as a creative consultant and in the process have confirmed my opinion that the end product heavily reflects the kind of research and conceptual thinking that is done in the pre-production phase. I think this is especially true when we are dramatizing a life within a historical context."

RC: One of the things I loved about the movie so much was how much airtime it gives to your parents' love story. It pays attention to their relationship in a way that a lot of the others, to that point, had not. Especially their dynamic. I mentioned to you last time that Ruby Dee didn't really love her performance as Rachel in *The Jackie Robinson Story* because she thought she had played Rachel as too passive. I love that one moment in *Court Martial* (because they had that brilliant casting idea of bringing Ruby back to play Mallie), where your parents had split up because Jackie was jealous about your mother being in the cadet corps, and Mallie tears into him. "You're just being a man and Rachel isn't like that. Rachel is too strong for that." I always see that speech as sort of Ruby's apology for the passive performance that she gave in *The Jackie Robinson Story*. I really love that moment in the movie.

SR: This is the advantage of when you serve as a consultant on these things; you get more authenticity. In her notes she clarified a number of times the depiction of that whole scene. There was an earlier draft with their wedding plans and the giving back of

the ring, and she had to clarify all that and make sure they understood it. So obviously she felt good about it at the end but still wanted to keep everything within a historical context. And that's always been important to us. To tell a story outside of the historical context is not a full story.

For example, a lot of people say, "Oh, your father was a Republican." Well, the majority of Black people were Republicans and that's coming out of Abraham Lincoln's days. The split started happening around Kennedy versus Nixon. And even with my father, he was a moderate Republican with the Rockefeller group and they got knocked out of the water in the 1960s. If you don't put it in context and you look at the voting record, you don't know. He was much more independent in his thinking, and it shifted, you know what I mean?

RC: Right, and by the time he died he had fully renounced Nixon and had voiced his disappointment in Nixon and his inability to follow through on his promises.

SR: Absolutely. Historical context is extremely important.

RC: Especially with film, it's a thing that historians are always battling, because film has this way of creating reality, right? People walk away from a movie thinking of it as fact, so it's important.

SR: And many people came up to us after seeing 42 and loving it and asking "Was that accurate?" And we felt good about being able to tell them it was, you know, basically, accurate. Certainly, there were some Hollywood components. When he asked her to marry him on the telephone after meeting with Branch Rickey, that kind of thing. There was more that went into that. But that's where Hollywood stepped in.

RC: What was the timing on that? The story that commonly gets told is that Rickey said, "Marry that girl because you're going to need her," and then history just jumps straight forward to the wedding.

SR: Exactly. No, they were engaged in 1941. They were engaged for five years. They tend to skip all of that. She was going to finish college and have a year or two to work and he was going to have a job; he would be employed. It happened in a recent interview, the guy had it backwards. He didn't have it that she had stated what she wanted to achieve before she got married, but what she expected of him to achieve. But both sides were equally important.

RC: During the 1990s and the early 2000s, there were multiple attempts to make a big-budget film. We talked about the Spike Lee one. I know that Robert Redford was trying to get one put together where he would play Branch Rickey. Were there any other attempts to make a big-screen adaptation, high profile or not, before *42* was made in 2013?

SR: Not to my memory.

RC: What do you think is the main reason that Lee and Redford weren't able to get these movies made?

SR: Spike ran into trouble getting support financially and getting the studio to be behind it. That's the same thing with Redford. So, you have this idea and you bring it forward but if you don't have the studio. They didn't think it was the time. That was before some of the major celebrations that have changed the legacy

But [producer] Thomas [Tull] already had the studio connection. And this was a passion project for him. He had made big films, made it big for the studios. And he was "It" right then. So he was the hot one able to pull it off. He came to us with, "I can get it done. I can get it done before/within the year and it will get done" and he never backed off that and he had the studio behind him.

RC: How involved were you and Rachel in the making of that?

SR: Oh, very. Very. Mom certainly more. Mom was the main person involved. Again, she was the consultant. But, you know, we were all – David and Mom and I all read scripts and Dave and I made our comments and Mom turned it in along with her comments.

RC: What was some of the feedback that she gave that changed the script and made its way into the movie, do you know?

SR: Oh gosh. Some even didn't totally make its way in. I think the overarching things in getting the story straight was to show his strength of character, the strength of their partnership, the clarifying relationship between he and Branch Rickey, you know, more employer to employee and then developing a friendship of sorts. He actually came to Dad's induction, when Dad was elected to the Hall of Fame, Branch was still alive, and he came. Those kinds of factors were important to us, getting that relationship as close to correct as possible.

RC: Let me ask you about Chadwick Boseman. I read an article where Boseman said that the first time he met your mom, she said to him, "Who are you and why do you get to play my husband?" And by the time the meeting was over he had earned her trust. What was it about him for you or your mom? What won you over to the Chadwick Boseman camp?

SR: First of all, he is smart. He understood history. He wasn't just a young actor coming in there who hadn't studied. He had studied both for the role but also studied Jackie Robinson, so he had his questions. With my mom he was – my mother is, you know, she's a very sharp business woman. I'm much more emotional [laughs]. She had to make sure that he was the right person. Because we were concerned that the material that's done be historically accurate. So if you've got an actor who comes in and already studied and understands the importance and the significance, that's part of the battle right there.

But he's also very charming and he meets you honestly. He meets your eye. He is open on his side too, you know, he wasn't a closed person. So, when you meet him and talk to him, he will share about his family as well as wanting to know about yours. That leads to a sense of trust about someone, you don't feel like they're hiding. He was Southern-born, which was important to us given the fact that dad was Southern-born, even though basically raised in California, still raised by a very Southern mother, so he understands that aspect again, historically as well as familiarly. It's a very familiar person for him to play. And he was very respectful of my mom, he was always respectful of the family. We embraced him. And then even before we saw his actual performance on the screen, we had embraced him as a person.

RC: Was your mom on set? Did she see him working?

SR: She was on set one time. Thomas arranged to pick her up and fly her to the set, I don't exactly remember where they were shooting that particular scene, but I know they had to fly, and she spent the day on set. So yes, she did see all of them work.

RC: The end of the Chadwick Boseman story is just so sad. [*Note: Boseman died of cancer at the age of 43, just a few weeks before Sharon Robinson and I spoke.*]

SR: We lost the man, which is very heartbreaking, but he produced so much in his short time. I always remembered from Jesse Jackson's eulogy of my father, the thing that struck me most, because I was young, I was 22. I'd seen my dad age very rapidly but I didn't understand how somebody could just die like that. Even though I knew he was sick, and I knew he had a heart attack. Jackson helped put it in context. I didn't hear it at the funeral, but I went back and listened to the eulogy after, when I could hear. It was on the radio so there were no distractions. What got me most was when Jackson talked about a life. That you don't measure it by how many years, but by what you've accomplished in that period of time. It always helped me throughout my life. We've both had young people die in our family. Mom and I each have lost a child. It forces you to actually get beyond the real grief of it. I'm six years out of mine and I'm just able to look back and find, you know, really wonderful parts of our life together. I was just thinking about that today. It really takes a long time to get to that level so you can understand what Jackson was saying that day. Don't try to measure it by the number of years. As devastated as we felt about Chad's passing, I am just so grateful for the work he left behind and the fact that he just kept working.

RC: After 42 there was one more movie, which is the only film that's fully captured the enormity of your father's story. It's really only Ken Burns's documentary that has been able to look at the full scope of his story because Burns has that luxury of four hours to work with. Did Burns approach your family first or did you all reach out to him?

SR: Both. My mother approached him. Years ago, I mean years before it actually happened, she told him that she wanted him to do the documentary.

RC: I remember he had initially talked about doing a film right after his baseball film had come out, but he had actually gotten a lot of push back from folks like Spike Lee who were concerned about a White man telling a Black man's story and he bailed on it. Do you have any idea what brought him back?

SR: I don't know about that, the comment you just made. I don't know. I thought it was that he had certain projects he was committed to, because he does these long-term plans. But, he wanted to get it done because he really wanted to be able to interview Mom for it and he was worried about her getting older.

That was part of what got him. So, he interviewed us: Mom, Dave, and I first. He did it before he got heavy into the interviewing process because they wanted to take advantage of when David was in the United States and while Mom was still able to remember the facts and stuff. And so, we just made it happen. I don't know the timing of that, but I know we were the early people in the interview process.

RC: I love every single interview he has with your mother in there. It's astounding to me, the eloquence, the story she tells about the fried chicken, about the subverted honeymoon because they got kicked off the flight. Her delivery in that story, I can hear it in my head, and I've only seen the Burns movie twice. There is just something indelible about her delivery of that. She is such a brilliant interview subject.

SR: We were all so grateful that he did it and that we have that interview.

RC: Was it just the interviews or did your family provide him other things like photos and other items like that?

SR: They had total access to what we had. They found things that we never found.

RC: That was my big question actually, my last question about the Burns film – was there anything about your father that you learned from working on the movie?

SR: So much! I can't think of all the things, but I'll give you one example. He clarified something that had been troubling me about the Pee Wee Reese incident, because I had written about it. I had grown up with it, the fantasy or fable or whatever it was. And yet when I went to write about it for kids, I never saw anything that was documenting that. Why wasn't there a newspaper article, you know? And then when we started working on the statue with Joe Black and some of his former teammates, I was like, "you don't remember anything about this story?" I was troubled by it. And then to hear him explain why it became this lore, I thought oh my god of course it makes total sense.

RC: Sure, the American public always seems to need that White savior to come in and sort of help make it palatable. One last question for you. There have been some wholly fictionalized characterizations of your father. Donald Honig and Robert Parker have written a couple of mystery books where your father is a character. He has even been very recently depicted in the new HBO show *Lovecraft Country*. Have you seen that at all by any chance?

SR: Nope.

RC: The very first episode of that show begins with the main character having a dream. And the dream starts with sampled narration from *The Jackie Robinson Story*, that voiceover that begins the movie, "this is the story of a boy, an American boy..." They sampled that. That's in it, and then your father appears, and he takes a baseball bat and uses it to defeat Cthulhu, Lovecraft's famous monster.

SR: Oh my god that's great!

RC: My question for you is what do you think of those fictionalized versions of your father where they're not really attempting to tell history? They're obviously telling a fictionalized story but they're using the mythos, the legend of your dad to help convey that story. What do you think of that and what do you think that says about the artistic desire to do that?

SR: Remember for me it's all about showing his strength of character. So, when you tell me what you just told me – that is showing his strength. I love when people do it right. I love the creative process, so anybody that does it in a really creative way, creative but honest, still keeping it historically correct, I think it's great. It also keeps his name out there. It makes a kid today say, "Who was Jackie Robinson that he has the power to defeat Cthulhu," you know what I mean?

RC: The eternal problem with Lovecraft's writing is how racist it is, right? But the beautiful thing about *Lovecraft Country* is that Jordan Peele, who is behind the show, is turning those racist tropes on their heads. He is attacking Lovecraft's racism so it's significant to me that he begins the story with Jackie. He's the first character in the first episode. And he is only there for a moment and it's a dream, but the demon that he's defeating with his baseball bat is the demon of racism. It's incredible how artists can take that and transport to that higher message that your father had all along.

SR: Exactly, that's my point. That higher message, yup.

RC: Sharon, thank you so much for taking the time to talk to me about your father's artistic legacy. It has been an illuminating pleasure.

SR: It was great having a chance to speak with you.

Sharon Robinson. photo by John Vecchiolla

Cold Warrior
The Jackie Robinson Story

By Tom Lee

In the typical telling of the Jackie Robinson life story there are two acts. The leading figures in both acts are White men. Act I is the run-up to White baseball: Pasadena, UCLA, the United States Army, the Kansas City Monarchs, the scouting of Clyde Sukeforth. This Act concludes in Branch Rickey's Ebbets Field office in 1946, golden light filtering through venetian blinds, as Mr. Rickey opens the door to Organized Baseball. The venerated moment is the famous turn-the-other-cheek conversation in which Mr. Rickey, not Jackie Robinson, sets the terms for the drama to come.

Act II is the entry into White baseball. This narrative sends Robinson to segregated Florida for spring training with the Montreal Royals, a season in the International League, the 1947 spring training Dodgers protest, and, finally, the call-up to Brooklyn. Robinson is defined by his silence in the face of his White racist teammates and his White racist competitors. The salvific moment in this Act is Pee Wee Reese's mythic embrace of Jackie, signaling Robinson's acceptance in the White man's game. Reese, not Robinson, steals the scene.[1]

Baseball's petition of Jack Roosevelt Robinson is nearly biblical. Since April 15, 1997, baseball asks each player to put on his number 42. On that day, baseball offers up each home run, each daring act on the basepaths as a living prayer to its suffering servant, as the prophet Isaiah wrote, "wounded for our transgressions, crushed for our iniquities." For us.

A movie centered on that redemptive story would be well worth the price of the popcorn. It would speak of Organized Baseball's deliverance from its stubborn past through Robinson's strength of character, his redoubtable will, his relentless insistence on the Right Thing, his perseverance despite the breakdowns of time, racism, and age. It would recast each 94-mph fastball aimed at his ear as another doomed pharisaic examination, refuted by the parable of a 90-foot charge from third to home. It would be undiluted and true.

In short, about him.

Spike Lee understood this in 1989, when he wore the Brooklyn 42 in *Do the Right Thing*. In a country where White people rarely confront race and privilege outside the context of violence, Jackie Robinson *is* the right thing.

The Jackie Robinson Story does not understand this. At every key moment, a White person is the cause, Jackie the effect. Once he reaches the major leagues, something *no* Black man had accomplished in the twentieth century, it is Branch Rickey, the hundredth-something White man to run a major-league club, at the film's active center. The passive voice is relegated to Robinson.

This essay proposes to understand Jackie Robinson—and Hollywood's attempt in 1950 to redefine him in *The Jackie Robinson Story*—on his terms, by taking him at his word. "I admit freely that I think, live, and breathe black first and foremost," he wrote.[2]

No wonder he never had it made.

Context: Television and Paul Robeson

The making of *The Jackie Robinson Story* in 1950 is a story of timing amid baseball's transformation from national pastime to nationwide media phenomenon. In 1949, Robinson hit .342 and stole 37 bases, both league-leading. The Dodgers won a thrilling pennant race on the season's final day. Robinson was the National League's Most Valuable Player and, for the first time, an All-Star.

At season's end, he would become a TV star. Nineteen forty-nine was the first year that every existing television network had the opportunity to broadcast the World Series. Local stations able to access a national feed could show the games live, too.[3] Major-league baseball was no longer the province of New York. The World Series now belonged to the world.

In St. Louis, newspaper ads promised shoppers at Baldwin Piano Company "WORLD SERIES TELEVISION VALUES!"[4] In upstate New York, Chappell's department store urged Syracusans to "See the World Series on your own set!"[5] The Associated

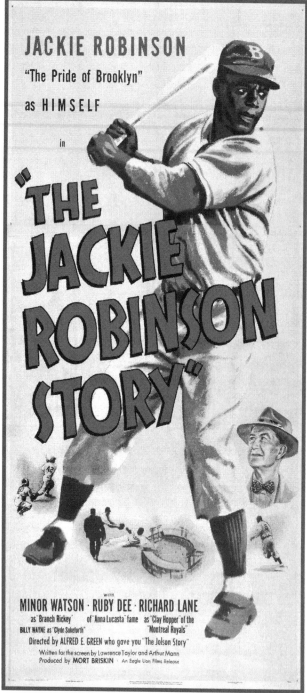

The poster for The Jackie Robinson Story.
photo by LMPC via Getty Images

Press reported 20 million people watched the World Series and declared 1949 "the year television became a national institution."[6]

Venues otherwise empty in the daylight hours used the Series broadcast to build crowds. The art-deco Fox Theatre in Brooklyn interrupted showings of Jimmy Cagney's *White Heat* to open its doors at 9:15 A.M. for those who wished to watch the games on "our own big screen... for the first time in any theatre."[7] Tavern owner Sam Atkins in New York opened at 11 A.M. and set drink minimums: "We don't allow people not to drink. It's either drink or get out for the World Series."[8]

It wasn't just the sets and the venues that were new. The Dodgers' Game One lineup was one-third Black, a World Series first. Robinson, Campanella, and Don Newcombe showed America something it had never seen, in any field of endeavor. Facilitated by new technology, and accompanied by the delights of tavern pours, movie theater popcorn, and the shared experiences they make possible, the country saw Black men and White men working together.

Hollywood judged they wanted to see more.

But more of what, exactly?

In a 1997 essay, Gerald Early, a distinguished professor and director of African and Afro-American Studies at Washington University in St. Louis and an authority on Robinson, gave his answer to that question.[9] Early argued *The Jackie Robinson Story* marked a turning point in American cinema—the first time White America recognized a Black man as a movie hero.

"Films of a given era or epoch," Early wrote, "no matter how ineptly made or far-fetched or how seemingly removed from reality, are about what is on a society's mind at the time, a dramatization of that society's fears and hopes, its obsessions and conventions."[10] Early argued that Robinson the movie character was a new prototype, an aspiring Black hero "trying to make it on merit in a sometimes hostile, sometimes concerned, white society that doubts his ability."[11]

If Robinson was a pop culture prototype, he was by no means alone. Campanella, Newcombe, and Larry Doby joined Robinson in the 1949 All-Star Game, the first time four Black players participated in the Mid-Summer Classic. Minor-league baseball, likewise, was undergoing its own dramatic racial transformation.[12]

1949 also was a breakthrough year in movies and music. A spate of feature films featuring Black leads confronting racial discrimination, the so-called "Negro Problem" films, all released that year.[13] The be-bop of Charlie Parker, Dizzy Gillespie, Miles Davis, and other Black artists pushed aside the wartime big band sounds.[14] *Billboard* created its first rhythm and blues chart in 1949. Antecedents of the rock-n-roll explosion—Louis Jordan's jump blues, John Lee Hooker's "Boogie Chillen," Paul Williams' "The Hucklebuck," and the doo-wop of the Orioles—dominated the original charts.[15]

Everyone, though, was merely catching up to Paul Robeson.

Robeson owned every stage he inhabited: son of a fugitive slave, Phi Beta Kappa, four-sport letterman, valedictorian at Rutgers, and graduate of Columbia University law school. He changed the way theater audiences understood Shakespeare and O'Neill. His baritone performance in the London staging of *Showboat*, as well as MGM's 1936 film version, made "Ol' Man River" a twentieth-century standard. His concerts packed theater halls on two continents.[16]

As Robeson became a citizen of the world, he adopted the world's causes. He championed the Spanish loyalists and spoke up against Nazism years before the United States entered World War II.[17] He fought for integration in baseball two years before Robinson signed with the Dodgers, taking a meeting with Commissioner Kenesaw Mountain Landis in 1943.[18] Appreciative of the Soviet Union's war against fascism and hopeful of the egalitarian promise of communism, he learned Russian and moved to Moscow.

Unwilling or unable, he never squared Marxist thought with Stalinist reality. That proved his undoing. His indifference, hostility even, to the "red scare" that gripped America in the late 1940s meant few Americans were surprised when, in April 1949, it was reported that he had assured attendees at a Paris conference that Black Americans would never take up arms against the Russians.[19]

It mattered not that Robeson protested he never said such a thing.[20] American politicians took full advantage. They turned a rare racial triple play off Robeson's slow roller, exploiting White fears of Red barbarians at the gate and a Black insurrection within.

Having injected the supervirus of race—specifically, the ancient variant of rebellion—into the global pandemic of communism, American politicians turned to manufacturing the cure. On July 8, 1949, the Associated Press reported that Georgia Democrat John Wood, new chair of the House Un-American Activities Committee, had invited a panel of "leading Negroes" to testify before his committee: "I think the principal purpose is to give the lie to the statements of Robeson that American Negroes wouldn't fight in case of a war against Russia."[21]

The witnesses included Lester Granger, executive secretary of the National Urban League; Charles Johnson, a sociologist from Fisk University in Nashville; and the Rev. Sandy Ray, of Brooklyn.[22] Sociologists and ministers of the gospel were not going to give Wood the press attention he sought. For that, he needed a cleanup hitter: Jackie Robinson.

"It might give the American people an idea how the Negroes stand," Wood said, "in the event of a war we hope will not develop."[23]

The next day, Robinson tried testifying from the Dodger clubhouse. "Paul speaks only for himself," Robinson told reporters.[24]

It didn't work. Wood wanted Robinson on *his* home field.

For a week, the parties danced about. Mail encouraging Robinson in every direction poured into the Dodger clubhouse. Wood opened his hearings.[25] Jackie kept playing. Nine days later, having beaten the Reds of Cincinnati, Mr. Robinson went to Washington.

Spoiler Alert: Robinson Before the House Un-American Activities Committee

Jackie and Rachel Robinson flew together from New York to Washington on July 18, 1949. Photographers posed them in front of the bronze "House Un-American Activities Committee" sign in the Cannon House Office Building as the "Hearings Regarding Communist Infiltration of Minority Groups" began.[26]

The Robinsons, political neophytes, were already known to their government.[27] The Federal Bureau of Investigation had monitored Robinson's political affiliations since Rickey signed him, linking him to various groups and causes the Bureau believed to be communist.[28] Whether Wood sought to use this information to accuse Robinson is unknown. It didn't matter. From a witness's standpoint, one either appeared and satisfied the committee, typically by ratting on a friend, or one was labeled a communist himself. Once labeled, your popular and commercial viability was at an end.

Robinson's appearance and testimony, however reluctant, suggested he understood the rules of this game, too. He could not have followed them more scrupulously.[29]

"There's been a terrific lot of misunderstanding on this subject of communism among the Negroes in this country," Robinson said, "and it's bound to hurt my people. Negroes were stirred up long before there was a Communist Party, and they'll stay stirred up long after the Party has disappeared—unless Jim Crow has disappeared by then, as well."[30]

Robinson's testimony linking the paranoia of the Red scare to the fate of the Black man was a work of art. The *New York Times* printed it in full. No other media outlet even noted it. They wrote what Robinson said next: "I've been asked to express my views on Paul Robeson's statement in Paris to the effect that American Negroes would refuse to fight in any war against Russia because we love Russia so much. I haven't any comment to make on that statement except that if Mr. Robeson actually made it, it sounds very silly to me.

"I can't speak for 15 million people any more than any other one person can, but I know that I've got too much invested for my wife and child and myself in the future of this country, and I and other Americans of many races and faiths have too much invested in our country's welfare, for any of us to throw it away because of a siren song sung in bass."[31]

It wasn't much, a couple lines buried in an earnest twelve-minute statement. But it did the job. And it's virtually all anyone read the next day in the metropolitan dailies.[32]

New York Daily News: "Jackie Hits a Double—P. Robeson, Jim Crow."[33]

Los Angeles Times: "Jackie Robinson Brands Robeson Claims 'Silly.'"[34]

Miami Herald: "Jackie Robinson Calls Robeson Song Off-Key."[35]

Spokane Spokesman-Review: "Infielder Gives Lie to Robeson."[36]

Knoxville News-Sentinel: "Robinson Says Race Doesn't Need Commies."[37]

Press outlets on the margins, those that had championed Robinson's journey and might have appreciated his larger message, also bit on the Robeson news hook—and took Robinson to task.

"Jackie Robinson fell into a trap of defilement," editorialized the *Daily Worker*, press organ of the American Communist Party. "The net effect of Robinson's playing ball with the Ku Kluxers of the Un-American Committee was to help them against his own people and his country."[38]

"Frankly, the main idea of these hearings was to get Jackie Robinson to testify," wrote the *Pittsburgh Courier*. "The Committee was banking on the publicity Jackie Robinson would get for the idea that Negroes are generally loyal."[39]

Robinson would have to defend his testimony for as long as he played. "Because of baseball," he wrote upon his retirement, "I was able to speak on behalf of Negro Americans before the House Un-American Activities Committee and rebuke Paul Robeson for saying most of us Negroes would not fight for our country in a war against Russia."[40]

Nearer the end, Robinson re-examined his participation.

"I have grown wiser and closer to painful truths about America's destructiveness," he wrote in his 1971 autobiography. "And I do have increased respect for Paul Robeson, who, over a span of that twenty years, sacrificed himself, his career, and the wealth and comfort he once enjoyed because, I believe, he was sincerely trying to help his people."[41]

It was too late. America long since had purged Robeson from its future.

Jackie Robinson had helped.

"Now you can fight back"

Congressman Wood wasn't the only impresario searching for a leading man in 1949. Hollywood wanted a movie. More, it wanted a sequel.[42]

Film creatives had recognized the artistic and commercial potential in a Robinson biopic from Jackie's big-league arrival in 1947. Robinson, himself, had sold the film rights to *Jackie Robinson: My Own Story,* an instant biography ghostwritten in 1949 by Wendell Smith of Pittsburgh's *Courier.* Robinson's newly hired financial advisor, Martin Stone, took one look at the deal and got Jackie out of it.[43]

Separately, a moderately successful Hollywood screenwriter named Lawrence Taylor was shopping a script to studios with Jackie as the central character. "Two of the big studios were interested," Taylor told *Ebony* magazine in 1951, "if the story could be changed to show a white man teaching

"Property of National Screen Service Corp. Licensed for display only in connection with the exhibition of this picture at your theatre. Must be returned immediately thereafter."   "THE JACKIE ROBINSON STORY" with Jackie Robinson, Minor Watson and Richard Lane   An Eagle Lion Films Release   Made in U.S.A.   Copyright 1950, AN EAGLE LION FILM. Permission granted for Newspaper and Magazine reproduction. (Made in U.S.A.) "Copyright 1950, RKO Radio Pictures, Inc."   50/330   JR-58

A publicity photo from *The Jackie Robinson Story*, featuring Robinson and co-star Ruby Dee.

Robinson to be a great ball player. Of course, that was out of the question."[44]

On the heels of Robinson's breakthrough popularity in 1949, however, Hollywood was newly intrigued. Taylor sold his script to producer William Heneman whose obscure British studio, Eagle Lion, agreed to make the film.

Word of Taylor's script traveled east to Brooklyn. In the Ebbets Field office where he had so famously scripted Jackie Robinson's entrance into White baseball—and his own role in the same—Branch Rickey appreciated the risk posed by a feature film offering a different narrative. Furious, Mr. Rickey took steps to protect himself. He put his longtime aide—and biographer—Arthur Mann on the case.[45]

"I went out to Los Angeles in mid-January with the picture in my pocket," said Mann. "This was in the form of a directive wherein the Brooklyn club and Branch Rickey were protected against misuse or abuse

of the situation. This was necessary because never before had a baseball club extended the right to film such a player-situation, added to which the right to portray the part of Branch Rickey."[46] Put differently: Hollywood tried to meddle with Brooklyn Dodger property; Branch Rickey, the great emancipator, would have none of it.[47]

Eight months after the HUAC hearings, five months after the World Series, *The Jackie Robinson Story* began shooting in Hollywood, starring Jackie Robinson as himself. The White press immediately greeted news of the film with skepticism.

"Most often, in telling a story about Negroes, the film people allow sentiment to run away with common sense," wrote *Hollywood in Focus* columnist William Mooring. "To patronize the Negro is to enlarge racial differences between blacks and whites."[48]

Mr. Mooring ought not to have worried.

Eighty minutes long, with 49 scenes, *The Jackie*

Robinson Story is a soap opera, a series of bite-size vignettes, capable of being learned each morning by a rookie actor and filmed in an absurd three-week production schedule.

That's not how the Hollywood trade press treated it. They gave every indication of a blockbuster in the making. Studio-leaked falsehoods.[49] Behind-the-scenes juicy bits from production.[50] Knowing observations from columnists on the inside. "Robinson wears success well," one whispered, "he realizes that he, as a man, has been favored by fortune."[51]

Fortune did not favor the Jackie Robinson portrayed on the screen. Denials of coaching applications, subtly racist slights at UCLA, the hardships of Negro League ball, Robinson's brother's employment as a street-sweeper despite an Olympic silver medal fill the first two-thirds of the film.[52] Despite their frequency, these vignettes were merely stones skimming the pond, racism without racists. They failed to bring the audience face-to-face with the responsible parties.

That happened only twice in the film.

The first occurred when Robinson and his Negro League team take an overnight bus ride. When they stop at a roadside diner, Jackie's teammates send him, the rookie, inside to buy dinner for them all. The scene is not violent, but it is accurate. Jackie meets Jim Crow face to face in the dishonest denials of service and the brushoff of the White patrons. The direction of the action is genuinely uncertain until a cook appears with an offer of sandwiches to go.

But that's it. In the next scene, Clyde Sukeforth appears out of nowhere and offers Robinson a train ride to Brooklyn. We never again see the Negro League team.[53] The Robinson-Rickey meeting scene is faithfully told, albeit with Rickey as the protagonist, and Act II is underway.

The second confrontation grew from Robinson's International League season with the Montreal Royals. Two White men in the grandstands strike up a conversation with a third, who identifies as a Brooklynite acquaintance of Rickey's.

"Tell Rickey you spoke with a couple of friends of his n_____ ballplayer."[54]

"Yeah, friends," the other says, making a throat-cutting sign with his thumb, "we're gonna call on Robinson after the game is over."

In the next scene, the "friends" approach Jackie and Rachel Robinson at the ballpark gate. Their demeanor and body language suggest they mean

physical harm. Robinson hears Rickey's disembodied voice, "you can't fight back" and, voila, two Whites arrive to hustle the Robinsons to the team bus, and the "friends" scatter.

There is one other moment in the film: a montage of racial taunts, in which minor-league fans and opponents say ugly things to no one in particular, but presumably to Robinson, such as "gimme a shine," "sambo," and "liver lips." But this montage stands alone. It is bracketed by a comic relief scene and an unconcerned Rickey scheming in his office with the president of the International League. Whatever the taunts are, they don't seem connected to anything else in the picture, except perhaps the racial awareness of Jackie's minor-league manager.

And then they are over.

That is the archetypal metaphor for *The Jackie Robinson Story*. The discrimination Robinson experiences is undersold, genuine but gentle. When confronted directly, Robinson prevails—but only with a helping White hand.[55] White coaches give him a prized baseball glove, Whites with big hearts admit him to college, Whites scout him, sign him, manage him, and mentor him. Whites tell him when he can and can't fight against racism.

The only scenes in which a willful Jackie Robinson runs counter to this motif are on the basepaths in the ballgame scenes. Daring and claiming, Robinson does not so much overcome racism in these moments, as outfox and outrun it. There are no White coaches giving the steal sign. Robinson steals home when he decides home is to be stolen.[56]

If *The Jackie Robinson Story* gave us nothing more than that, they would be gifts to cherish. One could watch 80 minutes of Robinson at his most daring. Alas, the filmmakers had other ideas. In the final scenes, having clinched the 1947 National League pennant, Rickey inexplicably appears in the Dodger dugout to congratulate Robinson, and the movie's message comes into focus.

"By the way, Mr. Rickey," Robinson says, "there's something bothering me. About that invitation to Washington, do you really think I should go?"

There has been no prior discussion of an invitation to Washington in the movie. There does not have to be. Every theater patron knows.

"Yes, Jackie, I do," Rickey says. "To the Senate, to the House of Representatives, to the American people. You've earned the right to speak. They want you to speak, about things on your mind, about a threat to peace that's on everybody's mind, Jackie. Now you can fight back."

Swelling music. An exterior of the Capitol dome. Robinson at a table, dressed in a business suit, reading from a script, five sentences from his 1949 testimony.

Except, it's not.

Below is the film's depiction of Robinson's HUAC testimony, side by side against the historical record. Note how *The Jackie Robinson Story* edits the story Robinson told.

The Jackie Robinson Story "testimony"	July 18, 1949 testimony
"I know that life in these United States can be mighty tough for people who are a little different from the majority."	"And just like any other colored person with sense enough to look around him and understand what he sees, I know that life in these United States can be mighty tough for people who are a little different from the majority."
"I'm not fooled because I've had a chance open to a very few Negro Americans."	Same.
"But I do know that democracy works for those who are willing to fight for it, and I'm sure it's worth defending."	Jackie never said this.
"I can't speak for any 15 million people. No one person can."	Same.
"But I'm certain that I and other Americans of many races and faiths have too much invested in our country's welfare to throw it away, or to let it be taken from us."	"But... I and other Americans of many races and faiths have too much invested in our country's welfare, for any of us to throw it away because of a siren song sung in bass."

Actual Robinson said nothing of the Cold War in his testimony.[57] Movie Robinson speaks of little else. The talk of democracy, of fighting for it, of letting it be taken from us, the splicing of the 1947 pennant to the 1949 testimony, were mere Hollywood artifices. So, too, was the unspoken suggestion against the film's persistent can-do-ism that systemic racism was unreal and that Robinson had nothing to say on the subject. He did:

> The white public should start toward real understanding by appreciating that every single Negro who is worth his salt is going to resent any kind of slurs and discrimination because of his race, and he's going to use every bit of intelligence, such as he has, to stop it. This has got nothing to do with what Communists may or may not be trying to do.
>
> And white people must realize that the more a Negro hates communism because it opposes democracy, the more he is going to hate any other influence that kills off democracy in this country—and that goes for racial discrimination in the Army, and segregation on trains and buses, and job discrimination because of religious beliefs or color or place of birth.[58]

But Jackie Robinson—son of sharecroppers, court-martialed by the Army for refusing to give up a bus seat, denied his most productive years in the major leagues—did not get to tell that story in *The Jackie Robinson Story*. Mann's reworked script whitewashed it out.

One may well conclude Robinson knew the truth behind Hollywood's fiction.[59] As his character finishes his "testimony," we see Robinson's image half-dissolve into that of the Statue of Liberty. He looks into the camera. Everything he actually said about race has been edited out. That which he didn't say about the Cold War has been added in.

The camera lingers on him, one, maybe, two seconds too long.

He shifts his jaw to the right. He is pensive and uncertain.

"Certainly not a good film"

Gerald Early said it best in 1997: "*The Jackie Robinson Story* is certainly not a good film."[60] Many films are not good. They can be under-budgeted, hastily shot, or sloppily written. They can skip central aspects of the subject's life and rearrange others to fit their narratives. These are all characteristics of *The Jackie Robinson Story*. As Early wrote, they make the film "a white-washed version of Robinson's life as most Hollywood biopics are white-washed versions of their subjects."

Contemporary White critics, no doubt relieved by the film's light touch on racial matters, were more kind. Kate Cameron of the *New York Daily News* gave the film 3 ½ stars. "His innate courage shines through this picture," Cameron wrote of Robinson, "and it is that quality that gives the film biography its special appeal to the heart of the beholder."[61] Jane Corby of the *Brooklyn Eagle* wrote Robinson "doesn't act in *The Jackie Robinson Story*, he's just natural."[62]

Louella Parsons, known as William Randolph Hearst's Hollywood hatchet-woman, gushed, "I don't know when a picture has left me with such a good feeling and real pride in being an American as *The Jackie Robinson Story*."[63] And no less than Eleanor Roosevelt wrote, "Mr. Robeson does his people great harm in trying to line them up on the Communist side of the political picture. Jackie Robinson helped them greatly by his forthright statements."[64]

Robinson's old allies would have none of the whitewashing. The *Daily Worker* called the movie "not only misleading but dangerous." The film "tried to rob progressives, Negro and white, of the history of their struggle against Jimcrow, to use Jackie Robinson against the unity that won him his place in baseball, and to report this story, with a brave air, yet all the while not only distorting it but lagging behind the real struggles against Jimcrow."[65]

The singular fault in *The Jackie Robinson Story* has nothing, however, to do with filmmaking or criticism of it. *The Jackie Robinson Story* is a bad movie because it isn't Jackie Robinson's story.[66] It denies him himself. His Blackness. The terror he knew for it. The beauty that shone for it. The heartache and joy he experienced because of it. The heights he reached because, and in spite, of it.

The Jackie Robinson Story is a bad hero movie because the hero does not fight his fight. In the end, a Black man is hired out, made a means to White persons' ends.[67] The film sends Jackie Robinson on an errand for a White status quo.[68]

But this is the final irony of a picture rich with irony. Its subject matter remains Jack Roosevelt Robinson. He is why the film endures. He is why this essay was written. He is why any reader has read this far. No matter the film's flaws, it is timeless because Robinson is timeless.

But timelessness is not the same as importance. The film's significance is in our hands. It is up to us to decide, more than 70 years later, whether *The Jackie*

Robinson Story continues to stand for the proposition that the sublimation of Black personhood is not too great a burden to bear against White self-interest and a nationalist agenda, or whether it can be relegated to the dustbin of history.[69]

"It isn't a perfect America and it isn't run right," Robinson wrote, "but it still belongs to us."[70]

An imperfect America can make *The Jackie Robinson Story* a period piece. All we need do is stop sending Robinson out there on our errands.

For as long as we do, *The Jackie Robinson Story* will forever be a bad movie, no matter the number we wear.

Notes

1   For a sport rich in iconography, the Reese embrace of Robinson has a unique place. A 2007 *New York Times* op/ed claimed the embrace likely never happened. Stuart Miller, "Breaking the Truth Barrier," *New York Times*, April 14, 2007 (accessed June 6, 2021, at https://www.nytimes.com/2007/04/14/opinion/14miller.html). Roger Kahn, writing in his 80s, slammed Miller as "an obscure journalist" and flatly asserted, based on his own numerous interviews with Reese, the embrace occurred in Cincinnati in 1947, as Reese sought to silence the taunts of his fellow Kentuckians. Roger Kahn, *Rickey & Robinson: The True, Untold Story of the Integration of Baseball* (New York: Rodale 2014), 272. A 2013 ESPN analysis, published to coincide with the release of the movie *42*, concluded the embrace occurred, but likely in Boston in 1948, not Cincinnati in 1947. Brian Cronin, "Did Reese really embrace Robinson in '47?," *espn.com*, April 13, 2013 (accessed November 22, 2021, at https://www.espn.com/blog/playbook/fandom/post/_/id/20917/did-reese-really-embrace-robinson-in-47). Jimmy Breslin wrote of Rachel Robinson's reaction at the 2005 dedication of a statue in Brooklyn commemorating Reese's embrace of Robinson. "She hated it. If there was one thing she and her husband despised, it was being patronized by whites." Jimmy Breslin, *Branch Rickey* (New York: Viking 2011), 120.

2   Jackie Robinson, *I Never Had It Made* (New York: Ecco Press, 1995), 168.

3   Ben Gross, "Looking and Listening," *New York Daily News*, September 15, 1949: 23C.

4   Advertisement, *St. Louis Globe-Democrat* (October 2, 1949): 3.

5   Advertisement, *Syracuse Post-Standard* (September 18, 1949).

6   Wayne Oliver, "Television Top Gift to Way of Life in '49," *Tennessean* (Nashville), December 27, 1949: 15. By comparison, only 9.6 million Americans watched the 2020 World Series. "2020 World Series draws 9.6 million viewers, an all-time low," *Los Angeles Times* (October 28, 2020)(accessed June 6, 2021, at https://www.latimes.com/entertainment-arts/business/story/2020-10-28/dodgers-win-but-the-2020-world-series-is-the-least-watched-ever).

7   Suzanne Spellen, "Walkabout: Brooklyn's Fox Theatre," Brownstoner.com (accessed June 6, 2021, at https://www.brownstoner.com/history/walkabout-brook-12/).

8   United Press, "Man Who Brought Back Nickel Beer Set To Collect On World Series Television," *Hartford Courant*, October 5, 1949): 20.

9   Gerald Early, "Jackie Robinson and the Hollywood Integration Film," in Glenn Stout and Dick Johnson, *Jackie Robinson: Between the Baselines* (Stroud, United Kingdom: Woodford Publishing, 1997), 99-102.

10   Early, 99.

11   Early, 101.

12   Jules Tygiel, *Baseball's Great Experiment* (New York: Oxford, 2008), 269-84.

13   The best-known film of this genre, *Home of the Brave*, examined the crippling injuries of a Black World War II veteran through the lens of the racism he experienced within his Army unit. Early argues in his essay that Robinson was "the obvious inspiration" for *Home of the Brave*. Early, 102; see generally "The Negro Problem Pictures of 1949," Black Classic Movies (accessed June 6, 2021, at https://www.blackclassicmovies.com/the-negro-problem-pictures-of-1949/).

14   Early, 100.

15   "From Race Music to Rhythm and Blues," *The Urban Daily* (accessed March 17, 2021, at https://theurbandaily.com/816655/from-race-music-to-rhythm-blues/).

16   See generally Martin Duberman, *Paul Robeson: A Biography* (New York, Knopf, 1989).

17   Duberman, 241, 282-96.

18   Robeson was more provocative than successful. Following Robeson's presentation, Landis famously told the owners, "Each club is entirely free to employ Negro players to any extent it pleases and the matter is solely for each club's decision without any restriction whatsoever." John Drebinger, "Owners Hear Robeson; Organized Baseball Urged to Admit Negro Players—Up To Each Club, Landis Replies," *New York Times*, December 4, 1943: 17. Recent history has more fully captured Landis' influence on maintaining baseball's color line.

19   A French journalist attending the conference quoted Robeson to have said that the wealth of America had been built

"on the backs of the white workers from Europe…and on the backs of millions of blacks…. And we are resolved to share it equally among our children. And we shall not put up with any hysterical raving that urges us to make war on anyone. Our will to fight for peace is strong. We shall not make war on anyone. We shall not make war on the Soviet Union."

Instead, the Associated Press reported Robeson said this:

"We colonial peoples have contributed to the building of the United States and are determined to share in its wealth. We denounce the policy of the United States government, which is similar to that of Hitler and Goebbels…. It is unthinkable that American Negroes would go to war on behalf of those who have oppressed us for generations against a country [the Soviet Union] which in one generation has raised our people to the full dignity of mankind…."

Duberman, 456-57.

20   "[N]o one seemed to be listening: his corrective remarks were not widely reprinted." Duberman, at 467.

21   Associated Press, "Negro Baseball Star Will Give Lie to Robeson," *Binghamton Press*, July 8, 1949: 12.

22   Associated Press, "Baseball's Jackie Robinson Called to Tell Off Robeson," *Los Angeles Mirror-News*, July 8. 1949: 10.

23   Associated Press, "Leading Negroes Refute Robinson," *Central New Jersey Home News*, July 8, 1949: 5.

24   Associated Press, "He'd Fight Russia for U.S., Says Bums' Jackie Robinson," *Rochester Democrat & Chronicle*, July 9, 1949: 5.

25   Associated Press, "Few U.S. Negroes Are Communists, Committee Told," *Troy Times Record*, July 13, 1949: 11.

26   See, e.g., "Noted Baseball Star Called," *Spokesman-Review* (Spokane, Washington) July 19, 1949: 2.

27   The American Communist Party made no secret of its interest in integrating organized baseball. For a thorough treatment, see Henry D. Fetter, "The Party Line and the Color Line: The American Communist Party, the "Daily Worker," and Jackie Robinson," *Journal of Sport History* 28, no. 3

(2001): 375-402; Tygiel, 36. Also, see generally Peter Dreier, "Before Jackie Robinson: Baseball's Civil Rights Movement" in *Jackie: Perspectives on 42*, Bill Nowlin and Glen Sparks, eds. (SABR 2021).

28   The FBI tracked Robinson's political activities from his presence at the opening of a Harlem office of the International Workers Order in 1946, to his plans to lead a march on Washington in 1966 to protest the shooting of University of Mississippi student James Meredith. Much of the file—though not the data—appears to have been gathered after Robinson's baseball career, while he was fundraising for the NAACP, given a 1958 memorandum referencing the "Suspected Communist Infiltration of the National Association for the Advancement of Colored People," at https://vault.fbi.gov/Jack%20Roosevelt%20%28Jackie%29%20Robinson. Accessed March 23, 2021 (search "Jackie Robinson").

29   The *New York Times* printed Robinson's HUAC testimony in full the next day. "Text of Jackie Robinson's Statement to House Unit," *New York Times*, July 19, 1949: 14 (hereinafter cited as "Robinson HUAC Testimony.")

30   In *Rickey & Robinson*, Roger Kahn recounted an exchange with Robinson about this portion of the HUAC testimony. "'A profound statement,' I said to him years later. 'For a second baseman,' said Jackie Robinson." Roger Kahn, *Rickey & Robinson* (New York: Rodale Press, 2015), 83.

31   Robinson HUAC Testimony.

32   A notable exception was *The Sporting News*. Its July 27 front page story, "Jackie, Under Oath, Says I Want Dough," chose to emphasize an offhand joke Robinson made as he began his testimony: "It isn't very pleasant for me to find myself in the middle of a public argument that has nothing to do with the standing of the Brooklyn Dodgers in the pennant race—or even the pay raise I am going to ask Mr. Branch Rickey for next year." The publication's coverage of Robinson's testimony regarding Robeson didn't begin until the story's 13th paragraph. *The Sporting News*, July 27, 1949): 1.

33   Ruth Montgomery, "Jackie Hits a Double—P. Robeson, Jim Crow," *New York Daily News*, July 19, 1949: 2C.

34   Associated Press, "Jackie Robinson Brands Robeson Claim 'Silly,'" *Los Angeles Times*, July 19, 1949: 1.

35   United Press, "Jackie Robinson Calls Robeson Song Off-Key," *Miami Herald*, July 19, 1949: 1.

36   Associated Press, "Infielder Gives Lie to Robeson," *Spokesman-Review*, July 19, 1949: 2.

37   Associated Press, "Robinson Says Race Doesn't Need Commies," *Knoxville News-Sentinel*, July 19, 1949: 6.

38   Fetter, 393.

39   Lem Graves, "Leaders Question Cause of Loyalty Probe Within Race," *Pittsburgh Courier*, July 23, 1949: 2. The NAACP also wrote Chairman Wood that it "failed to see the necessity" of the HUAC hearings. "See No Need for Hearings—NAACP," *New York Age*, July 16, 1949.

40   Jackie Robinson, "Why I'm Quitting Baseball," *Look* (January 22, 1957): 92.

41   Robinson gave his decision to testify lengthy treatment in his autobiography. "I thought Robeson, although deeply dedicated to his people, was also strongly influenced by his attraction to Soviet Russia and the Communist cause. I wasn't about to knock him for being a Communist or a Communist sympathizer. That was his right. But I was afraid that Robeson's statement might discredit blacks in the eyes of whites. If his statement meant that all black people—not just some blacks—would refuse to defend America, then it seemed to me that he had been guilty of too sweeping an assumption. I was black and he wasn't speaking for me." Robinson, *I Never Had It Made*, 83.

42   Athlete biopics, especially about baseball, were common movie fare in the postwar era. See generally James J. Donahue, "Review, The Baseball Film in Postwar America: A Critical Study," *NINE: A Journal of Baseball History and Culture*, vol. 21. no. 1, (Fall 2012), 158.

43   Arnold Rampersad, *Jackie Robinson: A Biography* (New York: Ballantine, 1997), 223.

44   Rampersad, 223.

45   Rampersad, 224.

46   Frank Eck, "Drama-Packed 'Jackie Robinson Story' Sticks to the Facts," *The Sporting News*, May 10, 1950: 9.

47   Mann stayed in Hollywood through shooting of the film. He wedged his way into the Eagle Lion production so thoroughly, he eventually took a co-writer's credit with Taylor on the final production. *The Jackie Robinson Story*, film credits.

48   William H. Mooring, "Jackie Robinson's Story," *Tidings*, (Los Angeles), March 10, 1950: 24.

49   An oft-reprinted early item claimed Lena Horne was "reported being sought" to play Rachel Robinson, see, e.g., *Hollywood Citizen News*, January 9, 1950: 17. The part eventually went to Ruby Dee.

50   One columnist claimed Jackie gained 25 pounds in two weeks of studio work "mainly because of the gallons of ice cream he consumed between scenes." Frank Neill, INS, "Jackie Robinson's Movie Viewed As 'Hit,'" *Cumberland (Maryland) Evening Times*, March 28, 1950: 5.

51   Darr Smith, *Los Angeles Daily News*, February 27, 1950: 19.

52   Not all the disappointments Robinson experienced are portrayed in the film. In keeping with the movie's patriotic message, there is no mention of the Army bus driver who ordered Lt. Jackie Robinson to move to the rear of a military bus in 1944—or of the young lieutenant's courageous refusal, court martial, and acquittal. See John Vernon, "Jackie Robinson, Meet Jim Crow," *Prologue*, Vol. 40, No. 1 (Spring 2008), accessed April 3, 2021, at https://www.archives.gov/publications/prologue/2008/spring/robinson.html; Breslin, *Branch Rickey*, 17-26 (reprinting witness statements from Lt. Jackie Robinson's 1944 court-martial hearing).

53   The only further mention of Robinson's teammates—or any other Black ballplayers—is when Rickey asks Robinson whether he had a contract with the ballclub. T.Y. Baird, the owner of the Kansas City Monarchs in 1945, claimed that Rickey induced Robinson to breach a contract with the Negro National League club. See, e.g., Associated Press, "Monarchs Head Assails Signing," *Philadelphia Inquirer*, October 23, 1945: 28). Negro League contracts were rare. No evidence of a written Robinson contract with the Monarchs has ever surfaced, nor has any evidence that the Dodgers organization compensated the Monarchs for signing Robinson. For a broader discussion of the business conflicts, see Duke Goldman, "1933-1962: The Business Meetings of Negro League Baseball, 1933-1962" in Steve Weingarten and Bill Nowlin, eds., *Baseball's Business: The Winter Meetings, Volume 2: 1958-2016* ((Phoenix: SABR, 2017), 390-458.

54   It is the only use of the n-word in the film.

55   Robinson seemed to understand the paradox. "It isn't even right to say I broke the color line," Roger Kahn quotes him from a 1952 interview. "Mr. Rickey did. I played ball. Mr. Rickey made it possible for me to play ball." Kahn, *Rickey & Robinson*, 173-74.

56   Robinson stole home 19 times in his career. No one in the 65 years since his retirement has stolen more. https://www.baseball-almanac.com/recbooks/rb_stbah.shtml. For a recount of all 31 times Robinson attempted a steal of home, see Bill Nowlin, "Jackie Robinson's Steals of Home," in Bill Nowlin and Glen Sparks, eds., *Jackie: Perspectives on 42* (SABR 2021), 230.

57   "The fact that the film severely edited Robinson's remarks suggests that systemic racism had no place in *Story's* narrative." Lisa Doris Alexander, "*The Jackie Robinson Story* vs. *The Court-Martial of Jackie Robinson* vs. *42*: Hollywood Representations of Jackie Robinson's Legacy," *NINE: A Journal of Baseball History and Culture*, vol. 24.1-2 (Fall-Spring 2015), 90.

58   Robinson HUAC Testimony. "Highlighting this portion of Robinson's testimony, which reads as quite frustrated and angry, would not have been in line with the stoic version of Robinson portrayed in the film; it would have complicated the us vs. them Cold War rhetoric that was prevalent at the time and would run counter to the "individual acts of discrimination" definition of racism the film projects." Alexander, 91.

59   To whatever extent Robinson couldn't articulate his unease in 1950, he had found his voice a generation later. "As I write this twenty years later, I cannot stand and sing the anthem. I cannot salute the flag; I know that I am a black man in a white world. In 1972, in 1947, at my birth in 1919, I know that I never had it made." Robinson, *I Never Had It Made*, xxiv.

60   Jackie had arrived at that judgment 25 years earlier. "Later, I realized it had been made too quickly, that it was budgeted too low, and that, if it had been made later in my career, it could have been done much better." Robinson, *I Never Had It Made*, 88.

61   Kate Cameron, "Jackie Robinson Story Touches the Heart," *New York Daily News*, May 17, 1950: 78.

62   Jane Corby, "Screenings," *Brooklyn Daily Eagle*, May 17, 1950: 12.

63   Louella O. Parsons, International News Services, *San Francisco Examiner*, May 6, 1950: 7.

64   Eleanor Roosevelt, *My Day*, (November 2, 1949), quoted in Duberman, at p. 482 n.60.

65   Henry D. Fetter, "The Party Line and the Color Line: The American Communist Party, the 'Daily Worker', and Jackie Robinson," *Journal of Sport History* 28, no. 3 (2001): 375-402.

66   Major League Baseball historian John Thorn once said, "I can think of no man having a more difficult road ahead of him than Jackie Robinson did in 1947." *Baseball: A Film by Ken Burns*, *Sixth Inning*, quoted by Fetter, 392.

67   "When the suggestion was recently made that the committee should investigate the activities of the Ku Klux Klan, which is beginning to raise its ugly head again in various parts of the country, [Wood] remarked jovially, brushing the idea of an investigation aside as absurd, that the Ku Klux Klan 'is an old American tradition, like that of illegal whiskey-selling.'" Robert E. Cushman, "Civil Liberties in the Atomic Age," in *The Annals of the American Academy of Political and Social Science* 249 (1947): 62.

68   White critics also praised the movie's "realism." In *The Sporting News'* review, Eck wrote little about Robinson. Eck focused on Mann's script and actor Minor Watson's portrayal of Rickey. "When BR sees the movie," Eck gushed, "he might even be surprised. It's as close to the real thing as any 'life story' to ever come out of Hollywood." Eck, 9; see also Fetter, 393.

69   Robinson understood the racial politics at play. "There are whites who would love to see us refuse to defend our country because then we could relinquish our right to be Americans." Robinson, 83-84.

70   Robinson, 84.

Jackie on TV

By Zac Petrillo

"Television is not only just what the doctor ordered for Negro performers; television subtly has supplied ten-league boots to the Negro in his fight to win what the Constitution of this country guarantees as his birthright."

- Ed Sullivan[1]

On the November 20, 1969 episode of CBS's *What's My Line?* Jackie Robinson was the surprise guest. One of the panelists, Soupy Sales, excitedly recounted that he watched Robinson play football for the UCLA Bruins way back in 1944. It's one of the "big thrills of [Soupy's] life and [he] gets a big kick out of telling people." Robinson debunks Soupy's story by saying softly, "Should I contradict him?" Robinson goes on, "I would like to have been in school in 1944," but Robinson played in the Bruins backfield in 1939.

The moment is gently comical, touching ideas of nostalgia and the trickery of memory.[2] More than anything it speaks to a fact of American life from the late 1940s through the early 1970s: Everyone believed they knew Jackie Robinson. His presence was ubiquitous because a generation grew up with him, not only in the news or on the baseball field, but on their television screens, out of uniform, giving batting tips in primetime, discussing beating the odds on talk shows, schmoozing with Hollywood stars at high-profile dinners, and even appearing in bit parts on scripted series.

Spurred by the public unveiling of television at New York's World Fair, the first broadcast of a baseball game was Princeton versus Columbia on May 17, 1939. Three months later, about 400 television sets in New York could watch Red Barber call the first televised major-league baseball games, a doubleheader between the Brooklyn Dodgers and St. Louis Cardinals on W2XBS (the station that became WNBC-TV).[3] It was nearly another decade before the league could take full advantage of the small screen.

World War II stymied consumer development because electronic companies focused their resources on assisting with the war effort. Television programming as viewers came to know it didn't proliferate American culture until roughly 1947 with such nationally syndicated shows as *Mary Kay and Johnny, Puppet Television Theater (Howdy Doody),* and *Meet the Press.* That same year, Jackie Robinson broke the color barrier in what was then known as major-league baseball.

The timing proved serendipitous as the first live World Series broadcast was Game One in 1947, which pitted Robinson's Brooklyn Dodgers against the New York Yankees. "Sunlight and shadows obscured NBC cameras' view,"[4] making the game hardly watchable, but the series still garnered nearly four million estimated viewers between Philadelphia, Washington, New York City, and Schenectady. People huddled around "7-inch and 10-inch screens"[5] at tavern gatherings that were responsible for double the audience of home viewership.[6] Over the next three years, television ownership exploded to approximately six million homes and as more sets entered the living rooms of average Americans, so too did Robinson.

Robinson's first major television appearance was on Milton Berle's NBC variety show, *Texaco Star Theater,* on September 27, 1949. He was amongst other celebrity guests such as W.C. Fields, Bela Lugosi, and, most notably, tap dancer Bill "Bojangles" Robinson. The sketches, including Berle and Bill Robinson performing "Take Me Out to the Ballgame," are light and baseball-themed, in line with Berle's comedic stylings transferred from radio a year earlier.

Less than two weeks later, the Dodgers lost to the Yankees in the World Series for the second time in three seasons. That offseason Jackie Robinson was named the National League's Most Valuable Player. Shortly after, Bill "Bojangles" Robinson died. Ed Sullivan, the columnist turned popular television host whom Jackie Robinson came to know well, arranged and paid for the funeral. Robinson attended in the company of Milton Berle and fellow television personalities such as actors Jimmy Durante and Danny Kaye. Babe Ruth may have been baseball's first major star, delivered to the public via national headlines, newsreels, and radio, but Robinson was, in just his third season, the sport's first star to come directly into households via the small screen.

To supplement his baseball income in the offseason of 1949, Robinson took a job selling television sets at Sunset Appliance Store in Rego Park, Queens. Joseph Rudnick, the store's owner, commented, "He's a natural salesman, with a natural modesty that appeals to buyers."[7] But Robinson himself, perhaps proving Rudnick's point, said, "If a customer is going to buy a set, he's going to buy it... You can't twist his arm." *The New Yorker* reported that Robinson's family owned a 16-inch television on which their only child (at the time) Jackie, Jr. liked to watch *Howdy Doody*, *Mr. I. Magination*, and *Farmer Gray*.[8]

In 1950, Robinson starred as himself alongside Ruby Dee in the film *The Jackie Robinson Story*. To promote the movie, Robinson made a May 20, 1950 guest spot on Dumont Television Network's *Cavalcade of Stars*. The skit begins with Billy, a boy who uses a wheelchair, reading *Life* magazine with Robinson on the cover. His dad enters bearing birthday gifts, trying to cheer Billy up with the promise of a party where celebrity guests will attend. It's not until his dad mentions that he will invite Robinson that Billy nearly jumps from his chair, exclaiming, "Jackie Robinson!" Before sinking, "Aw, he wouldn't come."[9]

After a series of failed attempts to sneak into Ebbets Field, Billy's dad, defeated, tells a concession stand worker that his kid is sick and wishes to meet Robinson. Another small boy overhears. The dad leaves to inform Billy their party will only be them. There's a knock at the door. Suddenly, the real Robinson is in their living room with the small boy. "I hope you don't mind our intruding, but my son told me that you wanted to see me," Robinson says.

He hands Billy a glove, but Billy says, "Where will I play baseball... in my dreams?" Jackie replies, "That's a good place to start..." before telling the story of how he started as a small Black boy amongst older White kids, so good that they couldn't help but give him a chance. Here is an example of Robinson stepping out from the television and literally into a fan's living room. The plot doubles in on itself, providing a glimpse into how television allowed fans, who previously only admired ballplayers at a distance, to now feel they knew them intimately.

Throughout the 1950s, Robinson remained a fixture on primetime shows. He appeared with his Dodgers teammates on such programs as Edward R. Murrow's *See It Now* and, for his first of multiple appearances, on *The Ed Sullivan Show*. He was also a solo mainstay on programs like *The Ken Murray Show*, *The Tonight Show* hosted by Steve Allen, and *On Your Way*.

On November 23, 1953, Robinson appeared on a CBS program called *Dinner with the President;* live coverage of a dinner marking the B'nai B'rith Anti-Defamation League's 40th anniversary. Prominent guests included senators, supreme court justices, Hollywood performers, and, most tellingly, television broadcasting luminaries David Sarnoff, Leonard Goldenson, and William Paley (heads of NBC, ABC, and CBS, respectively). While ostensibly meant to celebrate breakthroughs in freedom, the entire show was a coronation of television as a medium, as evidenced by a prolonged performance at the show's center by television's biggest stars, Desi Arnaz and Lucille Ball.

As with most of his early appearances, Robinson's time on screen was brief and innocuous, meant primarily to spotlight his courage amongst a racially-understanding crowd. While extolling the advancements in American civil liberties, Rex Harrison, one of the event's emcees, states there was "a lynching a week forty years ago," but while "there's still mob violence... in 1952 and in 1953, there has not been a single lynching in the United States." As politicians and television's newly-minted elite applauded progress, the fight was far from over, as Jackie no doubt knew. By 1956 another three Black people were lynched in America.[10]

Following the 1956 season, the Dodgers agreed to trade Robinson to the New York Giants. Rather than accept the trade, Robinson announced to *Look* magazine that he was retiring to pursue other ventures. "At my age a man doesn't have much future in baseball and very little security," Robinson said.[11] By that time the general public's acceptance of the civil rights movement was being tested as the Brown v. Board of Education decision, the murder of Emmett Till, and the Montgomery bus boycott made racial inequality national news and polarized public opinion, shaking the perceived postwar status quo by forcing all Americans to confront uncomfortable truths.

On January 9, 1957, just a day after the *Look* article hit newsstands, Robinson appeared on CBS's *I've Got a Secret*. In a rare departure from his normal experiences as a media guest, he was met with something other than warmth. The show's host, Garry Moore, brings Robinson out amidst a laundry list of his athletic accomplishments ("broad jump champion"; "shot a 71 in golf"), but the conversation turns to his decision to leave baseball and become the Vice President of Personnel at Chock full o'Nuts. Robinson says, "I'm very, very proud to be associated with the organization." Instead of having a panel of four people ask Robinson questions, Moore announces, "We decided to have a panel of 700, those in our studio audience." Robinson's eyes race left and right, uneasy at what might come next.[12]

Jackie immediately faces questions about whether he will miss baseball and why he quit the Giants even after saying he would play for them. For the first time in his television life, Robinson responds with frustration, firmly explaining that he had a "moral obligation to *Look* Magazine" for the exclusive story of his post-baseball employment. Next, a man asks if the trade to the Giants was why Robinson retired. Robinson, his voice rising, confirms, "It had absolutely nothing to do with my decision." Moore tries to defuse the moment by assuring, "Well, that answers that question once and for all." Still, the next audience member asks the same question: "Did the fact you were traded to the Giants have any bearing on your retirement?"[13]

As a cloud of discomfort hung over the rest of the show, Robinson graciously answered more questions about baseball. No matter how hard Robinson tried to direct the discussion to his plan to pursue a business career, it seemed the sheen of goodwill surrounding him had worn and fans had less room for adulation if he wasn't fitting their narrative.

For most of his adult life, Robinson's political stances aligned with the ideals of America's popular imagination. He was a supporter of Republican President Dwight D. Eisenhower, as evidenced by his appearance at the 1953 dinner. In the 1960 Presidential election, he strongly supported Eisenhower's Vice President, Richard Nixon. "Robinson had done everything that could be asked of him as an American Hero,"[14] but as the country shifted and the 1960s got underway, Robinson's politics transformed. He traveled to burned churches, spoke in support of the NAACP, and marched on Washington. He supported Nixon because he didn't feel John F. Kennedy was strong on civil rights. By the end of the decade, Robinson saw a different Nixon and did not support his run for office in 1968.

On May 20, 1962, Robinson, now squarely in the new phase of his public life, made what became his most well-known appearance, this time to offer "batting tips" to young ballplayers on *The Ed Sullivan Show*. By that point, Sullivan and Robinson had developed a close personal friendship, even co-chairing events such as a dinner honoring world heavyweight champion Floyd Patterson at the Commodore Hotel in 1960.[15] Before Sullivan hit it huge as the longest-running variety show host on television, he wrote a column during Robinson's rookie season that began: "Listen, kids" and celebrated Robinson "because he knocked Ignorance out of the park, tagged out Prejudice and trapped the pop-fly of Custom...."[16]

Robinson had joined his teammates on *Sullivan* in 1956. He was also spotted in the crowd on another episode, taking a bow during the host's customary celebrity audience-member introductions. In 1962, Jackie had just been inducted into the National Baseball Hall of Fame and been named UCLA's Alumnus of the Year. "We've got your model here," Sullivan tells Jackie, handing him a baseball bat. "My model... this is Willie Mays," Robinson responds to the laughter of the audience. And then, in another bit of Robinson's on-screen celebrity commenting on his real-world persona, Sullivan says, "Jackie, that's show business."[17]

Later, as Robinson encourages kids not to imitate professionals, to be themselves, and keep their eyes on the ball, he compares common batting mistakes to the same mistakes people make in golf. To which Sullivan playfully quips, "He's played with me, so he knows what I do."[18]

In 1966, Robinson starred in a minor role on an episode of *ABC Stage 67*. Titled "The People Trap,"

Robinson appears on *The Ed Sullivan Show* on May 20, 1962.
photo courtesy of Ed Sullivan estate

almost become stock for Robinson over two decades, the topic went to Robinson's efforts to improve Black construction businesses and then to Jackie, Jr.'s drug use and untimely death.

"We were quite proud that our son, in spite of a very serious heroin problem, overcame it," Robinson explains. "His automobile accident had absolutely nothing to do with drugs." Even during an uncharacteristically solemn moment, Robinson, a demeanor weathered by years of struggle and tragedy, tries to focus on positive change for the future. "It [drugs] is, to me, the worst problem that we have in this country today," Robinson continues. "Even worse than the race problem."[19]

Roughly nine months after *Dick Cavett*, Jackie Robinson died at 53 years old. Towards the end of his life, he said, "I guess I had more of an effect on other people's kids than I had on my own."[20]

Robinson not only broke the color barrier in major-league baseball but paved the way for integrating the military and public schools. He energized Americans to support the Civil Rights Act of 1965 and even promoted change within corporate America by becoming the first Black executive of a major company. This was largely because Americans had a relatable and rooting interest in a Black person doing something everyone loved: playing baseball. Even more so, Robinson's legacy endured because people got to see him as a flesh and blood human via the new medium of television. It was the perfect convergence of a moment. Jackie Robinson arrived along with a vessel by which America could experience him.

***

the science fiction story is set 100 years in the future (2067), when the United States is overpopulated, and land is scarce. He was one of many stars with bit parts in the show; others included Cesar Romero and Charlie Ruggles.

Two television appearances late in Robinson's life exemplify the complexities of his personality. First, in 1970, Robinson appeared on *Sesame Street* to recite the alphabet. It's pure Jackie. A careful charm in the precise enunciation of each letter. It's the Jackie that America thought they knew for over 20 years, the one they wanted to know, one that could make us comfortable with our differences and draw children into needing to learn.

In contrast, his final guest interview was on *The Dick Cavett Show* on January 26, 1972, less than a year after his oldest son died in a car accident at 24 years old. After a discussion about Jackie's experiences turning the other cheek in baseball, the kind that had

To research television history is to, at some point, land on YouTube. The space has become an invaluable archival resource thanks mainly to personal copies of early programs digitized for public consumption. As much as the videos are a treasure trove, the adjacent comment sections can be a cesspool of disparaging, hostile, if not downright vile opinions designed only to offend. One learns to keep their eyes up and never drift into the rabbit hole below.

It's encouraging that the comments on videos containing Jackie Robinson are an alternate universe from why you avert your eyes. Rather than the worst of humanity giddy to tear down an American hero, there are endless expressions of respect:

"The heroism and sacrifice of this prince of a man cannot be overstated."[21]

"One of the greatest amerericans [sic] who ever lived"[22]

"Jackie could've been the best politician ever! But I think being one of the best athletes in history will do!!"[23]

These comments give us a reaction to Robinson, not 70-plus years removed from his Dodgers debut but in real-time. Robinson's television appearances, most often short and far from subversive, provide the viewer with the way his presence changed the way the average American saw by changing *how* they saw.

Notes

1 Ed Sullivan, "Can TV Crack America's Color Line?" *Ebony*, June 1951: 58-65.

2 Rob Edelman, "'What's My Line?' and Baseball," *Baseball Research Journal, Society for American Baseball Research*, Fall 2014.

3 Roscoe McGowen, "First Day for the Small Screen," *New York Times*, August 26, 1939

4 Frank Fitzpatrick, "In '47, a different ball game," *Philadelphia Inquirer*, October 20, 2012: D1

5 Frank Fitzpatrick.

6 Joe Csida, "3,962,336 Saw Series on TV," *Billboard*, October 18, 1947: 4.

7 John Graham and Rex Lardner, "Success," *New Yorker*, January 1, 1950.

8 John Graham and Rex Lardner.

9 "Misc episode of 'Cavalcade of Stars', *Internet Archive*, https://archive.org/details/Cavalcade, August 17, 2008.

10 University of Missouri-Kansas City, School of Law, Lynching: By Year and Race, http://law2.umkc.edu/faculty/projects/ftrials/shipp/lynchingyear.html

11 James F. Lynch, "Jackie Robinson Quits Baseball; Trade is Voided," *New York Times*, January 6, 1957: 1.

12 rrgomes, "Joe E. Brown and Jackie Robinson on "I've Got a Secret" (January 9, 1957) – Part 3 of 3, *YouTube*, https://www.youtube.com/watch?v=7i0uqS4xWyM, August 15, 2011.

13 Joe E. Brown and Jackie Robinson on "I've Got a Secret" (January 9, 1957) – Part 3 of 3.

14 Sridhar Pappu, "An ill and unhappy Jackie Robinson turned on Nixon in 1968," *The Undefeated*, November 17, 2017.

15 UPI, "Today's Sports Parade," *Hugo Daily News* (Hugo, Oklahoma), July 17, 1960: 5.

16 Ed Sullivan, "Little Old New York," *Daily News* (New York), September 17, 1947: 59.

17 The Ed Sullivan Show, "Jackie Robinson "Batting Tips" on The Ed Sullivan Show, https://www.youtube.com/watch?v=hgIWwGXlgag, July 23, 2020.

18 "Jackie Robinson "Batting Tips" on The Ed Sullivan Show"

19 Pianopappy, "Jackie Robinson interviewed on the Dick Cavett Show," *Youtube*, https://www.youtube.com/watch?v=YCr0RAzf8ds, April 17, 2018.

20 "An ill and unhappy Jackie Robinson turned on Nixon in 1968."

21 Frank Russo, "Whats My Line Jackie Robinson," *YouTube*, https://www.youtube.com/watch?v=mvsSxxPoAHU, September 10, 2010.

22 LittleJerryFan92, "Sesame Street – Jackie Robinson Recites the Alphabet," *YouTube*, https://www.youtube.com/watch?v=KKSKQc9DmI4, June 3, 2007.

23 "Joe E. Brown and Jackie Robinson on "I've Got a Secret" (January 9, 1957) – Part 3 of 3.

Jackie on Stage
Jackie Robinson and his time in Vaudeville after the 1947 Season

By Adam Berenbak

Just across Florida Avenue, in the shadow of Griffith Stadium, home to both the Senators and the Grays in 1947, sat the Sportsman Inn. Joe Hurd, the new proprietor, had recently purchased the establishment from longtime DC radio DJ and baseball announcer Hal Jackson, who was in the process of moving to New York. On this occasion Hurd was hosting a party along with the District Theaters Group, owners of the Howard Theater, which sat across T street from the Sportsman Inn and still keeps its doors open to this day. The party included longtime vaudeville acts Tiny Bradshaw, Butterbeans and Susie, and a host of other Howard stage regulars. But the guest of honor, Jackie Robinson, had achieved stardom on a different stage that year.[1]

The most popular narrative in the life of Jackie Robinson centers around the year 1947, when he ended segregation in the National League. In that narrative, the year involves his momentous April 15 game, when he became the first Black man to play the sport at the major-league level since the 1880s, leading the Dodgers to a thrilling pennant chase and victory, becoming the first-ever Black player in a major league World Series, and culminating in his being awarded the first ever Rookie of the Year award. Though some biographies touch upon the 1947 post-season, including his salary negotiations and initial foray into film, few delve deeply into his post-rookie campaign activities. In his autobiography, Robinson makes no mention of this time, nor does Rachel Robinson in her *Intimate Portrait*.[2] The only mention of the offseason touches on all of the delicious food he ate on the southern speaking tour in January of '48, and how it led to him showing up to spring training overweight, which is where most of the narratives of his life pick back up.[3]

However, during October and November, Robinson traveled the US as part of a vaudeville act that toured traditionally African-American entertainment venues and may be referred to as Black vaudeville. Though baseball's biggest stars had been supplementing their income as vaudeville acts going back over half a century, Jackie Robinson's brief time on the circuit was scrutinized very much like his experience on and around the diamond during the first nine months of 1947, fraught with implications surrounding integration; his role as a Black ballplayer and exponent for social justice; as well as his standing in the Black community.

It begins with the ball dropping into Al Gionfriddo's expertly positioned glove. Jackie Robinson had driven in Pee Wee Reese in the third and crashed into Phil Rizzuto on second, providing some of the run support that made Gionfriddo's miraculous snag of Joe DiMaggio's monster smash all the more important, as it saved the game and set up a Game Seven of the World Series.[4] It was another first for Robinson in a season of firsts, but it would prove to be a letdown, as he went 0-for-4 and the Dodgers lost the game and the Series, the start of a near decade of Brooklyn frustration.[5] More important to the Dodger players was that they had lost out on the winners share, though they did take home a bonus that, in some cases, substantially supplemented their salary.

In Robinson's case, the Series losers share of roughly $4,200 nearly equaled his rookie salary of $5,000, the league minimum.[6] While papers such as the *Richmond Afro American* were quick to address that he had received the same share as his White teammates who had contributed as fully as he had, the total amount he had earned as a pro ball player during the full 1947 season fell far short of his contributions to the team and the game.[7] This was a problem not just of basic labor issues of major-league baseball at that time, but also of race and labor in the post-war period.

As so many Negro Leaguers, major leaguers, minor leaguers, and other pros had done since the advent of professional baseball, Jackie Robinson sought a livelihood outside of baseball once the season was done. While the majority of those players had found their sources of income in working-class labor and non-baseball jobs such as florists, policemen and running liquor stores, as well as winter ball south of the border, Robinson sought to utilize his notoriety and capitalize on his celebrity in the same fashion as other superstars had done as long as the game had existed. Given his position as a trailblazer, it would be a decision made under a microscope.

Though ballplayers had taken to the stage as early as the 1860s, one of the first well known acts was Cap Anson, cited so often as one of the primary drivers of segregation in baseball. After having appeared on Broadway once or twice in the 1890s, he made his debut on the vaudeville circuit in 1913, at the same time that more current stars of the game like John McGraw, Waite Hoyt, Christy Mathewson and Rube Marquard were moonlighting there as well.[8]

One reason for this was that vaudeville, as a forum, was relatively new at the turn of the century. It had its origins in Normandy during the sixteenth century, though in America the vaudeville of the twentieth century was much more closely related to traveling variety and medicine shows as well as the "concert saloons" of 1840's New York and Boston's Vaudeville Saloon.[9] The more modern iteration had begun in Boston in the late 1880s and offered more of a long-format variety show as an alternative to the large minstrel shows so popular on stages. By 1900 there were vaudeville houses all over the US that included both Black and White acts, as well as many of the minstrel acts it had supplanted.[10] For the most part, the main "act" of a famous ballplayer was to appear on stage and answer questions or read off a few quotes. Rarely was any singing or dancing performed – they were there just to be themselves.[11]

What became known as Black vaudeville began around the same time. While many Black performers joined vaudeville shows that included blackface and other hallmarks of minstrelsy performed before mostly White audiences, many others sought out Black audiences in churches and tents, as well as black-owned theaters known as the "Dudley Circuit,"

named for Sherman Dudley, or White owned T.O.B.A. (Theatre Owners Booking Association). By the 1920s and '30s, as Black business grew and became more profitable, a more expansive Black vaudeville circuit, sometimes referred to as the "Chitlin' Circuit," had developed, stationed at large venues such as the Apollo, in New York, and the Howard Theater, in Washington D.C., that had been built for that purpose.[12]

In October of 1947, after the announcement of his Rookie of the Year award, all the news about Jackie Robinson centered on his endorsements, most famously for Bond Bread, as well as a contract with General Artists Corporation.[13] GAC had arranged for him to earn extra income from a book as well as theatrical ventures, stops on the vaudeville circuit on his way to the West Coast, where he and his family would not only spend the holidays, but bring him close to film studios in preparation for a film produced by Herold Pictures, Inc called *Courage*, purportedly about juvenile delinquency.[14] The film never materialized, but his cross-country tour generated both the needed income unattainable through his salary and World Series loser's share, as well as a never-ending cavalcade of press and publicity, good and bad.

The press focused on the money he made from his off-season ventures – the many divergent accounts slyly implying greed as a motive, a narrative found often throughout the history of baseball players income. A few did so in aggressive terms that suggested racist overtones: "And the already wealthy Robinson isn't through. He is now sacking up the gold on vaudeville tours and personal appearances."[15] After he appeared on a few radio programs, it was announced that he would begin his string of vaudeville appearances at the Apollo Theater in Harlem, before hitting the stage at the Howard Theater in Washington, the Regal Theater in Chicago, and finally the Million Dollar Theater in Los Angeles.[16]

Much like John McGraw and myriad other ballplayers before him, his "act" was simply to show up and answer questions on stage, as he had done in his radio appearances.[17] Supporting him was Tiny Bradshaw and his band, along with longtime vaudeville comedians Butterbeans and Susie, and finally dancing acts like the Harris Brothers and the Three Hall Sisters. He was later joined by Monte Hawley.[18] As he was being celebrated for integrating baseball, Jackie Robinson was still scheduled to begin a tour on the chitlin circuit at the Apollo, a landmark that "after the demise of the Harlem nightclubs... continued the tradition of black vaudeville."[19] Though the Apollo was the apex of the Black stage, those who viewed Jackie as an integrationist may have perceived this as a step in the wrong direction.

On Saturday night, October 18, in front of a packed crowd in the Apollo, Robinson made his stage debut. Leading up to the performance, reporters had alternately highlighted the income he would attain as well as given generally positive reviews of his willingness to get on stage, and the quality of his supporting acts. Yet, nearly as soon as he had exited the stage, the critical reviews reflected the worries that a proximity to the minstrel tradition would cheapen his accomplishments, balanced with the desire to celebrate him properly. One of the first reviews came from the oldest black newspaper, the New York *Amsterdam News*. "The thought grows on you as you watch, 'What the hell is Jackie Robinson doin in this?' Clearly, 'money' was the right answer, but 'the idea persisted that there should be another way for him to earn the income he so richly deserves.'"[20] Doris Calvin, writing in the Baltimore *Afro American*, criticized the show itself as bringing Jackie "down to a far-beneath-him capacity," but wrote, "We're not saying Jackie shouldn't have made this tour. Too many proud folks want to see him in the flesh. But there's much room for improvement. The script, as it

now stands, should be burned and the writer shot at sunrise. The type of material Jackie needs is on the order of 'We the People.' In which he tells of his own life in a fascinating, idolized manner."[21]

The White press simply lauded the "hundreds upon hundreds of Harlemites" attending the show, claiming he had a "fine stage personality and appears to be just at home on the stage as first base."[22] And one of the few of his biographers to describe the tour, Arnold Rampersad, would focus much on Rachel's perception of the act, who "had reservations about this latest gambit. It seemed risky especially since 'Jack couldn't sing, and he was only a fair dancer. I couldn't imagine what he was supposed to do.'"[23] Another would point out that "some questioned if his appearance in a poorly run black vaudeville troupe undermined the public image of black dignity he had bolstered," but that "such criticism...only amplified the special burden for his race that he found himself carrying and the limited career opportunities for black males in postwar America."[24]

The reaction reflected both the importance for the community to celebrate him as an integrationist and hero, along with a worry that association with Black vaudeville would taint that role.

The week of the 25th saw productions of *No Exit* in Washington D.C., along with performances by Francescatti, Ted Lewis and his band, and movie house showings of Olivier's *Henry V*, *Crossfire*, and *Forever Amber*.[25] And at the Howard Theater, Jackie Robinson and his traveling show. The Robinson's stayed with local businessman Arthur Newman[26] while Robinson performed at the Howard, appearing on stage five times a day including the midnight "Night Owl Jamboree."[27] By the time of the party at the Sportsman Inn, it seemed that his publicity tour was in full swing, mixing weekly galas and performances as well as a lot of interaction with the press, who were included as guests at the Sportsman.

On the way to Chicago Jackie and Rachel Robinson, who were traveling with Jackie Jr., stopped off in Philadelphia to attend a

An advertisement for Robinson's October 1947 performance at the Apollo.

church banquet in his honor at the White Rock Baptist Church.[28] While there Robinson repeated a comment he had made during several press interviews during the tour – that he would spend only three more seasons in the majors.[29] Whether these were tactics aimed at gaining leverage with Branch Rickey in preparation for his 1948 salary negotiation that would take place in January, or simply his genuine feelings is not certain – later on the tour he would claim to have been misquoted. At the same time the *Richmond Afro American* was running a contest in its papers – asking readers who was more popular, Robinson or Joe Louis.[30] Regardless of the outcome, his position as the leading role model in the Black community was cemented.

Prior to Robinson's appearance in Chicago, the *Defender* ran a story about Abe Saperstein announcing he had offered Robinson a $6,000 contract to play basketball for Chicago's Harlem Globetrotters, at that moment coming into their own as a showcase of African-American sports talent.[31] Saperstein was intimately involved with Black baseball beginning in the late 20's with his affiliation with barnstorming tours and the Negro League East-West All-Star Game. Robinson's breaking of the color barrier was rejoiced by the Jewish community and seen as "a symbolic representation of their experience of assimilation into American society in the era immediately following World War II."[32] Yet Saperstein's role as part of a larger Jewish ownership stake in Black baseball was viewed as complicated, alternately as supportive and exploitative, and seen as promoting a "brand of comedic baseball based on vaudeville" that "played a role in making these 'showman' black players poor candidates for the serious game of major league baseball."[33] Though there is no record of Robinson's response, Saperstein's offer illustrates the challenges Robinson faced in deciding how to manage his status as role model, athlete, and entertainer.

Again, he and his wife were feted, this time at the Savoy Ballroom. Robinson took the occasion to honor Rachel, who was also presented with the "Smartest Woman of the Year" award.[34] Though the Savoy was a place where "race and class boundaries were blurred in ways that were undreamed of in other settings," Robinson continued to be honored mainly by Black organizations.[35] As the White press lauded him they still continued to speculate about his income from the tour – some said $100,000, Ed Sullivan quoted $25,000 – and generally posed him as an outsider.[36]

Booked into the Regal Theater, another stop on the "Chitlin' Circuit," for the week in Chicago, Robinson was presented with his Rookie of the Year Award by the Chicago Chapter of the Baseball Writers of America there on November 12.

On their drive to Los Angeles there was a small detour scheduled to take place in Oklahoma City, along with a meet-and-greet organized by sportswriter Fay Young. Months later an article came out in the *Chicago Defender* accusing Robinson of missing the gathering and disappointing a host of children eager to meet their hero.[37] Though he apologized and explained that he had been unaware of the meeting when they had passed through the city, he also criticized the tone of the reporting, it was another example of his complicated relationship with the Black press which peaked after his 1948 Ebony article criticizing the Negro Leagues and his appearance before the U.S. Congress' House Un-American Activities Committee (HUAC) the following year, where some accused him of selling out his community.

On Tuesday, November 18, Robinson and his tour arrived at its destination. Right away he went to work, attending a press junket at the Sports Club on South Hill before headlining the opening night of the Los Angeles leg at the Million Dollar Theater. The lineup was nearly the same, featuring Robinson and Monte Hawley, Johnny Taylor and Gerald Wilson, along with Little Miss Cornshucks, Mabel Scott, and Kay Starr, along with Herb Jefferies. They played the week before another well-known Robinson, Bill "Bojangles" Robinson, took over the stage beginning the 25th.[38]

The following week a "welcome home" reception was held at the First Methodist Church, with invitations sent to Happy Chandler, Branch Rickey, and fellow local National Leaguer Ralph Kiner.[39] There was no film, and it was rumored that final say laid with Rickey, who was "embarrassed" by the tour.[40] If so, it adds another layer to Robinson's decision making going forward, about future ventures on stage and screen, and how Rickey attempted to drive that narrative. *The Jackie Robinson Story*, made only a few years later, would be praised as groundbreaking in film integration, tapping into "cultural daydreams of American life, as Americans, both black and white, contemplated the possibilities of a society where blacks and whites would meet and interact completely as social equals."[41]

After the holidays the Robinsons began the slow journey east, this time on the 'southern tour' that gained so much attention for what Robinson gained in pounds. He continued the format of appearing publicly with music, though in a much less structured way, appearing at Wright's Playhouse in Waco Texas with an *a capella* choir called the Samuel Huston Collegians,[42] then with the Billy Banks orchestra in Chilhowee Park in Knoxville,[43] then Nashville with The 5 Bars at War Memorial Auditorium,[44] all while finding time to referee a "colored amateur boxing tournament' in Knoxville,[45] negotiating his salary with Branch Rickey, and eating too much good southern food. The challenges facing Jackie Robinson during the entirety of that 1947 journey, from Ebbets Field to vaudeville, epitomize the demands and triumphs of integration on so many different stages.

Notes

1   Louis Lautier, "Capital Spotlight," *Richmond Afro American*, November 1, 1947: 3.

2   Rachel Robinson, with Lee Daniels, *Jackie Robinson: An Intimate Portrait* (New York: Abrams, 1996).

3   Jackie Robinson, *I Never Had It Made* (New York: Putnam, 1972).

4   John Drebinger, "Dodgers Set Back Yankees 8-6 For 3-3 Series Tie," *New York Times*, October 6, 1947: 1.

5   "Baseball Reference"https://www.baseball-reference.com/boxes/NYA/NYA194710060.shtml

6   "Jackie's Series Share Estimated At $4,200," *Richmond Afro American*, October 11, 1947: 14.

7   "Jackie's Series Share Estimated At $4,200"

8   Elizabeth Yuko, "When Baseball Players Were Vaudeville Stars," *Atlantic*, April 6, 2017, https://www.theatlantic.com/entertainment/archive/2017/04/when-baseball-players-were-vaudeville-stars/521835/

9   Frank Cullen, Florence Hackman, Donald McNeilly, *Vaudeville Old & New: An Encyclopedia of Variety Performances in America* (New York, London: Routledge, 2006), xi.

10   John Strausbaugh, *Black Like You: Blackface, Whiteface, Insult & Imitation in American Popular Culture* (New York: Jeremy P. Tarcher/Penguin, 2006), 129.

11   "When Baseball Players Were Vaudeville Stars."

12   Strausbaugh *Black Like You*, 129.

13   "Jackie Robinson Prefers Bond Bread," *Richmond Afro American*, October 11, 1947: 11.

14   Jack O'Brian, "Broadway," *Sandusky Register Star News*, October 13, 1947: 4.

15   Al Lightner, "Sportslightner," *Statesman Journal*, October 12, 1947: 14.

16   Danton Walker, "Broadway," *Evening Independent*, October 9, 1947: 3.

17   "Robinson Packs Stage Wallop at Apollo Theater," *Brooklyn Eagle*, October 24, 1947.

18   "Jackie Robinson Launches Theater Tour at NY House," *Pittsburgh Courier*, October 18, 1947.

19   Brenda Dixon Gottschild, *Waltzing in The Dark: African American Vaudeville and Race Politics in the Swing Era* (New York: Palgrave, 2002).

20   Arnold Rampersad, *Jackie Robinson: A Biography* (New York: Knopf, 1997), 190.

21   Dolores Calvin, "They Made Him A Bum?" *Baltimore Afro American*, November 1, 1947: 6.

22   "Robinson Packs Stage Wallop at Apollo Theater."

23   Rampersad, *Jackie Robinson: A Biography*, 190.

24   J. Christopher Schutz, *Jackie Robinson: An Integrated Life* (Lanham, Boulder, New York, London: Rowman & Littlefield, 2016).

25   Advertisements, *The Washington Post*, October 26, 1947.

26   Lautier, "Capital Spotlight," 3.

27   "Robinson To Appear on Howard's Stage," *Richmond Afro American*, October 18, 1947: 15.

28   "Jackie Tells of Ambition to Help Boys," *Richmond Afro American*, November 8, 1947: 3.

29   "Jackie Robinson Plans Retirement in 3 Years," *The Washington Post*, October 25, 1947: 14.

30   Sam Lacy, "From A to Z with Sam Lacy," *Richmond Afro American*, November 15, 1947: 14.

31   "Globetrotters Make for Jackie Robinson," *Chicago Defender*, October 4, 1947.

32   Rebecca T. Alpert, *Out of Left Field: Jews and Black Baseball* (Oxford, New York: Oxford University Press, 2011).

33   Alpert, *Out of Left Field*.

34   "Robinson Lauded: Jackie and Wife Honored in Chicago," *Richmond Afro American*, November 15, 1947: 16.

35   Gottschild, *Waltzing in The Dark*.

36   Ed Sullivan, "Men and Maids and Stuff at Broadway and 42nd St.," *Hollywood Citizen-News*, October 27, 1947: 18.

37   "Dodgers' Jackie Robinson Denies Oklahoma Story," *Alabama Tribune*, December 24, 1947: 1.

38   "The Weekly Newsreel," *California Eagle*, November 20, 1947: 23.

39   "Civics Bodies to Honor Jackie Robinson at Reception Wednesday," *Metropolitan Pasadena Star-News*, November 23, 1947: 43.

40   Herbert Goren, "Jackie Robinson Increases Bank Roll Between Seasons," *The Muncie Star Press*, November 30, 1947.

41   Gerald Early, "Jackie Robinson and the Hollywood Integration Film," in *Jackie Robinson: Between the Baselines*, ed. Glenn Stout and Dick Johnson (San Francisco: Woodford Press, 1997).

42   "Jackie Robinson to be Interviewed by Maxey Here Thursday Night," *The Waco News-Tribune*, January 18, 1948: 13.

43   "Robinson to Show Here With Band," *Knoxville Journal*, January 25, 1948: 17.

44   "Jackie Robinson, Rookie of the Year, in Person With 'The 5 Bars'," *Nashville Banner*, February 4, 1948: 15.

45   "Negro Boxing Meet Opens Monday Night," *Knoxville Journal*, February 22, 1948: 17.

Comic Book Superhero

By Tom Hawthorn

A new publication appeared on magazine racks as the first game of the 1949 World Series neared. It had a bright yellow cover with garish red letters at a jaunty angle spelling out Jackie Robinson's name with a subdued subheading declaring him to be a "BASEBALL HERO." A colorized photo of the smiling player in a blue Brooklyn Dodgers cap was the dominant image, while the secondary art included a black-and-white photograph of Robinson

The cover of the second issue of the Fawcett Publication of *Jackie Robinson.*

after taking a practice swing. "True life story of the famous Brooklyn Dodger," read a tagline. The price was 10 cents.

The 36-page issue offered the player's biography in comic-book fashion, mixing the personal with the anecdotal, as well as statistics from his first two-and-a-half seasons in the National League. The book concludes with Robinson's selection to the 1949 All-Star Game, though does not mention his batting championship or Most Valuable Player award at the end of the season. The comic was likely rushed to the printing press before the season ended and the World Series got underway.

The comic book's tone is set in the first panel, which occupies two-thirds of a page. Robinson, "Marvel of the Baseball Diamond," is described as "the sharpest hitter, the speediest baserunner and the surest fielder in our national pastime!" The player "rose to fame the hard way, as he is also the first Negro in organized baseball. Hailed today as a new Ty Cobb, brilliant Jackie has overcome all handicaps to become a symbol of the fighting spirit of the American boy!"[1]

The story then follows a predictable biographical trajectory: birth in Cairo, Georgia followed by a move to Pasadena, California, where his single mother encourages his studies, while discouraging an obsession with baseball. The industrious boy sells newspapers on the street corner and hustles change as a bootblack. One day, Tony Lazzeri stops by for a shoeshine. Jackie asks if he is "the fellow who hit all those home runs in the Coast League last year," which places the fictional encounter in 1926, the year after Lazzeri hit 60 homers with the Salt Lake City Bees. Lazzeri helps young Jackie get a job at the baseball park.

Robinson's athletic exploits in football, basketball and track at Muir Technical High School, Pasadena Junior College, and the University of

California, Los Angeles are described. He meets nursing student Rachel Isum at university, enlists in the U.S. Army following Pearl Harbor before being commissioned as a 2d lieutenant, and then plays for the barnstorming Kansas City Monarchs of the Negro Leagues after the war.

He is scouted by Clyde Sukeforth of the Dodgers and signed by Branch Rickey, "maker of champions," who encourages the player to marry Isum. "The world was electrified with the news of Jackie's signing by the Dodgers," the book states. "Millions hailed Branch Rickey's courageous act — a few condemned him for breaking the Jim Crow code!"

The code is not explained in the comic, though a later panel includes a handwritten letter reading, "If you try to play ball down here, we'll ride you out of town. [signed] K.K.K." Another panel includes gentlemen with Southern accents condemning his hiring. The player later dutifully leaves the field at spring training in Florida when a sheriff in a cowboy hat puts a hand on his shoulder to say, "You git off'n this heah field right now! Our law says cullahd and white cain't play together!"

Later, the player endures taunts by opponents, including a rival player who holds aloft a black cat with the taunt, "Here's one of your relatives." The Phillies target Robinson with expletives shouted from the dugout (rendered in typographical symbols — @*#%$ — known as grawlixes) and a threatened strike by St. Louis Cardinals players.

A Dodgers exhibition tour of the South leads to a panel showing hooded Klansmen threatening to tar and feather Robinson and Black teammate Roy Campanella. Robinson's response is to deliberately strike a sitting Klansman sitting in the stands in civilian clothes with a foul ball.

The flavor of the hagiography is captured in the closing two sentences.

"He is loved by every fan in America for his courage, tact and brilliance, on the field and off," the comic book stated. "Long may Jackie Robinson, first Negro in Big League Baseball, star in his country's great national game!"

While the story does not avoid the racism faced by Robinson and the other early players who integrated major-league teams, it is a word that does not appear in the comic book. While the book acknowledges the limited career possibilities of a young Jackie Robinson — elevator operator or athlete — it does not address the unfairness of segregation.

Cathy Keen, an archivist with the National Museum of American History, reviewed the portrayal of Robinson as a comic-book hero in a 2013 article in which she found "the abuses he endured are addressed in a vague, sanitized way. Why were the sharp edges of reality so blunted in this comic book? There are many possible reasons — protecting children who idolize the players, avoiding offense, wishful thinking — but perhaps one was to focus on the game."[2]

The comic certainly does not spare in idolizing Robinson's skill as a hitter, fielder, and, especially, baserunner. The message from Robinson to his youthful readers is one of promoting good citizenship. The inside front cover included a signed letter from the player urging children to join an organized baseball team. "Keep yourself in fine physical trim," Robinson urged. "Don't smoke and don't touch alcoholic liquors."

The inside back cover included an autographed, full-page photograph of the player after taking a practice hack. The back cover got into the nitty-gritty of selling mail-order merchandise with an image of the player with a message balloon reading, "C'mon, kids! These items are a hit with all my fans!" The player is depicted wearing a Jackie Robinson cap ($1) and a Jackie Robinson T-shirt ($1). Cotton sweatshirts were also available for $1.75, while a 27½-inch girl's scarf cost $1. The mailing address for orders was in Woodmere, a hamlet on Long Island, about 16 miles east of Ebbets Field in Brooklyn.

While there was limited news coverage of the release of the comic book, its origins can be traced to Robinson's desire to make an income in the offseason. He had led Jackie Robinson's All-Stars, a barnstorming team, but there was a financial risk in backing a traveling team, while being on the road kept him even longer from his wife and son, who was born five months before his father made his major-league debut.

In 1949, Robinson was hired as a floor salesman by Sunset Appliance Stores, a company with a storefront in Queens about to open a second location in Times Square. Robinson's first day on the job came at the new store on the evening of October 8, when he was assigned to greet admirers and well-wishers. Incredibly, he had gone 1-for-3 with a run scored and a run batted-in that afternoon as the Dodgers lost Game Four of the World Series to the New York Yankees by 6-4. (The second baseman also helped complete an oddball, 5-2-4 double play in the first inning.) The afternoon following his debut at the appliance store, Robinson was once again on the field at Ebbets Field, going 1-for-3 with a single and an RBI sacrifice fly as the Yankees won the championship with a convincing 10-6 victory.

Robinson's offseason professional life changed with a visit to the penthouse offices of Kagran Corp. at W. 58th St. and Fifth Avenue in Manhattan's Theatre District. He met with company president Martin Stone, a lawyer four years older than the ball player. Stone had clerked for U. S. Supreme Court Justice Benjamin Cardozo and had served as an unofficial adviser to President Harry Truman, yet he would find success in broadcasting as an agent, producer, and licensor.

Stone and a friend had started a radio program called *Author Meets the Critics* on a station in Albany, New York. The concept, though highbrow, was simple. Two reviewers would evaluate a bestseller before being joined by the author for unscripted conversation. After serving in the Navy during the war, Stone decided to go into show business as an entertainment lawyer. He brought his radio program to television, the growing media he correctly figured was soon to dominate the landscape.

Stone was agent for Bob Smith, the host of a children's radio program on WEAF in New York. Smith's trademark greeting was a bumpkin's hearty, "Oh, ho, ho, howdy doody." Stone wanted him to bring the program to television. *Puppet Playhouse* debuted on WNBT, part of the NBC network, just after Christmas in 1947. A year later, the renamed *Howdy Doody Show* was a marketing juggernaut, as some 95 products, with many more to come, had been officially licensed.

The actor Gabby Hayes, known as a sidekick in B-movie westerns, appeared on *Howdy Doody* and joined Stone's stable. One of the first of his many licensing deals was to lend his name to a regular comic book issued by Fawcett Publications. The ball player arrived in Stone's penthouse office at an opportune time. The lawyer's recent experience placed him in a position to exploit a lucrative marketing campaign aimed at children and adults.

"For five months, I worked at untangling a lot of Jackie's previous contracts — he's entirely too trusting a guy," Stone later told Tex McCrary and Jinx Falkenburg, a popular husband-wife team who hosted radio and television programs, as well as writing a column for the New York *Herald-Tribune*. "Then we brought out a book on his life, and negotiated a movie based on his life. Once the ball was rolling, we broke with full-page ads of Jackie Robinson dolls, T-shirts, comic books, etc. — about thirty franchises. Then I turned to WNBC again and worked out a Saturday morning radio show with Jackie. He's pretty happy about the whole thing — this way he has a chance to see his wife and boy during the offseason.

"The best proof, I guess, of the success of the merchandising of Jackie's name came when another ballplayer came in here and said, 'Hello, Marty, I'm Pee Wee Reese. Is there anything you can do with me?'"[3]

Stone's merchandising and licensing operations expanded to include such athletes as figure skater Sonja Henie, as well as the comedian Jackie Gleason and the television show *Lassie*. By the end of the 1950s, Stone estimated he had arranged about $500 million in licensing agreements.

He continued to serve as Robinson's attorney for the player's lifetime, notably arranging his hiring as an executive by the Chock full o' Nuts chain of coffee shops and sudden retirement from baseball. The decision was revealed in a *Look* magazine article, the news of which leaked on January 7, 1957, an exclusive for which the publication paid $50,000, more than any salary the athlete had ever made in a season. The Stone and Robinson families remained close for more than two decades, and Rachel Robinson attended Stone's funeral when he died in 1998, aged 83.

At the heart of the marketing campaign devised by Stone for his baseball client was the production of *The Jackie Robinson Story*, a Hollywood biopic written by Lawrence Taylor and Arthur Mann, the latter Robinson's official biographer. The ball player portrayed himself, while Ruby Dee played Rachel. It was filmed in California before the start of spring training in 1950 and released in May.

As a minor part of a larger strategy, the one-time comic magazine issue was likely not given much thought. The comic magazine was produced by Fawcett Publications of Greenwich, Connecticut, an independent newsstand distributor which also issued such popular magazines as *True*, *True Confessions*, and *Woman's Day*, as well as a line of pocket-book originals under the Gold Medal Book label. The publisher also produced a run of comic books and was best known for introducing Captain Marvel in *Whiz Comics #2*, released in 1940.

Jackie Robinson: Baseball Hero hit newsstands on September 23, 1949. The uncredited artwork was the responsibility of frequent Fawcett contributors Clem Weisbecker (pencils) and John Jordan (inks), whose work has been identified by experts in Golden Age comics. The script was the responsibility of baseball writer Charles Dexter.

The comic book's storyline was likely borrowed from Robinson's *Jackie Robinson: My Own Story*, released by the Greenberg publishing house in 1948. The as-told-to book was written by Wendell Smith, sports editor of the Pittsburgh *Courier*, who roomed with Robinson on the road in 1946 and 1947.

Either ignored or unknown by the publisher, let alone Robinson and his lawyer-agent, was Dexter's background, which could have proved embarrassing and potentially devastating for Robinson's financial and political future had it been revealed at an inopportune time.

Dexter was one of several pennames used by the writer, who had been a baseball reporter for the *Daily Worker*, a newspaper published by the Communist Party USA.

Dexter was born as Lewis Freiberg Levenson in 1895 in Rochester, New York, where his Russian immigrant father was a barber before opening a hair salon. Lew Levenson graduated from the Pulitzer School of Journalism at Columbia University before serving as a French translator with the rank of sergeant in the U.S. Army overseas during the First World War. After the war, he married Leola Brummer and worked as a movie and theatre press agent and wrote a few stage plays himself. Feature articles under his byline appeared in mainstream publications such as *McCall's*, the *New York Times*, the *New York World*, the *New York Herald-Tribune*, and the *Washington Post*.

In 1932, he was lured to the West Coast to work for Columbia Pictures. After losing his Hollywood job two years later, Levenson helped organize beet workers in the state's Imperial Valley, a time during which he likely became a Communist. He wrote an article for *The Nation* magazine describing dozens of incidents in which Latino labourers had been beaten by police and organized vigilantes during anti-Red raids. He also published *Butterfly Man: The Untold Story of a Strange Love*, a homophobic novel about a high-school athlete who succumbs to alcoholism after indulging in sexual decadence.

A page from one of the stories in *Jackie Robinson* comics, this one highlighting an August 1947 steal of home.

Back in New York by 1936, Levenson was hired by the *Daily Worker*, where he wrote reviews and arts features under his own name as well as such pseudonyms as "Annette Castle" and "Benjamin Cordozo." As a sports reporter, he wrote under the names "Scorer" and "Charles Dexter."

His identity as a Communist became newspaper fodder when he was hired as a publicist for the Federal Writers' Project as part of the New Deal's Works Progress Administration. His hiring was criticized by conservative dailies, notably the *Chicago Tribune*, as well as by the Republican Party. One typical headline in an Indiana newspaper read: "WPA Writers' project called hotbed of Reds."[4]

He hid out in New Hampshire until the controversy simmered down, emerging to abandon the name Levenson in favor of Dexter. He covered the 1940 World Series between the Detroit Tigers and Cincinnati Reds as a *Daily Worker* correspondent. The following season, he was said to be the only one among nearly 300 members of the Baseball Writers' Association of America to have correctly predicted the Yankees winning the American League and the St. Louis Cardinals, Dodgers, and Reds finishing in that order in the National League.

In 1948, Dexter was subject to a strange indignity while covering a game at Yankee Stadium. During a rain delay in the fifth inning, a U.S. Treasury Department agent arrested and handcuffed him in the press box before taking him to a precinct in The Bronx. The writer was released without charge and returned to catch the end of the game in what he described as a case of mistaken identity.

Dexter contributed articles to the Dodgers' yearbooks in 1941 and 1942, as well as selling articles about baseball to *Collier's*, *Baseball Digest*, and the *Saturday Evening Post*. He was, as Jerome Holtzman of the *Chicago Tribune* described him in 1997 column, a "a wonderfully qualified baseball writer."[5]

So, the business arrangement made sense. As well, the *Daily Worker* had been outspoken for more than a decade in promoting the integration of professional baseball. Even as Dexter was completing the comic book's script, Robinson was called to testify before the House Un-American Activities Committee (HUAC) on July 18, 1949, a week after the All-Star Game. Segregationists on the committee believed the civil rights movement was dominated by Communists and they sought Robinson's testimony as a rebuke to statements made overseas by the great actor and athlete Paul Robeson. In Paris, Robeson made an anti-war statement regarded by much of the American press as traitorous.

Robinson's testimony was widely praised, especially by White editorialists working for major daily newspapers. How different the reaction might have been had the committee asked about his business arrangements with a *Daily Worker* correspondent writing under a pseudonym.

The success of the first comic book led Fawcett to announce the title would appear as a regular bimonthly publication. Five more Jackie Robinson comics were issued, the final one appearing in 1952. *Jackie Robinson #2* included articles in comic form on the 1947 World Series, Wilbert Robinson as a "Dodgers of Yesteryear," a Robinson steal of home on August 29, 1947, his track career, and a two-page printed article about hitting technique without illustrations written by Dexter. Each issue was printed in the "hundreds of thousands," according to promotional materials.

In 1950, Fawcett also released biographical comic books written by Dexter featuring Dodgers teammates Campanella and Don Newcombe. One of the more remarkable historical notes of these eight comic books was that these baseball titles featuring African American players were published only two years after what is regarded as the first known comic magazine written and drawn by African Americans. *All-Negro Comics*, founded by the journalist Orrin Cromwell Evans and issued in July 1947, lasted only one issue, as he was unable to find a wholesaler willing to sell him newsprint for a second issue.

Earlier in the year in March, the Parents' Magazine Institute released *Negro Heroes #1* featuring stories about Harriet Tubman and George Washington Carver. The next issue, released in 1948, featured Jackie Robinson on the cover.

Dexter and Robinson also collaborated on Robinson's 1964 nonfiction book, *Baseball Has Done It*, in which he addresses baseball's integration by interviewing other baseball players. Dexter is credited as editor of the publication, which included oral histories from Campanella, Newcombe, Henry Aaron, Monte Irvin, and Larry Doby, as well as some White southern players such as Alvin Dark.

The final panel of *Jackie Robinson: Baseball Hero #6* features the player directly addressing the reader. He says: "There's only one way to play the game, fellows! Play hard, play clean, play to win until the last man is out!"

Bibliography

Rampersad, Arnold. *Jackie Robinson: A Biography* (New York: Ballantine Books, 1997).

Robinson Jackie, as told to Wendell Smith. *Jackie Robinson: My Own Story* (New York: Greenberg, 1948).

Robinson, Jackie, ed. by Charles Dexter. *Baseball Has Done It* (Philadelphia and New York: J.B. Lippincott Company, 1964).

Tygiel, Jules. *Baseball's Great Experiment: Jackie Robinson and his Legacy* (New York: Oxford University Press, 2008).

The six Jackie Robinson comic books issued by Fawcett can be read online here: https://comicbookplus.com/?cid=2885

Notes

1   *Jackie Robinson: Baseball Hero* (Greenwich, Connecticut: Fawcett Publications, [undated]). https://comicbookplus.com/?dlid=67936

2   Cathy Keen, "Jackie Robinson: Comic Book Hero," https://americanhistory.si.edu/blog/2013/06/jackie-robinson-comic-book-hero-42.html

3   Tex McCrary and Jinx Falkenburg, "TV showman plays to age groups." *Green Bay Press-Gazette* (Green Bay, Wisconsin), July 30, 1951.

4   "WPA writers project called hotbed of Reds," *Times* (Munster, Indiana), November 2, 1936.

5   Jerome Holtzman, "Cooperstown vote highly imperfect," *Chicago Tribune*, January 7, 1997: B6.

Jackie Robinson's Radio Shots

By Ralph Carhart

One of the more impressive aspects of his trailblazing life is that Jackie Robinson had a wide and varied interest in the world, and his career reflected that. As early as college, when he became a four-letter athlete, Robinson would not be pigeon-holed into one path. The all-encompassing nature of his talents could certainly be seen in his time on the diamond, when he could beat you with his bat, legs, and glove, but it was most starkly on display in his post-playing career. In the years after he left the Dodgers, he was a businessman, a philanthropist, and an activist—all in different fields, from coffee, to construction, to politics.

He also maintained an intermittent career in the media. He broke racial ground again in 1965 when he became the first Black member of a national network broadcast team on ABC's *Major League Baseball Game of the Week*. Yet, even before he regularly appeared in a television booth, he had a brief career as a radio host. Beginning in 1960, he sat behind the desk for a series of interviews produced by RCA for national syndication, called *Jackie Robinson's Radio Shots*. Roughly 90 episodes of this program survive, and a look at the roster of guests gives a keen insight into the eclectic nature of Robinson's interests. There are certainly interviews with some of baseball's more interesting names (more on them later), but this series of programs, most clocking in somewhere between two-and-a-half and three minutes in length, goes far beyond the diamond.

The athletic world is well-represented, including watersports. Professional fisherman Moe Hoffman appeared on the program three times. They spoke of the rising popularity of the sport, particularly amongst women and families, how a novice could get started and, of course, swapped stories about "the big one." Robinson also devoted two episodes to water-skier and boating expert Tom Dorwin who, along

with his sister Janie, was a hall of famer in his sport.[1] Today, the Tommy Dorwin Award is given annually to the outstanding judge at the national waterskiing championships.

There were also three episodes devoted to swimming, each with a different guest. These were particularly notable because two of those episodes featured women, whose athletic feats were often ignored by the press of the time. Greta Andersen, two-time Olympic medal recipient in 1948, spoke with Robinson about the training regimen for one of her upcoming crossings of the English Channel, a feat she ultimately accomplished six times. Robinson also spoke to legendary Olympian Alice Landon, who swam the Long Island Sound as a 13-year-old girl (in 1915!) before embarking on a hall of fame[2] career in the water.

Horse racing was of particular interest to Robinson, serving as the subject of 13 surviving episodes of the program, second only to baseball. As with the rest of his life, Robinson's interest in the Sport of Kings was not limited in scope. He dedicated episodes to a notable breeder (Noel Simpson), official (Jimmy Kilroe), trainer (Sasha Werner), announcer (Fred Capossela), and, of course, jockeys. He featured harness jockey Morris McDonald, as well as Ted Atkinson who, in 1957, became the first active jockey to be elected into the Racing Hall of Fame. Atkinson made multiple appearances on the show. Warren Mehrtens, who won the triple crown in 1946 (only the seventh jockey to accomplish the feat at that point in history), spoke with Robinson about the single-minded focus of most jockeys and how, for him, retirement offered the opportunity to pursue his other interests, a mindset that Robinson could certainly appreciate.

Robinson talked to experts on more esoteric pastimes, including bodybuilding, shooting, and wrestling. Mr. Universe champion Bruce Randall regaled Robinson with the story of how he went from 400 to 185 pounds in just eight months in his journey to become the strongest man on earth. Fred Ruff, president of Colt's Manufacturing Company, spoke of the varieties of guns that were used in American hunting, as well as the types of game that were popular targets. Robinson took the opportunity to approach the then-less controversial subject of the need for firearm training to cut down on accidents, a point Ruff agreed with (though he wouldn't go so far as to concede to a national skills test). Professional wrestler and actor Mike Mazurki (a two-time guest) dispensed with the myth that the sport was "fake," though he did discuss how it had evolved from "real" wrestling to its popular form, filled with "color" and "showmanship."

Mainstream sports, like boxing and golf, were given plenty of airtime. Tommy Armour, who won 25 PGA tournaments in the 1920s and 30s, appeared on three programs. Armour, who is credited with coining the term the "yips," after he was suddenly struck with an inability to make short putts, offered advice to parents of young golfers, reminisced about his childhood in Scotland, and explained why he believed golf is "a thinking man's game." Robinson kindly avoided the subject of Armour's record-breaking 18-over-par implosion at the 1927 Shawnee Open.

Boxer Ralph "Tiger" Jones appeared on the program twice. Jones shocked the boxing world when he defeated heavily-favored Sugar Ray Robinson in 1955, only the fourth time that had happened in Robinson's career, against 133 victories. Jones used his airtime to tease his defeated foe about the fact that despite Jones's urging, Sugar Ray Robinson refused to meet him in the ring for a rematch. When interviewing Chico Vejar (who also lost to Jones in 1957), Robinson steered the conversation to the state of boxing. Vejar expounded on Robinson's question by calling the period the "lowest ebb" in the sport's history, blaming bad publicity and a lack of quality fighters.

Robinson leapt off the starting point of his conversation with Vejar by dedicating an entire episode to an editorial, something he did four times over the course of *Radio Shots*. In that program, absent of the typical interview guest, Robinson offered the opinion that a national boxing commissioner, who could implement and enforce rules that would prevent the throwing of bouts and protect the fighters, would go a long way towards restoring public trust in the sport. He also offered his uninterrupted thoughts on creating a national lottery (a concept he favored, with the prescient idea of directing the funds to schools), the art of stealing home (with in-depth insights of his steal in Game One of the 1955 World Series), and on overcoming handicaps.

Ever-conscious of giving voice to society's underdogs, Robinson invited Junius Kellogg on the show. Kellogg helped expose the infamous CCNY collegiate basketball point-shaving scandal before joining the Harlem Globetrotters. He appeared on the program to discuss the Pan American wheelchair basketball team. Less than a year after joining the Globetrotters, Kellogg was in an automobile accident that damaged his spinal cord and left him paralyzed. He adapted to his injuries and became the coach of a basketball team, sponsored by Pan American Airlines, made up of youths that had all suffered paralyzing injuries as children. Kellogg called his charges the "most competitive" athletes he had ever seen.

Some of the program's most interesting conversations took place with people who worked behind the scenes in the world of sports, in the fields of production and sportswriting. Television producer Ted Raynor appeared on the program three times. Raynor dispelled the myth that the airing of sports on television was hurtful to a professional team's financial bottom line, instead arguing that the benefits of an increased media presence far outweighed lost ticket sales. A pioneer in the world of bowling, Raynor also made certain to highlight how his programming brought more women into that sport than ever.

Legendary sportscaster Bill Stern appeared on the program to give advice to aspiring announcers. He also related some of his most memorable experiences in sport, including his most favorite, the 1939 Rose Bowl, when underdog Southern Cal overcame undefeated Duke 7-3, with a touchdown in the closing seconds. Dick Young, winner of the BBWAA Career Excellence Award in 1978, and a vocal advocate of Robinson's when he integrated the Dodgers, had a frank conversation with his host about the personality conflicts that can sometimes separate professional athletes and the writers who cover them.

Robinson also looked outside of the world of sports for subject matter. He frequently spoke with entertainers, including songwriter Gordon Jenkins, whose music was sung by the likes of Frank Sinatra,

Louis Armstrong, Billie Holiday, and Johnny Cash. Superstar singer Johnny Mathis appeared on the program to discuss his large family and his collegiate athletic skills, including his connection to fellow high-jumper (and future NBA Hall of Famer) Bill Russell. One of the most adorable episodes in the whole *Radio Shots* series was when Robinson interviewed young star Paul O'Keefe, who took over the role of Winthrop Paroo in Broadway's *The Music Man*, the part that would be played by Ron Howard in the film version. In his high-pitched voice, O'Keefe delighted Robinson as he spoke of his love for boats and his desire to leave acting to play football when he grew up.

Impresario, and former sportswriter, Ed Sullivan appeared on the program in an interesting role reversal. Despite having been friends since Robinson's earliest days on the Dodgers, the two had never sat down for a formal interview. Even though Robinson was the host of the show, Sullivan instead chose to use the opportunity to ask Robinson a pair of questions he always wanted answered. Who was the toughest pitcher Robinson ever faced? Ewell Blackwell. Who was the greatest hitter he ever saw? Ted Williams. Robinson also took the time to remember an early article of Sullivan's in which he asked fans to set their prejudices aside and appreciate the wonder that was Robinson, the multi-talented ballplayer.

Predictably, it was baseball that saw the most airtime on the program, with 16 of the surviving episodes dedicated to the sport that made Robinson a legend. "The Clown Prince of Baseball," Al Schacht, appeared on the show three times, where he launched into some of the routines that made him famous even after his days as a player and coach were over. Don Drysdale, who had played besides Robinson during the latter's final season in

A natural on the radio, Robinson spent a fair amount of time behind the microphone.
photo by NBCU Photo Bank/NBCUniversal via Getty Images

Brooklyn, discussed the unexpected success of the 1959 Dodgers squad. Monte Irvin lamented with Robinson over the years he lost to segregation, which kept him from joining the New York Giants until 1949, when he was 31 years old. In a minor slight to his former teammate, Robinson took the opportunity to tell Irvin that he should have won the 1951 MVP Award instead of Roy Campanella.

Two of the most intriguing conversations from the world of baseball were with Branch Rickey and Satchel Paige, both of whom appeared on the program twice. At the time of their interview, Rickey was entrenched in his plan to start the Continental League, and he and Robinson discussed some of the ideas that would separate the doomed league from the current world of organized baseball. They also spoke of the hope that a third league would bring to the burgeoning world of Little League, and the additional employment opportunities it would present. Buried in Rickey's enthusiastic proselytizing for his league, these episodes are tinted with a warmth between the two old colleagues that is felt across the decades.

When talking with Paige, Robinson, who had already famously spoken of his dissatisfaction with his brief time in the Negro Leagues, recalled the grueling schedule of the league, including their shared season together on the 1945 Kansas City Monarchs. They also discussed Josh Gibson, who Robinson called "the greatest hitter baseball has produced," and the friendly rivalry that existed between the two Negro League greats. In his own words, Paige recalled the iconic tale of walking three batters on purpose, just so he could strike out Gibson with the bases loaded. Another entertaining anecdote from the interview included the story of the derivation of the nickname "Satchel." In this telling (the answer often varied), Paige claimed it was because as a child he always carried his baseball equipment with him in a bag, and if the other boys wouldn't let him play, he would leave and take all of the equipment home. Paige also advised Robinson on how to deal with stomach troubles. His miracle cure? Goat's milk.

There are dozens more guests who appeared on *Radio Shots*, including: Charles Start, the head of a program to coach amateur athletes; General Omar Bradley, the first Chairman of the Joint Chiefs of Staff and the architect of the Korean War; Ann Eastham, an entertainer who appeared at the Steel Pier in Atlantic City, where she rode a high-diving horse which leapt from a height of 75 feet to a tank of water below. Seemingly no subject was off the table for the polymathic Robinson. *Radio Shots* is a rarely discussed part of Robinson's legacy, but it offers an interesting glimpse into the curious mind of one of America's greatest heroes.

Author's Note

There are multiple ways to listen to Jackie Robinson's Radio Shots online, including purchasing them for your own collection. One site that has them available for streaming is Old Time Radio Downloads: https://www.oldtimeradiodownloads.com/sports/jackie-robinsons-radio-shots

Notes

1   Wisconsin Water Ski Federation Hall of Fame: https://www.waterski.org/hall-of-fame-inductees/dorwin-family

2   International Swimming Hall of Fame: https://www.ishof.org/honoree/?_sf_s=landon

The First
A Broadway Musical

By Luisa Lyons

"You know what would be a great musical? The story of Jackie Robinson." So said film critic Joel Siegel to writer Martin Charnin at a chance meeting at their business manager's midtown office in April, 1980.[1] Director and lyricist Charnin was an established theatre veteran whose biggest musical success was *Annie,* which opened on Broadway in 1977 and went on to become a world-wide sensation. Siegel was a well-known writer and film critic, who later became the long-running entertainment editor for ABC's *Good Morning America.*

Charnin and Siegel immediately got to work writing *The First.* Charnin's long-time assistant Janice Steele recalled that the Charnin and Siegel met each day to write, and the script came together very quickly.[2] Charnin brought on young composer Bob Brush to write music for the show. Brush had written a musical adaptation of E.B. White's *Charlotte's Web,* but was unable to acquire the rights. Charnin heard the score, and tried to secure the rights on Brush's behalf, but was also unsuccessful, and instead suggested the pair work on another project.[3] When Charnin proposed the idea of *The First,* Brush was at first hesitant. He recounted saying to Charnin, "Wait a minute, you and I, and Joel Siegel are going to do a musical about Jackie Robinson? Three White guys from the burbs...?!" Charnin replied "It's going to be great." Despite his reservations, Brush recalled that he "was young and enthusiastic and wanted a Broadway musical, so off we went."[4] A young creative working on one of their first Broadway shows would be a recurring a theme on *The First.*

Charnin, Siegel, and Brush were not the first White creative team to take on a musical centered on Black or African-American characters and stories.[5] *The First* wasn't even the only musical of that description in the 1981-82 Broadway season, with *Dreamgirls* opening shortly after *The First* in December 1981.

Part of the team's enthusiasm in taking on the project was that they were all avid baseball fans. According to Janice Steele, Charnin had even participated in the Broadway Show League, playing softball in Central Park.[6] Additionally, Charnin felt that being Jewish, he somewhat understood what Jackie had endured and that in writing *The First,* he thought he could make a difference.[7]

In January 1981, the *New York Times* announced that Charnin, Siegel, and Brush had been at work on *The First.*[8] The musical was set to be produced by Michael Harvey and Peter A. Bobley in association with 20th Century Fox. Choreographer Peter Gennaro, costume designer Theoni V. Aldrege, and scenic designer David Mitchell were announced as part of the creative team.

While most Broadway musicals usually have a development period of several years, Charnin opted not to do any out-of-town try-outs and instead go straight to Broadway.[9] Due to a theatre shortage, *The First* was "on standby" for two theatres, the Lunt-Fontanne (which was home to the Black-led and surprise hit *Sophisticated Ladies,* a revue featuring the music of Duke Ellington) and the Martin Beck.[10]

The Martin Beck Theatre suddenly became available when *The Little Foxes* closed, and Broadway preparations went into full swing.[11] Rehearsals commenced in August 1981, and save for Charnin, Siegel, and Brush, a new creative team was in place. It is not entirely clear why a new team were hired, though Janice Steele recalled time conflicts came into play.[12] The new team included scenic designer David Chapman, costume designer Carrie Robbins, lighting designer Marc B. Weiss, sound designer Louis Shapiro, musical director Joyce Brown, musical supervisor and orchestrator Luther Henderson, and stage manager Peter Lawrence. Zev Bufman, Neil Bogart, and Roger Luby had also joined the producing team. Bufman had been a producer for just over two decades, and his credits included the Broadway revivals of *Peter Pan, Oklahoma!, West Side Story,* and *Brigadoon,* along with *Buck White* starring Muhammed Ali, and *The Little Foxes* starring Elizabeth Taylor.

Brown and Henderson were the only Black members of the creative team. According to stage manager Peter Lawrence, the team had initially approached Charlie Blackwell, a Black stage manager, to work on the show. For unknown reasons, Blackwell turned it down, though his son David Blackwell was brought on as second assistant stage manager.[13] Choreographer Alan Johnson hired an African-American associate, Edward M. Love Jr., a dancer who had appeared on Broadway in *Raisin, A Chorus Line,* and *Dancin',* in the touring company of *The Wiz,* and was later the choreographer on the film *Hairspray.*

A *New York Times* report from September 1981, specifically discusses dance rehearsals and the issue of White creatives telling a story about Black baseball players, but fails to mention Love's role or presence.

"In another room in the studio, meanwhile, Alan Johnson, the choreographer, was rehearsing the actors who were supposed to be the Kansas City Monarchs, the black baseball team. In fact, Mr. Johnson, who is white, was teaching the actors, who were in their 20's, how blacks were supposed to sing and dance in the 1940's."[14]

Henderson and Brown, along with Robbins, were the most experienced of the new team. Robbins and Henderson each had over 20 Broadway credits to their name, along with multiple awards or nominations.[15] Brown had been a conductor for the Alvin Ailey American Dance Theater company, a guest conductor with the Boston Philharmonic, conductor or assistant conductor on eight Broadway shows, and was the first female African-American musical director on a Broadway musical, *Purlie,* from its opening night.[16] Minus those exceptions, Charnin had surrounded himself with a young and inexperienced creative team, and though many went on to illustrious careers on Broadway or in Hollywood, at the time of *The First* some of those creatives felt

The First star David Alan Grier, as Robinson, along with costar David Huddleston (Branch Rickey). photo courtesy of David Chapman

unable to express concerns about the problems posed by predominately White artists telling Jackie Robinson's story.[17]

With a creative team in place, the next step was to cast the show. Early in development, the team had reportedly tried to bring on Michael Jackson to play Robinson, but Jackson was "unfortunately... unaffordable."[18] The team conducted hundreds of auditions over two five-week sessions to find their leading man and chose David Alan Grier, fresh out of Yale Drama School, and reportedly the first person to audition for the role.[19]

Lonette McKee was cast as Rachel Robinson and Darren McGavin as Branch Rickey. The other cast members included Bill Buell, Trey Wilson, Ray Gill, Sam Stoneburger, Thomas Griffith, Paul Forrest, Steven Bland, Luther Fontaine, Michael Edward-Stevens, Rodney Saulsberry, Clent Bowers, Paul Cook Tartt, Steven Boockvor, Court Miller, D. Peter Samuel, Bob Morrisey, Jack Hallett, Thomas Griffith, Bonciella Lewis, Janet Hubert, Kim Criswell, Margaret Lamee, and Stephen Crain.

By the start of rehearsals in August, Rachel Robinson, Jackie's widow, had also been brought on as a consultant. Mrs. Robinson, as she preferred to be called,[20] was initially skeptical of a musical about her husband — "I thought it was ridiculous... I called my lawyer about it. Could you imagine Jack singing and dancing on Broadway?"[21] Charnin reportedly won Mrs. Robinson over by explaining that musicals "didn't have to be *No, No, Nanette*, and could depict the socially significant."[22] David Alan Grier later recalled that Mrs. Robinson gave her blessing after watching a run through of the show, and witnessing Charnin's and Siegel's love for the Dodgers.[23]

According to the actors and creatives interviewed for this chapter, Rachel Robinson was an inspired presence in the rehearsal room. Across all interviews, Mrs. Robinson was spoken of with great reverence and awe. She was described as "lovely, very supportive,"[24] "steady, gorgeous, single-mindedly protective of Jackie Robinson,"[25] "classy, so cool, a benevolent presence."[26]

Rachel Robinson also gave David Alan Grier access to the Robinson family scrapbooks. The books were enormous, two feet by three feet, and chronicled Robinson's career all the way to his retirement. They are loosely referenced in the musical — when Robinson boards a New York bound train to meet with Branch Rickey, Rachel tells him, "If your meeting with Mr. Rickey makes the papers, send me the clipping."[27]

Rachel Robinson was used to give gravitas to the project in press leading up to the show's opening. The *New York Times* quoted Robinson as stating, "They really worked hard to get it authentic... I think there has been a great effort to get the facts straight, to give it an air of authenticity."[28]

Another real-life character brought on was Dodgers announcer Red Barber, who provided voice overs for the final scenes, and also did television commercials for the musical.[29] Stage manager Peter Lawrence recounted one performance where the voice over track wouldn't play, and he switched on the god mic and did the voice overs himself, much to the consternation of Martin Charnin who was watching from the back of the house.[30]

The rehearsal period lasted six weeks. According to all interviewees, the topic of race, or the fact that a predominantly White creative team was telling the story of a Black man, were not directly addressed in rehearsals. According to Janice Steele, during the dress rehearsal, a scene featuring Black cast members in zoot suits caused consternation amongst the actors. They went to Steele, and she arranged for the costumes to be cut.[31] Rehearsals for difficult scenes between David Alan Grier and Casey Higgins were limited to the two actors and the creative team, but these seem to be the only accommodation for addressing racially-sensitive topics.

Peter Lawrence described Charnin as "the godfather of the show," but noted how he receded during its development and lost faith in the book.[32] Both Lawrence and composer Bob Brush spoke to the fact that Charnin was not collaborative throughout the development or rehearsal process,[33] though David Chapman "adored working with him" and felt there was a "free flow of ideas."[34]

One such idea Chapman had was to open the show with actor Kim Criswell, dressed as Kate Smith, standing on a small platform that would ascend above the stage while she sang "God Bless America." Charnin rejected the idea, though the show did open with the players, umpires, and coaches singing the final two lines of "Star Spangled Banner." It is ironic that almost 40 years later, Kate Smith's recordings were taken out of rotation by the Yankees and Philadelphia Flyers due to the discovery that she had recorded songs that contained racist lyrics in the 1930s.[35]

On October 19, 1981, a year and a half from its initial conception, *The First* began previews at the Martin Beck Theatre (now the Al Hirschfeld Theatre). The run was immediately beset with problems. Darren McGavin, playing the pivotal role of Branch Rickey, left the production. Sources differ as to whether he was fired, or resigned by choice. The *New York Times* reported that McGavin had resigned due to a "reduction in Rickey's material."[36] However, Peter Lawrence recalled Charnin asked McGavin to leave due to "trouble with lines,"[37] and Lawrence and Janice Steele both corroborated that McGavin didn't portray Branch Rickey as the writers saw him.[38] Lawrence also recounted that Charnin desired to make Branch Rickey more approachable and that McGavin pushed back, causing tensions to arise.[39] Replacing McGavin delayed the show's opening by five days.[40]

In early drafts of the script, and into previews, the show was framed by "bar scenes" featuring three Brooklyn fans. The fans served not only as comic relief, but in Lawrence's view, also provided a wider view of the cultural perspective of 1947 by acting as social commentators.[41] Criswell and Lawrence both remembered the scenes fondly, feeling that they contained some of the heart and humor of the show.[42] David Chapman meanwhile felt the scenes didn't land, as they required the viewer to be intimately acquainted with the Dodgers to understand the subtleties.[43] The bar scenes were cut by opening night, with more focus placed onto Branch Rickey, and the story of his "racial heroism" in bringing Robinson onto the team.[44]

In the orchestra pit, musical director Brown also left the show. Mark Hummel, who had been the rehearsal pianist, and was the keyboard player in the pit, was asked to replace her. According to Hummel, Brown was let go as she was "not capable" for the role and made kissy sounds from the pit to get the actors' attention which were being picked up by the floor mics.[45] Janice Steele also recalled of Brown, "although wonderful, [she] had problems remembering things at that time. She was older and having issues keeping up."[46] *The First* was Brown's final Broadway show.

During previews, the creative team had sensed they had not done enough to court a Black audience.[47] As had been done with *Purlie* a decade earlier,[48] a consultant was retained to help bring in the African-American community.[49] Entrepreneur and innovator Gene Faison was the creator of *The Black Shopper's Guide for Better Living*, which included music and

lifestyle coupons, and was marketed to a network of over 3,000 churches around the US. Faison had reached out to the Producers Association for Theatre seeking deals for the magazine, and was connected with Steele, Charnin's assistant.[50] Unfortunately, the show closed before word could get out. Faison recounted in his interview that there had been no integration in other formats that could have been used to promote the show.[51] He also felt that while the show was successful in portraying the legend of Jackie Robinson, it failed to adequately touch on the Black or African-American experience.[52]

The First officially opened on November 17, 1981, and, despite the setbacks, the creative team felt that the show was in good shape.[53] Upon walking into the theatre, the audience saw a show curtain made to look like a real-life scoreboard. According to designer David Chapman, the curtain was so heavy the walls of the Martin Beck Theatre had to be reinforced.[54]

The opening night crowd, which included baseball luminaries Leo Durocher, Duke Snider, Larry Doby, Ralph Branca, sports writer Dick Young, and Rachel Robinson, was reportedly enthusiastic.[55] The official reviews were yet to come in. David Alan Grier recalled briefly leaving the opening night party with some friends, and returned to be refused entry by the bouncer. Furious, Grier's friends attempted to tell the bouncer that Grier was the lead of the show being celebrated inside. The bouncer replied, "I've seen your notices. You don't have a show."[56]

The notices were indeed dismal. Frank Rich, in the all-important *New York Times* review, stated "While this show offers about five minutes of good baseball and a promising star in David Alan Grier, its back is broken by music, lyrics, book and direction that are the last word in dull."[57] Douglas Watt, writing for *Daily News* stated the show "never gets to first base... and it really has nothing more to tell us than what is implicit in the title, that Robinson broke the racial barrier in major league baseball...."[58] In a review for the *Journal News*, Jay Sharbutt opined the musical "has about as much passion, fire and complexity as your average TV movie, maybe less."[59] *Daily News* sportswriter Dick Young criticized the show for its lack of historical accuracy in how Dodgers' fans treated Robinson, and in its depiction of jealous Dodger wives.[60]

Actor Kim Criswell felt that some of the negativity in the reviews was directed at Joel Siegel because he had dared cross the line from being a critic to being

Scenic elevation of the Ebbets Field set, by designer David Chapman. image courtesy of the artist

a creative.[61] Despite McGavin reportedly leaving the show due a reduction in Branch Rickey's role, several commentators also noted that Branch Rickey, instead of Robinson, appeared to be the star of the show.[62]

In Robinson's first solo, and fourth number of the show, "The First," he shares in a plaintive "I want" ballad, about longing to participate in the world as a child, but being told by his momma that climbing, swimming, and playing are all only "for the white man."[63] Throughout the script, Robinson only ever talks about wanting to play baseball, not being allowed to play baseball, and how the color of his skin has caused difficulty- "...I'm some kind of sideshow freak. I just want to be another ballplayer."[64]

Being limited by skin color is also explored in the show's second song, "The National Pastime," a satirical doo-wop number sung by the Black players of the Kansas City Monarchs when Sukeforth asks Robinson to meet with Branch Rickey in New York. The number contains the line "this year's n__", about all-White teams using Black players for show, but not actually signing them as full-time players. Composer Brush attempted to make the music as over the top as possible, to make it come across as a joke.[65] David Alan Grier described the song as "amazing," a "delicate mix" of the vernacular of the day, and the

feelings of other Black players when Robinson was promoted to the major league. David Chapman felt that the song "hit the audience between the eyes," and that they weren't quite sure how to respond to hearing the n-word being sung on stage.[66]

Casey Higgins, Hatrack Harris, Swanee Rivers, fictional amalgams of several real-life players who are portrayed as not-too-smart bigots, later repeat n__ multiple times in the song "It Ain't Gonna Work" — "It ain't gonna work/ Don't care how good we get/ No n__'s worth the sweat...."[67]

Act one closes with a scene reminiscent of the opening, culminating with crowds at the stadium repeatedly yelling "Jungle bunny! Jigaboo!" at Robinson. An angry fan yells, "Get the n__ off the field!" and a watermelon is thrown at Robinson's feet. In rehearsals, the item thrown was a prop black cat, but was switched to a watermelon to look better on stage.[68] The portrayal of poor treatment of Robinson by Dodgers fans was contested by Dick Young, who stated "It is scandalously slanderous to the good people of Brooklyn. It is my memory that 99% of The Flatbush Faithful rooted for Jackie Robinson...They supported him, admired him, and were ready to fight for him."[69]

Bob Brush recalled that during the writing process, there was pressure to make Jackie Robinson likable, rather than the "brave and fierce competitor that he was."[70] Brush felt that perhaps Broadway wasn't ready for the harder story in 1981, and wondered if anyone else apart from Charnin could have even gotten the story to stage at that time. Brush noted "People thought, this is the guy who wrote *Annie*, it's going to be safe. He's not going to tell us things we don't want to hear."[71] Whilst Charnin had insisted that musicals didn't have to be *No, No, Nanette,* he shied from portraying the gritty realness of Robinson's story.

Five years earlier in 1976, Leonard Bernstein and Alan Jay Lerner tried to save their problematic *1600 Pennsylvania Avenue,* a musical that told the story of a present-day theatre group rehearsing a play about the history of the Presidents' Black serving staff, by hiring a Black production team, Gilbert Moses and George Faison.[72] As historian Allen Woll noted about *1600 Pennsylvania Ave*, "a white vision was… out of place in the context of the 1970s." Although the restructure didn't save the Bernstein and Lerner musical, *The First* could have also used more creative input from Black artists.

Black artists such as Langston Hughes, Vinnette Carroll, and Clarence Jackson, had been creating musicals in the 1960s and 1970s that boldly focused on societal issues and Black stories.[73] Musicals with Black creative teams such as *Don't Bother Me I Can't Cope* (1972), *Your Arms too Short to Box with God* (1974), *Purlie* (1970), and *The Wiz* (1975) were all hits, and had contributed to the growth of a Black audience on Broadway.[74] The other White-driven Black musical of the 1981-2 season, *Dreamgirls,* had far greater success than *The First,* and this can possibly be attributed to the fact that the Black cast members had made significant contributions to the show's script and development.[75]

Despite the lack of love from the critics, *The First* was nominated for several awards, including the 1982 Tony Awards for Best Book of a Musical (Charnin and Siegel), Best Featured Actor in a Musical (Grier), and Best Direction of a Musical (Charnin); and the 1982 Drama Desk Awards for Outstanding Featured Actress in a Musical (McKee) and Outstanding Set Design (Chapman). Grier won the Theatre World Award.

After 33 previews, and 31 performances *The First* closed on Broadway. It had been scheduled to make a cast recording the day after opening night, but the recording was canceled following the poor notices.[76]

The musical was not recorded for the New York Public Library's Theatre on Film and Tape Archive, and has not been revived since.

Despite its lack of success, the cast and creative team deeply believed in *The First*. The production was an incredibly special and impactful one for the performers and creatives who worked on it. According to Janice Steele, there was a belief that *The First* "was so much bigger" than just a musical, that they were going to change the world with the show.[77] Similarly, David Chapman felt that there was an "unspoken belief" that "the show was for freedom and the American way."[78] David Alan Grier noted that despite the show only accounting for a few months of his life, "it felt like an entire year," and "life had been perfect for those few months." On closing night, Grier walked through the stage door to be greeted by "stage hands, the cast, publicist, costumers, maintenance crew, all who enveloped me in this hug. It was so healing." Grier also noted that he still has his costume.[79]

For some of the White creatives and cast members, the show was a wake-up call to the realities of racial prejudice that still existed in America.[80] Steele noted that *The First* changed her life entirely, that she became more vocal about challenging racism as a result of what she learned.[81] Chapman recalled that *The First* was one of his favorite theatrical projects. He stated it was the first time he was able to "work in abstractions, rather than realism," and he enjoyed the challenge of creating multiple settings, Ebbets Field, locker rooms, Branch Rickey's office, Union Station, and a farmhouse outside St. Louis, and employing a dynamic design that would not leave the audience waiting for long set changes.[82]

Ultimately, *The First* did not make the great musical Siegel had hoped for. Despite the presence of Rachel Robinson, the predominantly White creative team were not able to capture Jackie Robinson's story beyond the surface level ideas that he was Black and the first African-American in the major leagues. Given that Charnin and Siegel have both passed away, and the strong reawakened movement for Black stories told by Black creatives, it is unlikely *The First* will be revived.

Notes

1   Carol Lawson, "BROADWAY; Jackie Robinson story returning as 'The First.' a musical," *New York Times*, January 16, 1981: 2.

2   Janice Steele, telephone interview, October 12, 2021.

3   Bob Brush, telephone interview, September 24, 2021.

4   Brush interview.

5   Allen Woll, *Black Musical Theatre: From Coontown to Dreamgirls* (Baton Rouge and London: Louisiana State University Press, 1989), 267.

6   Janice Steele, telephone interview, October 12, 2021.

7   Steele interview.

8   Lawson.

9   Peter Lawrence, telephone interview, October 20, 2021; Steele interview.

10   Liz Smith, "Moving, shaking, and tucking in," *Daily News* (New York), March 15, 1981: 8.

11   Lawrence interview; Steele interview.

12   Janice Steele, email correspondence, December 6, 2021.

13   Lawrence interview.

14   John Corry, "Rachel Robinson Recalls When Jackie was First," *New York Times,* September 22, 1981: 12.

15   https://www.ibdb.com/broadway-cast-staff/carrie-f-robbins-25256#Credits; https://www.ibdb.com/broadway-cast-staff/luther-henderson-11837#Credits

16   Lisa Nicole Wilkerson, "Raising the baton: How Dr. Joyce Brown became a pioneering Broadway maestro," *ESPN*, June 10, 2017. https://www.espn.com/espnw/culture/feature/story/_/id/19602110/how-dr-joyce-brown-became-pioneering-broadway-maestro. The entity was presented as Boston Philharmonia in the article.

17   Mark Hummel telephone interview, October 20, 2021. Lawrence interview; Brush interview.

18   Claudia Cohen, "Jackie Robinson Story to B'way?" *Daily News*, September 10, 1980: 156.

19   Uncredited, "From Yale to Broadway," *New York Times*, August 11, 1981: 11.

20   Gene Faison, telephone Interview, October 19, 2021.

21   Corry, "Rachel Robinson Recalls When Jackie was First."

22   Corry, "Rachel Robinson Recalls When Jackie was First."

23   David Alan Grier, telephone interview, October 15, 2021.

24   Mark Hummel, telephone interview, November 3, 2021.

25   Lawrence, interview.

26   Kim Criswell, telephone interview, October 14, 2021.

27   Joel Siegel and Martin Charnin, *The First: A Musical*, French's Musical Library (S. Franch, 1983): 24.

28   Fred Ferretti, "A Musical Celebrates an Athlete," *New York Times*, November 8, 1981; Section 2, 1.

29   Jay Sharbutt, "Charnin took charge of 'First' by chance," *Journal-New*, (White Plains, New York), November 22, 1981: G8.

30   Lawrence interview.

31   Steele interview.

32   Lawrence interview.

33   Lawrence interview; Brush, interview.

34   David Chapman, telephone interview, October 8, 2021.

35   Stefan Bondy, "Yankees dump Kate Smith's 'God Bless America' from rotationover signer's racist songs," *New York Daily News*, April 18, 2019. https://www.nydailynews.com/sports/baseball/yankees/ny-kate-smith-god-bless-america-20190418-wfkyednrvrherh57sfmb4h7s5y-story.html. Accessed December 7, 2021.

36   Ferretti.

37   Lawrence interview; Steele interview.

38   Lawrence interview; Steele interview.

39   Lawrence, interview.

40   Ferretti.

41   Lawrence interview.

42   Criswell interview.

43   David Chapman interview, October 8, 2021.

44   Lawrence interview; Steele interview.

45   Hummel interview, November 3, 2021.

46   Steele interview.

47   Steele interview.

48   Woll, 257.

49   Gene Faison, telephone interview, October 19, 2021; Steele interview.

50   Faison interview.

51   Faison interview.

52   Faison interview.

53   Faison interview.

54   Chapman, interview.

55   Dick Young, "Opening night audience likes 'The First,'" *Gettysburg Times*, November 20, 1981: 13.

56   Grier interview.

57   Frank Rich, "STAGE: 'FIRST,' BASEBALL MUSICAL," *New York Times*, November 18, 1981: 25.

58   Douglas Watt, "'The First,' new musical, strikes out," *Daily News*, November 18, 1981: 65.

59   Jay Sharbutt, "'The First' Bows," *Journal News*, November 20, 1981: 55.

60   Dick Young, "Brooklyn Rooted for Jackie," *Daily News*, November 19, 1981: 155.

61   Criswell interview.

62   Young, "Brooklyn Rooted for Jackie." 155 and Watt.

63   *The First: A Musical*, 27-28.

64   Siegel and Charnin, Martin, 72.

65   Brush interview.

66   Chapman interview.

67   *The First: A Musical*, 41-42.

68   Criswell interview; Lawrence interview,

69   Young, "Brooklyn Rooted for Jackie."

70   Brush interview.

71   Brush interview.

72   Woll, 267-8.

73   Woll, 247.

74   Woll, 249, 251; Caseen Gaines, *Footnotes: The Black Artists Who Rewrote the Rules of the Great White Way* (Naperville, Illinois: Sourcebooks, 2021), 361-2.

75   Woll, 275-6.

76   Brush interview.

77   Steele interview.

78   Chapman interview.

79   Grier interview.

80   Criswell interview.

81   Steele interview.

82   Chapman interview.

Youth Theatre

By Bryan Dietzler

Not only has Jackie Robinson been made popular in print and on the big screen but he also has been well represented on stage. That is, he has been well represented on the "smaller" stage. Robinson's remarkable story has become a part of many different forms of entertainment, including youth theater. There have been several children's plays written and produced featuring Robinson as either a central or secondary character. The message that each play ventures to put forth is clear. They want to pass on the legacy of one of the greatest baseball players in the history of the game, as well as one of the best people of his time.

In the Year of the Boar and Jackie Robinson

A few of these plays are based upon books that are geared towards children. One such story is called, *In the Year of the Boar and Jackie Robinson*. The play is based off the book by Bette Bao Lord, and was adapted by Mark Branner. The original production premiered in November 2019, and because of the COVID pandemic the new work has not had much of an opportunity to make the rounds. However, it was produced by the Hawaii Theater for Youth in Honolulu, Hawaii.[1]

Becky Dunning, who is the Managing Director of the Honolulu Theater for Youth, said of the play, "The show was very well received."[2] The total attendance for the play was 10,041.

The theater collected testimonials and several recorded remarks about the play that signaled its popularity, not only with students, but with educators. One person commented that they "Really enjoyed the play! It was clever. For us in particular, we do topical studies on human rights and Jackie Robinson so it was a wonderful tie into both!"[3] In terms of the educational value of the play, one comment stuck out. "Everything is via video or the internet nowadays, and for my students to have empathy for human beings who are bravely performing on stage right in front of them, that is essential."[4] The creators capitalized on children's familiarity with video, as the part of Jackie Robinson was "played" by a projection, while the part of the little girl central to the story, Shirley, was played by a live actress.

Jackie And Me

Yet another play for youth that featured Robinson was *Jackie and Me*, adapted by playwright Steven Dietz. The story is based on a series of books written by Dan Gutman that feature a time-traveling youngster. Holding a baseball card in his hand, the youth can travel back in time to meet the player featured on that card. In this book, he travels back to meet Robinson.

Jackie and Me premiered in 2010 and has proven to be a popular show among children. It helps provide them with not only a history lesson, but a lesson in American culture. It shows children what things were like back in the days when Branch Rickey decided to take a stab at ending segregation in baseball and bring in the first African-American player to the big leagues. It continues to be a part of youth theater around the country although, like *In the Year of the Boar*, the number of productions were minimized due to the coronavirus pandemic.

After a showing of the play at the Chicago Children's Theater in the Ruth Center for the Arts, the ChicagoCritic.com website had several great things to say about the play. "The 80-minute show is truthful, fun and filled with worthy life lessons for kids." Critic Tom Williams (somewhat sexistly) suggested that you "take your kids and grandkids (especially boys) to see this fun show. The actors knock it out of the park."[5]

The play attempts to give a first-hand look at several social issues including racism and equal rights. Its educational value for youth cannot be denied.

Jackie and Me has made it onto the stage in several cities and towns across the country and has developed into one of the more popular plays about Robinson. Yet another production premiered at the Knoxville (Tennessee) Children's Theatre in March 2022.

MVP: The Jackie Robinson Story

Yet another play that places Robinson at the center is *Most Valuable Player: The Jackie Robinson Story*. This youth play has appeared at several venues in the past and has become a popular show. The play was written by Mary Hall Surface. Surface had previously written such theatrical works like *Forward, 54th*, and *The Sorcerer's Apprentice*.[6]

According to Surface, "*Most Valuable Player* was created collaboratively at a theater company in the Bay Area of California, the now closed California Theater Center." She talked about the actor who starred in the play, Dorien Wilson, whose acting credits include *The Steve Harvey Show* and *The Parkers*. She said, "In 1984, we had an especially strong group of actors, including Dorien Wilson, who has had a successful television career. As a company, we were committed to creating theater for young audiences that expanded their perspectives and deepened their understanding of the of the world around them, both the past and the present."[7]

When talking about the origins of the play, Surface said, "While I am credited as the playwright, the play was born through research and improvisations crafted by our director, J. Steven White." About the process of coming up with the "body" of the play, she stated that, "As a company, we all read biographies and other research about Robinson, Rickey, and more. We'd bring our research into the rehearsal room and improvise scenes based on historic moments that we felt were inherently theatrical and essential to Robinson's story." Surface then explained that she "would then craft the improvisations into the scenes that ultimately became the play."

As Surface recalls, "the play was the most successful project of their theater company, touring across the United States, to a festival in Peru, and on an 11-week tour of American military bases." What kind of impact did the story of Jackie Robinson have on the audiences? "Robinson's story of both living with and confronting racism resonated deeply with audiences of both adults and young people worldwide."

The play was welcomed outside of the United States, including in Japan. Surface directed the play at the Theater Seigei. She stated that it was an "extraordinary experience given the love of Japanese for baseball and their unease of confronting racism."

It's interesting to note that the play catered to a whole new generation of children who did not know the story of Robinson. The writer stated, about Robinson, in her final comments, "As far as the value of the play, we were honored to introduce his story to a new generation. His courage and strength in facing racism in baseball and beyond inspired us to encourage young audiences to not only revere but embody his qualities." She concluded, "We also, at the time, felt that we were opening new conversations around the toll that racism takes on us all – African American and white – and on our society's health. I sincerely hope that the play planted the seeds of a deeper understanding and a desire to move us forward as a nation in the hearts and minds of our audiences."

The play is a take on Robinson's life from his growing up in California all the way through his playing days with the Brooklyn Dodgers. Despite the fact it was a children's play, the script does contain the use of derogatory language, which one theatre chose to immediately address. At a showing at the Children's Theater in Madison, the derogatory word is explained up front to help ease its impact.[8]

Black Diamond

The play *Black Diamond* is not completely about Robinson, but does feature him in it. The show is part of the "Greatest Stories Never Told" series, which introduces youth to stories from the past that aren't often told to children, in an effort to allow them to learn about the lesser-known past.

Some of the famous baseball players featured in the play include, along with Robinson, Satchel Paige, Josh Gibson, Andrew "Rube" Foster, and Moses "Fleet" Walker. The names remind baseball fans of a time when White and Black players played in different leagues. The focus on Robinson centers around his breaking the color barrier in baseball.

The Smithsonian Associates Discovery Theater produced the show and when asked about the play, Company Director Roberta Gasbarre stated that "We are very proud of *Black Diamond*." She explained, "It was created in 2002 from a script written for the Smithsonian (Institute) by Raquis D'Juan Petree, and was produced each year from 2002-2007, and again in 2011, 2018-19. The script was updated almost every year it was produced, notably by Michael Bobbitt, now Executive Director of the Massachusetts Arts Council, who also played Satchel Paige."[9]

When asked how many attended the play, Ms. Gasbarre said, "It is difficult to estimate how many people have seen the interactive museum theater piece since we have performed it, both at the Smithsonian; on tour in schools, museums and art centers as far as Greensboro, North Carolina; at the Library of Congress; and even on the field of the Washington Nationals Baseball Stadium." She went on to say, "Although we have incomplete records, we have confirmed a number of 76,323 people, youth and adults, who have seen it. The likelihood is that it is close to 90,000."

When asked about how popular the play was, Ms. Gasbarre replied "The play was a huge hit each time we produced it, and audiences consistently cited Jackie Robinson as their most favorite character, who is the youngest among the veteran players featured, and the character young audiences most connect(ed) with. He is well-educated (a character calls him a "war-fighting college boy"), idealistic and not accepting of the systemic racism present in the sport he loves."

She goes on to say that "His final scene uses his own words in first-person, direct address to demonstrate his extraordinary place in baseball history". In this quote, Robinson said "I'm not concerned with your liking or disliking me…, All I ask is that you respect me as a human being… A life is not important except in the impact it has on other lives."

Ms. Gasbarre said that "*Black Diamond* poses a question to the audience at the end of the play, which asks them to put themselves into the story of Jackie Robinson and the Negro Leagues." Gasbarre explained that "The characters ask, 'What do you do when they won't let you play? Do you run away and cry? Do you get mad and let yourself hate yourself and the world? Do you stop playing a game you love? Or…do you go and start your own game… and get so good that they ask *you* to play, and then you decide…. Whether you want to play with them.'"

She continued, "That's what Jackie Robinson did. In *Black Diamond*, Jackie and the other historic figures ask this of the young people in the audience, who always respond with a roar. They know the answer. And they take it home with them—with Jackie teaching them the lesson from the stage." A teacher

who viewed the show said that she, "loved that the show was interactive and engaging. My kids are huge sports fans and teaching history through sports was perfect for them."

Jackie Robinson

There are a host of smaller plays that have cropped up over the last few years. One that is still being staged by the Bright Star Touring Theatre Company is simply called *Jackie Robinson*. This play is aimed at children from kindergarten to fifth grade, covers Robinson's life, and teaches children about how tough it was for him to survive as a baseball player. The play has been shown both in the theater and online and is still touring today. In fact, one can go to the theater company's website (https://www.brightstartheatre.com/book-a-show/) and see the pricing that they charge for each of their shows, including *Jackie Robinson*.

The play, like so many of the others we have looked at, teaches children about the fascinating life of Robinson and all that he had to go through. As the accompanying study guide explains, "It's always so much fun to learn about ordinary Americans who accomplish extraordinary things. Jackie Robinson began his life humbly, and was able to become a ground breaker in professional sports. In addition to being the first Black major league baseball player in modern times, Robinson was a symbol of hope and inspiration for young people across the United States. We know young audiences will find inspiration in Jackie Robinson even today."[10]

Plays like this help to not only show youth how tough and complicated Robinson's career was, but it also fosters the hope that if they work hard, they can eventually live out their dreams. Robinson's dream was to be a professional athlete, and through a lot of hard work, he was able to reach the highest point of his dreams. Eventually, following his baseball career, he became an important part of the Civil Rights movement helping to earn freedoms for people of color.

Jackie Robinson: A Game Apart

Another play is called *Jackie Robinson: A Game Apart*. The play was written by Mike Wiley and is a story about Robinson's life in the big leagues. The play takes the viewer back to the time and place that

Publicity photo from the Chicago Children's Theatre production of *Jackie and Me*, featuring l. to r.: Kamal Angelo Bolden (Jackie), Patrick DeNicola (Ant), Sean Cooper (Flip), Phil Biedron, Vanessa Greenway (Mom), Rania Manganaro, Tracey N. Bonner (Rachel) and Tyler Ross (Joey). photo courtesy of Chicago Children's Theatre, Michael Brosilow photographer

Robinson lived in and gives them a chance to see how life was for a man of his race and his position in life.

As the website for the play states, "Witness the hopeless humiliation of a star player who was showered with adulation on the field and became a second-hand citizen when he walked off the diamond." The description goes on to say, "Meet Jackie's compatriots fighting the same battles between the end zones, inside the ring and around the track. *A Game Apart* is a powerful lesson in courage through dedication, perseverance and leadership."[11]

Play To Win:
The Jackie Robinson Story

Finally, yet another play that involves Jackie Robinson is, this time, a musical, called *Play to Win: The Jackie Robinson Story*. This show featured a book written by Charles Cleveland and James de Jongh. The music was composed by Jimi Foster. The *New York Times* reviewed the play and stated "There are painful memories in the Jackie Robinson story, but on the whole, it is one of the best stories Americans can tell

about themselves. "Play to Win" tells it economically, with a lot of feeling.".[12]

An interview with the musical director of one of the touring productions, Laura Brenneman, gives a look inside the musical and what it was all about. Ms. Brenneman directed the music for the company Theater Works USA, based out of New York City. The musical also went on a national tour.[13]

She remarked that "the play is really geared for kids" and that it has been "revived a number of times," including the year that she was the musical director for in 2005. The play has a small cast. Some of the memorable players include Branch Rickey, Robinson, and his wife Rachel. "There were a handful of other players," Ms. Brenneman said.

In preparation for the play, in order for the theater company to go out on the road an execute the play with success, according to Ms. Brenneman, "it involved a three-week process." When asked how many people saw the show, she stated that "it was very well attended."

The author asked Ms. Brenneman what she thought the message of the musical was and she said, "It's one of standing up for what you believe in. It's one of perseverance despite having so many obstacles. The biggest meaning is in the title. Playing to win. This is a play that supports people who are facing oppression." She stated, "It sends a positive message. It's a message of fighting against implicit biases."

Notes

1   "In the Year of the Boar and Jackie Robinson," *Honolulu Theater for Youth*, February 21, 2021, https://www.htyweb.org/boar/

2   Rebecca Dunning, interview with the author, January 14, 2021

3   "In the Year of the Boar and Jackie Robinson Collected Comments," Rebecca Dunning January 14, 2021

4   "In the Year of the Boar and Jackie Robinson Collected Comments," Rebecca Dunning January 14, 2021

5   Tom Williams, "Jackie and Me, by Stephen Dietz," *Chicago Critic*, February 11, 2021, https://chicagocritic.com/jackie-and-me/

6   "Most Valuable Player," Plays Available for Production, *MaryHallSurface.com*, March 26, 2021. https://www.maryhallsurface.com/plays

7   Mary Hall Surface, interview with the author, February 18, 2021. All quotations attributed to the playwright come from this interview.

8   Amelia Cook Fontella, "Children's Theater of Madison's Inspiring 'Most Valuable Player' tells Jackie Robinson's Story," *Isthmus.com*. March 22, 2021, https://isthmus.com/arts/stage/childrens-theater-of-madisons-inspiring-most-valuable-player-tells-jackie-robinsons-story/

9   Roberta Gasbarre, interview with the author, May 5, 2021. All quotations attributed to Ms. Gasbarre come from this interview.

10   "Jackie Robinson," *BrightStarTheatre.com* June 26, 2021. https://www.brightstartheatre.com/wp-content/uploads/2016/03/JACKIE-ROBINSON-PDF-2014-.pdf

11   Mike Wiley, "Touring Performances," MikeWileyProductions.com, July 12, 2021. http://mikewileyproductions.com/touring/

12   "Review/Theater: Play to Win a Musical About the Integration of Baseball", *New York Times*, February 15, 2021. https://www.nytimes.com/1989/07/21/theater/review-theater-play-to-win-a-musical-about-the-integration-of-baseball.html

13   Laura Brenneman, interview with the author, May 8, 2021. All quotations attributed to Ms. Brenneman come from this interview.

The Plot to Kill Jackie Robinson
Historian Donald Honig Plays 'What if?'

By Ray Danner

Consider this quote from eminent baseball historian Donald Honig's 1985 book *Baseball America*:

> For those who cared to pay attention, Robinson's style of play should have been both threat and warning, for this was not merely an athlete expending brutal amounts of energy to win baseball games; this was a black American releasing torrents of pent-up rage and resentment against a lifetime portion of bigotry, ignorance and neglect: this was a messenger from the brooding, restless ghettos. Only Cobb had played with the same unbuckled zeal that Robinson displayed, and Cobb was psychotic.[1]

In the myriad ways Jackie Robinson's historic achievement in Brooklyn is framed, the words "threat" and "warning" aren't typically included. Determined, maybe, or courageous. Barrier-breaking. A hero. But a threat. And a warning. To whom? Clearly Honig did not mean only the Dodgers' National League opponents. Baseball's longstanding conservative "traditions"? All White America?

In Honig's 1992 foray into fiction, *The Plot to Kill Jackie Robinson*, Honig provides one possible answer in the form of a White man from Queens. The fictional Quentin Wilson, an easily contemptible New Yorker with serious anxiety about the furious rate of change he sees in the country he went overseas to defend during the Second World War.

With regards to Honig's quote in *Baseball America*, he created a character, Wilson, who *is* paying attention and who thinks he uniquely recognizes Robinson's "threat" as indeed a message from the "brooding, restless ghettos." Wilson believes in conspiracies. Blacks are hiding from census takers in Harlem to hide their numbers, plotting to take over. What is

Wilson going to do about it? How can he stop what he sees as an inevitable revolution? Well, the answer is the title of the book.

But first, before discussing Quentin's plot, let's stop and assess something. Donald Honig wrote fiction?

While Honig is perhaps just behind the historians and storytellers that make up a Mount Rushmore of contemporaries like John Thorn, Roger Angell, or Bill James, his writing looms large for any reading into baseball's past. If Lawrence Ritter's *The Glory of Their Times* stands as a desert island baseball book,[2] then it is Honig who picked up the oral history mantle. Honig's first work of non-fiction, 1975's *Baseball When the Grass Was Real*, repeats the formula, if not exactly the magic, of *Glory*.

Crossing the country to meet in person with the men who populated the game 20 to 40 years earlier, Honig interviews mega-watt stars like Bob Feller, Johnny Mize, and Lefty Grove along with lesser-known role players such as Max Lanier and Elbie Fletcher. As is common in oral histories, the lesser-known players provide the real gems with a view just outside of the clubhouse media scrum.

Fletcher stands out. As Honig reveals in his 2009 memoir *The Fifth Season: Tales of My Life in Baseball*, Fletcher was Honig's brother's unlikely favorite player when they were kids. A lifetime .271 hitter on some mediocre Boston Braves and Pittsburgh teams for 12 seasons, Honig waxes poetic about the "statistical gravity" of the long season, evidenced by Fletcher's 1941-43 stretch batting .288, .289, and .283 in successive seasons. "Did you know that from 1917 through 1919 Ty Cobb batted .383, .382, .384? He was in the same rut you were," Honig says. "Except for that little '3' in front," Fletcher replies.[3]

Honig's mid-life transition to baseball history followed a bibliography of fiction writing that included a short story featured on *Alfred Hitchcock*

Presents ("Man With a Problem"), a hockey player questioning the violence in the game (*Fury on Skates*), an 1850s covered wagon journey (*The Journal of One Davey Wyatt*) as well as several early forays into baseball fiction. One of these hard to find, out of print stories is 1971's *Johnny Lee*; the story of a young, Black minor-leaguer from Harlem facing racism in small-town Virginia.[4]

Before returning to his fictional roots, Honig earned the eminent in his informal title, cranking out 43 books about baseball history over the ensuing decades, according to his online bibliography.[5] *Baseball Between the Lines* came a year after *When the Grass Was Real* and repeated the oral history formula for stories from the 1940s and '50s. With straightforward titles, Honig covered the history of managers (1977's *The Man in the Dugout: Fifteen Big League Managers Speak Their Minds*), positional rankings (*The Greatest First Basemen of All Time* and *The Greatest Pitchers of All Time*, both from 1988,

The cover of *The Plot to Kill Jackie Robinson*, illustration by Steve Carter & jacket design by Todd Radom.
image courtesy of Penguin Random House

followed later by catchers and shortstops), and so on through the World Series, league histories, great teams, and more.

In 1992, at the age of 61, Honig returned to his fictional roots with *The Plot to Kill Jackie Robinson*. In this speculative historical fiction, Honig largely stays away from the man himself and takes his readers to the bars and seedy hotel rooms of Manhattan, a quiet neighborhood in Queens, amongst the sporting crowd in Havana, Cuba, and to a deserted beach on Long Island for target practice.

Honig's surrogate is jaded *Daily News* sportswriter Joe Tinker, just back from the war and sliding into a role he could easily play for the rest of his life: hard-drinking womanizer rubbing elbows with athletes and celebrities at Toots Shor's. Perhaps like Honig himself, Tinker has ambitions beyond the sports pages. Or he's just bored with the job.

"A sportswriter. Stamped and labeled," Honig writes of his protagonist. "Doomed forever to write about the antics of the toy department."[6] Elsewhere, Honig has Tinker say to his editor, "Writing sports can be great – it is great – if that's what you want to do with your life. But ... it's limiting, confining." He continues, "The drama is artificial because it's programmed to happen. We make it happen. It occurs because we're there. But in reality it's banal, because it's going to happen again tomorrow, or next week. It's *scheduled* to happen."[7]

But what if this ambitious sportswriter is handed something meatier to write about? Oddly, Tinker doesn't even seem to recognize the opportunity the imminent arrival of Jackie Robinson portends. Robinson has just finished a successful minor-league season in Montreal and seems destined to crack Brooklyn's 1947 roster. Tinker knows that Branch Rickey plans to install Robinson in Brooklyn the following season and isn't shy about saying so. For most of the novel, he sees this mainly as a baseball story. How will Jackie transition to first base on a loaded Brooklyn roster.

Instead, it's a November murder in the apartment across the street from his own that gets his attention. A White man is shot dead with a Black prostitute and her pimp in the room. The White man, Harry Wilson, is a cop and former high school baseball legend from Capstone, Queens. It's an avenue for Tinker to stick his nose into investigative reporting, pursuing "background" on Harry Wilson, and ultimately crossing paths with Wilson's brooding younger brother, Quentin.

It's Quentin who immediately voices the main theme of the novel – resistance to change. It's Quentin who says, "They're out to take everything we've got. They're even coming into baseball, for Christ's sake, with that black son of a bitch the Dodgers got up in Montreal. They'll be in our jobs, our neighborhoods, our homes. It's changing...everything's changing. Somebody better do something before it's too late."[8] Honig has created a character who keenly feels Robinson's arrival as a "threat and a warning" and is ready to do something about it.

The apprehension around change is elsewhere in the novel, if not expressed with Quentin's vehemence. Harry Wilson's old baseball coach laments the buses that will soon replace the trolleys in Queens. "Progress," Tinker offers. "Changes, changes," the coach says. "I don't like 'em. Leave things as they are. We've been managing just fine." Regarding veteran Tinker, he suggests "You weren't out there fighting for changes, were you? You were fighting to keep things as they were."

Tinker, ever the realist, thinks "I was fighting the biggest change of them all – becoming dead."[9]

Harry's old teammate Cornelius Fletcher, repeats the chorus while reflecting on the milk bottle plant where he works: "Everybody's going to be switching over to cardboard containers before you know it." His co-workers are "worried about their jobs. The people who unload the empties, put them in washing machines. You know how it is. Something new comes in, something old goes out."[10]

Even Tinker, presented by Honig as a non-judgmental, live-and-let-live man, is not immune to pondering his fate in a changing world. "Tinker turned around for a moment and surveyed his own dark bedroom. This building was what – fifty, sixty years old? Who knew what might have taken place right in this room...But all those strangers in the light and the dark of their lives had left behind not a sound, not a trace. Human transience was probably the most puzzling and disheartening of all realities; it was the mockery of all effort and all passion."[11]

Resistance to change is a theme deeply explored in countless fictional narratives. Wasn't it Woody's fear of losing his place as Andy's most favored toy to Buzz Lightyear that sets the plot of Toy Story in motion? The boy in The Sixth Sense may see dead people, but it's the reluctance of the dead to accept their fate that sets up one of the great twist endings in movie history. Stepping back to baseball non-

fiction, where would modern baseball be without Michael Lewis' Moneyball and the inevitable fallout of scouts versus spreadsheets?

What takes Honig's examination of change out of the neighborhood and into America itself is the symbol at the center of the story. This isn't the plot to kill Jack Johnson or Jim Brown. The Plot to Kill Whitey Ford would be a story of an obsessed fan who wants his team to have a shot at beating the Yankees for once, but it says nothing larger about society itself.

It's the symbolism of Jackie Robinson in the most myth making of American sports, in the nation's most emblematic metropolis, that leads to an idea that stopping one man may just stop an entire people. Robinson, the man, is a symbol on par with the unsinkable Titanic, the grandest ship in the world, doomed on its maiden voyage from Southampton to New York City while steaming recklessly through a field of ice in the mid-Atlantic without adequate lifeboats. It's the mayor opening his beaches on Amity Island to tourists to save the summer season while a killer shark swims offshore. "It's all psychological. You yell barracuda, everybody says, 'Huh? What?' You yell shark, we've got a panic on our hands on the Fourth of July."[12]

Honig's choice of Robinson as Quentin's target is necessary and appropriate. It's Robinson who stands alone at the gate between the Negro Leagues and White major-league baseball. Visible over his shoulders are Roy Campanella and Don Newcombe and Larry Doby. Hank Aaron and Willie Mays. Dick Allen and Doc Gooden. Robinson's success, we already know, means 11 of the next 14 National League MVPs will be Black men and the balance of power in baseball will switch to the National League, generally more welcoming to Black players in the late '40s and '50s.

But more importantly to Honig's purposes, and what he has pursued in this novel that largely stays away from Robinson's direct presence, is what Robinson's arrival signals.

As Cornelius Fletcher states, "Well, I know a hell of a lot of people who'll never go to Ebbets Field again... Real Dodgers fans too. People got feelings, you know."[13]

Quentin Wilson laments, "It would be the old pattern, like in a neighborhood: as soon as 'they' began moving in, people began moving out. Only this time the neighborhood was Baseball. The big leagues...And of course the grandstands would be filled with them too. You wouldn't be able to go to a major-league baseball game anymore. The death of baseball meant the death of summer, and people were sitting complacently and letting it happen, letting themselves be deluded, because they didn't realize how many of them there were and that once the tide began to flow it would be unstoppable."[14]

Honig may be subtle as a hammer, but Quentin lays it out. The mechanics of how he plans to stop Robinson and whether he's successful aren't necessary to discuss here, expect to mention that the finale of the book bears no small resemblance to Frederick Forsyth's *Day of the Jackal*, notably a novel and film focused on resistance to change, in *Jackal's* case the recent liberation of Algeria by French President Charles de Gaulle. The Jackal's ingenious method of smuggling his weapon close to his target clearly inspired Honig, as did the geography of the final shootout.

So, what does one take away from a historical fiction written over 40 years after the fact where one can assume that the bad guys fail and Robinson fulfills his destiny?

For Honig, it may be another look at the power of sports writing. Near the conclusion, Tinker's girlfriend pushes back on his continued apathy towards his profession and his writing on Robinson's rookie season:

> You've got a forum. A couple million people in this city read you every day. And don't tell me that what you write is simply an account of a baseball game. A sportswriter – a good one, one who is perceptive and can write – has a hell of a lot of scope. It may be baseball games that you are writing about, but those are human beings that are out on the field. What you say about them is going to influence how people are going to feel about them and react to them. This story is just beginning and you have an obligation to see that it's told fully and fairly.[15]

In his 70s, Honig said in an interview with Marty Appel, "I'm a novelist at heart – I started as a novelist and went back to it after '94. The last baseball books I did, I felt sort of detached. My head was drifting to other subjects, to fiction."[16]

In another interview, Honig said about Tinker: "I've made him a guy who's a little bit jaded by sports.

He's had this horrendous experience in World War II, and it's helped put sports in perspective for him. Frankly, he's bored by it all."[17]

In Honig's book, Jackie Robinson barely makes an appearance but he's the presence, the spark, that looms over the action. It's his impending arrival that stirs bigots to action and creates an idea in Honig's fictional stand-in that he's writing about more than just baseball. Honig, Tinker, and baseball fans in general have Robinson to help develop "a social conscience through baseball."[18] It wouldn't be giving away too much to say that, much like in *Day of the Jackal*, the assassination fails and history proceeds uninterrupted.

Jackie Robinson the character may have escaped Honig's fictional sniper to go 0-for-3 on April 15, 1947, and Robinson the man may have played 10 Hall of Fame-caliber seasons in Brooklyn, but Robinson the symbol and myth may well live on in stories that outlast the game itself.

Notes

1   Donald Honig, *Baseball America: The Heroes of the Game and the Times of Their Glory* (New York: Macmillan Publishing Company, 1985), 258.

2   Mike Durell, "The Glory of Reading The Glory of Their Times," Seamheads.com, June 1, 2015, https://seamheads.com/blog/2015/06/01/the-glory-of-reading-the-glory-of-their-times.

3   Donald Honig, *The Fifth Season: Tales of My Life in Baseball* (Chicago: Ivan R. Dee, 2009), 201.

4   Honig's book *Fury on Skates* was published in 1974 by Four Winds Press. His *The Journal of One Davey Wyatt* was a 1972 book published by Franklin Watts. *Johnny Lee* was published by McCall Pub. Co.

5   "Bibliography," http://donaldhonig.com/Bibliography.html.

6   Donald Honig, *The Plot to Kill Jackie Robinson* (New York: E.P. Dutton, 1992), 215.

7   Honig, *The Plot to Kill Jackie Robinson*, 104.

8   Honig, *The Plot to Kill Jackie Robinson*, 15.

9   Honig, *The Plot to Kill Jackie Robinson*, 48.

10   Honig, *The Plot to Kill Jackie Robinson*, 52.

11   Honig, *The Plot to Kill Jackie Robinson*, 117.

12   Richard D. Zanuck, David Brown, Steven Spielberg, Peter Benchley, Carl Gottlieb, John Williams, Roy Scheider, et al., *Jaws* (Universal City, California: Universal), 1975

13   Honig, *The Plot to Kill Jackie Robinson*, 54.

14   Honig, *The Plot to Kill Jackie Robinson*, 44.

15   Honig, *The Plot to Kill Jackie Robinson*, 260.

16   Marty Appel, "Sports Collectors Digest: Don Honig & David Voigt," appelpr.com, http://www.appelpr.com/?page_id=311.

17   Jocelyn McClurg, "Baseball Writer Hits New Hot Streak," *Hartford Courant*, July 11, 1993: G1.

18   McClurg, "Baseball Writer Hits New Hot Streak."

The Court-Martial of Jackie Robinson

by Dr. Milbert O. Brown, Jr.

Seventy-five years ago, Jackie Robinson broke major-league baseball's modern-day color barrier, ushering himself into the history books and helping open the doors for so many more. A few years earlier, while in the U.S. military, Robinson endured a life-altering situation—an unexpected court-martial. If Robinson had been found guilty of any charges from his court-martial, he would have been presented with a dishonorable discharge. With this negative mark, he would certainly have been denied a chance at a major-league baseball career.

In his two-hour TNT movie, *The Court Martial of Jackie Robinson,* filmmaker Larry Peerce produced a classic. Peerce had experienced several box-office flops in the past, but this 1990 made-for-TV movie was a success. Actor Andre Braugher eloquently portrays a young and intense Jackie Robinson in the film. Two other outstanding performances included veteran thespians Ruby Dee, who plays Jackie's mother, Mallie, and Bruce Dern, who plays a fictional Dodger scout. The repeat bookend characters that offer the young Robinson advice and support through the movie were J. A. Preston, who plays Wendell Smith and Stan Shaw, the movie's Joe Louis. Smith was a reporter for the *Pittsburgh Courier,* one of America's most influential Black newspapers. Louis, the heavyweight boxing champion, was Robinson's Army buddy whose fame helped gain Robinson's acceptance into the Army's Officer Candidate School.

The film opens with Rachel Isum, played by Kasi Lemmons, chatting with Wendell Smith as she waits for Jack Robinson, one of the University of California-Los Angeles (UCLA)'s star athletes, and her love interest. Smith was a former star baseball player who wanted to join the majors but was denied because of the color blockage, so he became a sportswriter after college. He later recommended Robinson as the primary candidate to break baseball's racial barrier with the Brooklyn Dodgers.

The film shows the courtship of Jackie and his girlfriend Rachel, holding hands and walking on the UCLA campus, before their lives changed as part of their remarkable history. The innocence of their love resembled a frozen moment often welcomed in the imagery from a Norman Rockwell painting. We witness their relationship endure uncomfortable discussions when Robinson threatens to drop out of college to help his mother financially. He tells Rachel, also a student at UCLA, that "a colored man with a college degree is still colored." Robinson's mother (Dee) had a limited but powerful voice in the film, as she tells her son she works hard for him to be able to enjoy the benefit of a college education. The creative license in the film presents Robinson being drafted while still an enrolled student as mother and Rachel wished. According to historical accounts, Robinson dropped out of school and was then drafted into the Army.[1] The romance of Jackie and Rachel is again compromised when Rachel joins the Cadet Nurse Corps. She returns Jackie's engagement ring after his disapproval of her cadet service commitment. The U.S. Cadet Nurse Corps was established in 1943 by President Franklin D. Roosevelt to help ease the nursing shortage during the World War II years. The pair is later reunited before Robinson returns to Ft. Riley from leave.

While at Ft. Riley, Lt. Robinson, now the morale officer for colored troops, had a strong will for insisting on fairness for Black soldiers under his command. Robinson got involved when Black soldiers complained to him about their inability to receive adequate service and seating at the mess hall. During his tenure at Ft. Riley, Robinson quits the football team after not being permitted to play in some games because of racial restrictions. Because of Robinson's defiance he is sent to Camp Hood. Upon receiving his transfer orders, he talks to Joe Louis about the unfair transfer. One of Jackie's and Joe's best movie moments comes when Louis tells an irritated Robinson about the reality of the south and when to fight as a Black man. "Just because you're an officer and a gentleman ... you can't just walk into the club."[2] He lands at Camp Hood, known as one of the Army's most racist environments and the worst place for a Black soldier. Robinson is initially labeled as troublemaker hours after arriving on the Texas base, but still he is assigned as the tank commander for the Black soldiers.

In the film, *The Court-Martial of Jackie Robinson*, before Army Lieutenant Jack Roosevelt Robinson stepped on the bus that served as the stage for this important event, a fellow Black officer, Lt. Gordon Jones, welcomed him. Lieutenant Jones introduced Robinson to his wife, Loretta, as played by Nancy Cheryl Davis. After his courteous acknowledgment,

Andre Braugher (Robinson) and Ruby Dee (as Mallie Robinson) in *The Court Martial of Jackie Robinson*. image courtesy of Alamy

Robinson walked on the bus and sat next to Lt. Jones' spouse, Loretta, in the middle section of the bus. There may have been a cause for alarm as Mrs. Jones was a fair-skinned Black woman often mistaken for being White.[3] In the Turner Network Television (TNT) movie, Lt. Jones, played by Peter Parros, mentioned that he had to secure off-base housing because many thought the Joneses were an interracial couple.

In reality, on July 7, 1944, Lieutenant Robinson caught the Southwestern Bus Company bus operated on the Texas Army Base-Camp Hood. Robinson sat in the middle of the bus with Mrs. Jones. After a few blocks, the bus driver stopped and told Robinson to go to the back of the bus. When he refused, that was the beginning of problems for the young lieutenant. It was alleged that Lt. Robinson was unruly-- a code for Black people stepping out of place when they reject the southern White value system. With no regard for Robinson's officer insignia, the driver told the dispatcher, "There's the n____ that's been causing the trouble."[4] The lieutenant reminded the driver about the Army regulation against separation on Army buses during the ride. Robinson was aware that the War Department was finalizing a transportation order stating that race would not be a factor on military installations.

At the Texas base, desegregation of buses was a post regulation, but Jim Crow transportation laws still held their strength even on bases.[5] It was the customary practice that bus drivers made Blacks go to the back of the buses. Like slave patrols that retrieved runaway slaves in the 1830s, bus drivers were designated as special policeman and had the power to arrest Black passengers.[6] "All states gave the white man who operated these vehicles the power to determine when, where, and whether any Black person could secure a seat on their buses."[7] Jackie Robinson was not the first Black person to be humiliated for refusing to move to the back of the bus, but he was the first known Negro officer to be court-martialed because of his defiance.

For years Blacks had wrestled with the restrictions of travel on buses. In Texas and throughout the south, Black passengers were banned from riding if that made White patrons uncomfortable. "By 1929 Black residents of Austin and several other Texas cities were petitioning the Texas Railroad Commission to require all holders of bus company certificates to transport Negroes on their lines."[8] W.H. Mitchell, a Black man, was arrested for attempting to board a Houston bus in 1925.[9] "Likewise, in Portsmouth, Virginia colored people were barred from riding on the bus lines."[10]

According to Mia Bay's (2021) book, *Traveling Black: A Story of Race and Resistance*, it was logical for Blacks to be positioned to the back of the bus following Jim Crow attitudes of "separate but equal."[11] But, seating in the back of the bus was far from equal. Lyman Johnson, a civil rights activist, commented, "Every time we hit a pothole; in the road ... the people in the back were bumped up and down. It was rough as riding an old mule. These undesirable rear seats, which might have otherwise been difficult to fill, were assigned to Blacks passengers, often noticed and resented. I didn't like having to pass empty seats in the front to go to colored seats in the back."[12] Georgia and South Carolina had the unique idea of establishing real segregated seating for colored passengers, by having them facing backward and having Whites facing forward. Many of the Black patrons' bodies flung back as they suffered from motion sickness and swallowed the exhaust of the smoky bus fumes.[13] At the turn of the century and during WWI, Jim Crow policies strengthened public transportation segregation in America's southern states. "More than four hundred state laws, constitutional amendments, and city ordinances legalizing segregation and discrimination were passed in the United States between 1865 and 1967. Several states even prohibited hearses from carrying both races. Even the dead could not be transported equally."[14]

The bus policies in southern states were strictly enforced even after Jackie Robinson began his Hall of Fame career as a professional baseball player. In March 1955, shortly after a young minister, Reverend Martin Luther King, Jr., moved to Montgomery, a 15-year-old girl refused to give up her seat. The arrest of the young Claudette Colvin fueled the fire for another more mature rider by the name of Rosa Parks. Parks' arrest resulted in launching a national civil rights movement known as the Montgomery Bus Boycott. "The inaction of the city and bus officials after the Colvin case would make it necessary for them in a few months to meet another committee, infinitely, more determined."[15] *Plessy v. Ferguson* (1896), a landmark U.S. Supreme Court case, presented America with the "separate but equal" doctrine. Yet, the Montgomery Bus Boycott was an economic challenge as it altered segregationally travel practices against Montgomery's Black citizens-the bus company's most loyal patrons.

Even Black soldiers dressed in their uniforms shared the heavy burden of second-class citizenship concerning the segregated transportation laws. In 1944, Corporal John W. Childs took a bus from Macon to Savannah, Georgia, and was forced to wait for over an hour to ensure no other White passengers needed his seat.[16] In 1942, "a Black soldier was shot and killed in Mobile, Alabama, by a white bus driver, while Texas police shot at least two others for riding in the white section of the bus."[17] According to unfair bus segregation rules, Black women, men, soldiers, or citizens were not treated any differently.

Private Sarah Keys, a Women's Army Corps (WAC) member, got leave from Ft. Dix, New Jersey, and hopped a bus home to North Carolina on August 1, 1952. Around midnight, the bus stopped in North Carolina, and a new bus driver took over. Before the beginning of the trip, the driver started re-ticketing the passengers. He awoke the young 22-year-old Keys and told her to move to the back of the bus.[18] She was to give up her seat for a White marine, but she refused. Private Keys was arrested and escorted to the police station. Keys' action was not well-known, but she helped to fuel the fight for bus travel a few years before the Montgomery Bus Boycott ignited by the fire from Rosa Parks. In the court case *Sarah Keys v. Carolina Coach Company* that was settled in 1955, the Interstate Commerce Commission ruled in favor of Keys. The Interstate Commerce Act "outlawed the segregation of Black passengers in buses traveling across state lines."[19]

When Jackie Robinson refused to move to the back of bus, it infused a hunger within him. Like other Black patrons, he wanted to be respected and not dismissed as a human being. It was noted when the bus driver called Lt. Robinson a n____, Robinson became enraged, and several Whites began to gather near the upset Lieutenant. The driver, supported by a crowd of White citizens, demanded action against the angered Robinson.[20] Because of Robinson's uneasiness about the volatile circumstance he faced, and possible court-martial, he wrote Truman K. Gibson, the Assistant to the Secretary of War. A few days after Robinson sent the letter to Gibson's attention, a court-martial charge sheet was produced at Camp Hood on July 17, 1944. The first of three charges against Lt. Robinson was the Violation of the 63rd Article of War. The charge was that Lt. Robinson had disrespected Captain Peeler L. Wigginton, his superior officer, after dramatically mentioning his problem with a White soldier. Peeler alleged that Robinson said, "Captain, any Private, you, or any General calls me a n____ and I'll break them in two." Wigginton said the colored lieutenant, spoke to him in an "insolent, impertinent and rude manner."[21] There were over a dozen negative sworn statements gathered on July 7 and 8 that reflected poorly on Lt. Robinson's conduct--which set up grounds for his court-martial.

After Gibson received Lt. Robinson's letter, he advanced it to the chain of command with a written note, "this man is the well-known athlete."[22] Jackie Robinson a former University of California-Los Angeles star, was one of the best athletes in the country. As a four-sport athlete, Jackie was denied an opportunity to run track like his brother, Mack, when the 1940 Olympics were cancelled because of the war.[23] Robinson was one of the football stars on UCLA's 1939 backfield known as the "Gold Dust Trio." One of Jackie's famous "Gold Dust Trio" teammates was Woody Strode, who played professional football after WWII and became an actor. One of his prominent roles was as the title character in the film *Sergeant Rutledge*, about a fictional Black soldier who endured an Army court-martial trial.

In front of 98,000 fans, Robinson scored a touchdown in the College All-Star Football game against the Chicago Bears.[24] The Bears, a professional football team, were impressed with Robinson's ability. Only a few Blacks played in the early professional football league that started in 1920, but they were reduced to performing on minor-league teams. The football league did not have an open-door policy for admitting Black players, but started adding more to their roster when baseball began integrating.[25] Robinson played in a few games for the integrated Pacific Coast Football League before entering the service in 1941. In 1943, while stationed at Fort Riley, Robinson tried to join the camp's baseball team, but the officer in charge had proclaimed, "I'll break up the team before I'll have a n____ on it."[26]

In 1944, the war was still in full swing. Robinson, a young second lieutenant, was the commander of Company B, 761st Tank Battalion, as part of the World War II effort. Like several thousand other Negro troops, he was restricted from direct combat duties. Even though Black soldiers had fought in the Revolutionary and the Civil War, White Americans discounted their service.[27] Whites openly questioned the Negro communities' commitment to American patriotism. In 1942, John J. McCloy, the Assistant Secretary of War referenced "an alarmingly large percentage of Negroes in and out of the army who do not seem to be vitally concerned with winning the war. If the United States does not win this war, the lot of the Negro is going to be far, far worse that it is today."[28] Contrary to the opinions of McCloy and many Whites, the African-American population wanted to solve two problems: one against war aggression in Europe and the other against racism in America. Jackie said, "I was in two wars, one against a foreign enemy, the other against prejudice at home."[29]

One of the rare sights in the military in 1940 was Black officers. The Army had only five regular Black officers, and three were chaplains.[30] The Navy still did not have any Black officers until 1944, when they commissioned 13 Black officers known as the "Golden Thirteen." Henry L. Stinson, the Secretary of War, believed that Blacks should not be placed in leadership roles and integration would destroy morale in the service.[31] Jackie Robinson, a college man with a few credits short of completion from UCLA, told Joe Louis that he and several other African American men were not allowed into the Officer Candidate School (OCS).[32] The boxing champion contacted Washington attorney Truman K. Gibson who had connections with the Secretary of War.[32] Shortly, after the call, Robinson and other Black soldiers were admitted into OCS class at Fort Riley.

An Army-appointed lawyer led Robinson's court-martial defense. Lt. William Cline was played by actor Daniel Stern in the film. Cline's "cross-examination of the prosecution's witnesses exposed the racist undertones of Robinson's arrest. For example, one corporal who took the stand admitted that he heard Private Mucklerath — a key prosecution witness — refer to Robinson with a racial epithet at the MP headquarters."[33] The trial's duration was over four hours, with Robinson testifying in his own defense. One of the strong character witnesses for the defense was Lt. Colonel Paul L. Bates, Robinson's commanding officer. Lt. Col. Bates praise of Robinson's leadership skills was so overwhelming that the court directed Bates to answer only questions pertaining to the arrest. From the beginning, Colonel Bates of the 761st Tank Battalion refused to issue court-martial charges against Robinson. The post commander ordered that Robinson be transferred to the 758th Tank Battalion to support the trumped-up charges, and the new commander signed the court-martial orders.[34]

Throughout the movie, it is easy to see Robinson's courage as he fought against the poisonous venom of racial prejudice. Robinson would emerge as one of America's pioneers in baseball and civil rights in later years. Robinson hurdled over bad episodes during his service experience, but it prepared him for a nasty climate, courtesy of an angry segment of White society and baseball.[35]

Jackie's wife, Rachel Robinson, said the 1990 movie was "not a documentary about baseball or Robinson's athletic career (but) about a man who refused to accept what he knew was wrong, both legally and morally, and fought against the prejudices of a Jim Crow atmosphere."[36]

Dr. Cornel West, a philosopher and Black intellectual, wrote the introduction of the 1995 edition of Jackie Robinson's autobiography, *I Never Had It Made*. Dr. West writes "more even than ether Abraham Lincoln and the Civil War, or Martin Luther King, Jr., and the Civil Rights movement, Jackie Robinson graphically symbolized and personified the challenge to a vicious legacy and ideology of white supremacy in American history."[37] In the book, Robinson adds that "the Army had barred this type of segregation. The incident was an attempt to frame me."[38]

In 1945, a few months after being cleared of an Army court-martial, Robinson signed a baseball contract with the Montreal Royals while proudly sporting his military uniform.

Notes

1   Laura Smith, "Jackie Robinson was once humiliated and court-martialed for sitting next to a Black woman people thought was white," *Timeline.com*, March 21, 2018. Retrieved from: https://timeline.com/jackie-robinson-wouldnt-go-to-the-back-of-the-bus-bd637b346c3f

2   Kenneth Clark, "Double jeopardy: Movie recounts ballplayer's fight with racism," *Chicago Tribune* October 8, 1990: A7.

3   James Endrst, "Trial of a hero chronicles on TV a nation's shame," *Hartford Courant*. October 15, 1990: B1.

4   Michael Lee Lanning, *The Court-Martial of Jackie Robinson* (Lanham, Maryland: Stackpole Books, 2020), 50.

5   Lanning, 50.

6   Mia Bay, *Traveling Black: A story of race and resistance* (Cambridge, Massachusetts: Harvard University Press, 2021), 154.

7   Pauli Murray, *States' Laws on Race and Color* (Athens, Georgia: University Press of Georgia, 1997). Also see Bay, 154.

8   "Ask for an Interpretation of Jim Crow Law," *Brownsville* (Texas) *Herald*, January 14, 1929: 13. Also see Bay, 165.

9   "Attempts to Ride Jim Crow Bus, Arrested," *Pittsburgh Courier*, February 28, 1925. Also see Bay, 165.

10   Bay, 165.

11   Bay, 165.

12   Bay, 165.

13   Bay, 165.

14   Marc Brenman, "Transportation Inequity in the United States: A Historical Overview," American Bar Association, July 1, 2007. Retrieved from: https://www.americanbar.org/groups/crsj/publications/human_rights_magazine_home/human_rights_vol34_2007/summer2007/hr_summer07_brenma/

15   Martin Luther King, Jr., *Stride toward freedom: The Montgomery Story* (New York: Harper & Brothers, 1958). 27.

16   Bay, 169.

17   Catherine Barnes, *Journey from Jim Crow* (New York: Columbia University Press, 1984: 40; "Soldier near death in Texas for riding in white section of bus," *Chicago Defender*, August 8, 1942.

18   "August 1, 1952: Sarah Keys refused to give up her seat on a bus." Zinn Education Project. Retrieved from: https://www.zinnedproject.org/news/tdih/sarah-keys-bus

19   Zinn, 1.

20   Lanning, 51.

21   Lanning, 176.

22   Lanning, 209.

23   J. M. Casper, "Lieutenant Jackie Robinson, Morale Officer, United States Army,", *Jackie Perspectives on 42* (Phoenix: Society for American Baseball Research, 2021), 51-60.

24   Casper, 51.

25   Bob Gill and Tod Maher, "Not only the ball was brown: Black players in minor league football, 1933-46. Professional Football Researchers Association, *The Coffin Corner*: Vol.11, No.5. 1989. Retrieved January 31, 2022. https://profootballresearchers.com/archives/Website_Files/Coffin_Corner/11-05-384.pdf

26   Lanning, 33.

27   Lanning, 32.

28   Lanning, 33.

29   Lanning, 33.

30   Lanning, 32.

31   Arnold Rampersad, *Jackie Robinson: A Biography* (New York: Ballantine Books, 1998).

32   Lanning, 37.

33   "The Court Martial of Jackie Robinson," The Faculty Lounge: Conversations about law, culture, and academic July 6, 2018. Retrieved from: https://www.thefacultylounge.org/2018/07/the-court-martial-of-jackie-robinson.html

34   Kareem Abdul-Jabbar and Anthony Walton, *Brothers in Arms: The Epic Story of the 761st Tank Battalion, WWII's Forgotten Heroes* (New York: Broadway Books, 2004), 57.

35   Casper, 51.

36   Shav Glick. "Jackie Robinson's Verdict of Honor. *Los Angeles Times*. October 14, 1990: 3.

37   Henry Louis Gates, Jr., "Was Jackie Robinson Court-Martialed?" PBS.org, Retrieved from: https://www.pbs.org/wnet/african-americans-many-rivers-to-cross/history/was-jackie-robinson-court-martialed/

38   Rick Du Brow, "Jackie Robinson vs. Another Racial Barrier," *Los Angeles Times*, June 19, 1990: F7.

Mr. Rickey Calls a Meeting

By Peter Dreier

In 1947, concerned about the firestorm that could erupt once he went public with his plan to break baseball's color barrier by hiring Jackie Robinson, Brooklyn Dodgers president Branch Rickey believed that his effort would not succeed without the full support of the Black community. In Ed Schmidt's play, *Mr. Rickey Calls a Meeting*, Rickey invites Robinson and three beloved and prominent Black Americans -- heavyweight boxing champion Joe Louis, entertainer Bill "Bojangles" Robinson, and actor-activist Paul Robeson -- to a secret meeting in a room at New York's Hotel Roosevelt on April 9, 1947, to solicit their public support.[1] The entire one-act play takes place in that room, as each character voices his views about Rickey's plan.

During the meeting, Rickey tells Louis, Robeson, and Bill Robinson that he won't proceed with his plan without their unanimous support. The play revolves around Rickey's effort to persuade the three men, who represented different and overlapping segments of the Black community, to embrace his plan.[2] Each figure in the play had some history with the others. Each of three invitees was also facing personal problems at the time. As the play unfolds, Louis and Bill Robinson express support for Rickey's plan, but Robeson raises objections regarding Rickey's motives and his control as well as the potential demise of the Negro Leagues. The play pivots to the others' reactions to Robeson's ideas.

Schmidt's play, written in 1989, debuted the following year at the Ironbound Theater in Newark, New Jersey. It was also staged at San Diego's Old Globe Theatre and at the Pasadena Playhouse, in Robinson's hometown, in 1997, the 50th anniversary of his breaking the color line. LA Theatre Works sponsored a live radio version of the play in 2004.[3]

Jackie Robinson

Rickey picked Robinson, a four-letter athlete at UCLA and a rookie with the Kansas City Monarchs, to integrate the major leagues over other more-established Negro League stars not only because of his athletic talent but also because he was young, educated, religious, and had experience dealing with inter-racial situations. Rickey knew Robinson had a hot temper and strong political views, but believed that he could handle the emotional pressure.

After signing Robinson to a minor-league deal in August 1945, Rickey assigned him to the Montreal Royals, Brooklyn's top minor-league team, for the 1946 season, believing that he would face less racism in Montreal than in other minor-league cities. During the season, however, the Royals traveled to segregated cities like Louisville and Baltimore, where Robinson couldn't stay in the same hotel or eat in the same restaurants as his white teammates.[4] After Robinson led the International League with a .349 batting average and led the Royals to a triumph in the minor league World Series, Rickey intended to bring him up to the Dodgers for the 1947 season. He even moved the Dodgers' spring training camp to Cuba, where Robinson would face less racist hostility than in Florida, where they usually trained.

Branch Rickey

Rickey was an unlikely candidate to dismantle baseball's segregation system. He was politically and socially conservative. He opposed swearing or drinking alcohol. In his youth, he was active in the Anti-Saloon League, a temperance group. He occasionally made anti-Semitic and anti-Catholic comments.

Soon after he joined the Dodgers in 1942, Rickey began strategizing about challenging baseball's color line. The question of *why* he did so has been the subject of much debate. Rickey viewed baseball in almost missionary terms, as a sport that enhanced American democracy and opportunity. He believed that segregation violated Christian principles.[5] But Rickey often publicly denied that he was on a moral crusade. "My only purpose is to be fair to all people and my selfish objective is to win baseball games," he explained.[6]

There were financial reasons motivating him as well. "The greatest untapped reservoir of raw material in the history of the game is the black race. The Negroes will make us winners for years to come."[7] Rickey believed that hiring Black players would boost attendance among the growing number of Black Americans who were moving from the South to the New York area during and after World War Two. Negro League teams were attracting large crowds when playing at the Polo Grounds and Yankee Stadium. The Brooklyn Bushwicks, a popular semipro team, drew their biggest crowds when they played Negro League teams.[8]

Rickey was a fervent anti-communist. In the late 1940s, he condemned ballplayers who jumped to the rival Mexican League for better pay as a "communist plot." During the 1930s and 1940s, the Communist Party had gained influence in progressive circles, particularly among Black Americans in New York.[9] Rickey knew that the Communist Party, its newspaper the *Daily Worker*, and leftist-led unions had been agitating to integrate baseball since the 1930s. He viewed the Negro press, led by the *Pittsburgh Courier*'s sports editor Wendell Smith, as allies in the cause. But Rickey did not want leftists to get credit for breaking the color line or to force his hand and his timetable.[10]

Rickey wanted to wait until early 1946 to make his announcement, but his hand was forced by New York Mayor Fiorello LaGuardia's Committee on Baseball, which was about to issue a report calling on the three New York teams to hire Black players. Rickey did not want it to appear that he had signed Black players under pressure. He arranged for the Royals to introduce Robinson as the team's newest member at a press conference in Montreal on October 23, 1945.

Joe Louis

Joe Louis reigned as heavyweight champion from 1937 to 1949. In 1938 he became a national hero for defeating German Max Schmeling, a symbol of Hitler's Nazi ideology of Aryan supremacy, in a first-round knockout. Although the military was segregated during World War Two, Louis raised money for war bonds and helped recruit Black Americans to enlist. He first met Robinson when they were stationed at Fort Riley, Kansas, a segregated Army base. Fort Riley officials refused to accept Robinson's application for Officers Candidate School. Louis used his influence and within days after arranging a meeting for Robinson and other Black soldiers with a representative of the Secretary of War, Robinson was enrolled in OCS. That incident, not mentioned in the play, led to a personal relationship between Louis and Robinson.

His managers promoted Louis as "Bible-reading, mother-loving, God-fearing ... and not... too black," according to historian Jeffrey Sammons.[11] Louis once remarked that his public image "made some whites begin to look at colored people different."[12]

By 1947, at the time of the fictional meeting, Louis was still champion, but, at 32, well past his prime, overweight, and virtually broke. He saw only $800,000 of the $5 million grossed in his title fights. His handlers skimmed much of his income. Louis donated many of his purses to the war effort, but the IRS claimed that his income from those charity fights was taxable and harassed him for unpaid taxes.

Bill Robinson

Tap dancer Bill "Bojangles" Robinson was the most highly paid Black entertainer in the country during the first half of the twentieth century. He was sometimes criticized for performances that reflected undignified racial stereotypes, an accusation he strongly resented given the limited roles available to Black performers in his day. He was a racial pioneer – breaking barriers on Broadway, Hollywood, and radio. He often played to mixed-race audiences, was the first Black dancer to star in White vaudeville circuits, one of the first Black headliners to refuse to perform in blackface, and the first Black performer to appear in an interracial dance team in a Hollywood film – with Shirley Temple in *The Little Colonel* in 1935. (That scene, in which the two dancers hold hands, was removed for screenings in the South.) Robinson used his influence -- persuading the Dallas Police Department to hire its first Black policeman, staging the first integrated public event in Miami, and lobbying President Franklin Roosevelt to improve the treatment and pay of Black soldiers during the war.

Robinson was a fervent New York Yankees fan. The team even enlisted him to quell the anger of New York's Black residents after a Yankee player made overtly racist comments.[13] In 1936 he was an original part-owner of the New York Black Yankees, a Negro League team that played most home games at Yankee Stadium. He was also one of two Black Americans that LaGuardia appointed to the 10-member committee to investigate racial segregation by the city's three major-league teams. The committee's work was stymied because one member (Yankees President Larry MacPhail) opposed the very idea and another member (Rickey) wanted to integrate the Dodgers on his own timetable without pressure from outsiders.[14]

Paul Robeson

Born in 1898 to a former runaway slave, Robeson starred in four sports at Rutgers, was twice named to the All-American football team, won Rutgers' oratory award four years in a row, was elected to Phi Beta Kappa, and was valedictorian of his 1919 graduating class. He played professional football to pay his tuition at Columbia University law school but gave up practicing law to pursue a theater career. A highly successful film and stage actor, he also sang opera, show tunes, Negro spirituals, and international songs in 25 languages. His concerts drew huge audiences. During World War Two, he entertained troops at the front and sang battle songs on the radio.

Robeson was also a defiant radical. He gave free concerts for unions and progressive causes. He often refused to take roles that demeaned Black Americans, although some of his film roles reflected popular but negative stereotypes. In 1945 the NAACP awarded Robeson the Spingarn Medal, its highest honor.[15]

Robeson was an outspoken critic of European and American imperialism and a strong supporter of nations in Africa and elsewhere seeking to unleash themselves from the yoke of colonialism. He embraced the Soviet Union, which he believed had done more than his native country to battle racism and anti-Semitism. He denied being a member of the Communist Party, but he was clearly close to the party and shared many of its views.

In 1943 Robeson led a delegation of prominent Black Americans, including the owners of major Black newspapers, who met with baseball Commissioner Kenesaw Landis and team owners to demand the sport's desegregation. "They said that America never would stand for my playing Othello with a white cast, but it is the triumph of my life," Robeson declared at the meeting. "The time has come when you must change your attitude toward Negroes. Because baseball is a national game, it is up to baseball to see that discrimination does not become an American pattern. And it should do this this year."[16]

In 1947, at the time of the play's fictional meeting, Robeson was still a popular figure. but as the Red Scare widened, he became increasingly controversial. He was certainly aware that the walls were closing in on him. The FBI already had Robeson under surveillance for his outspoken views and his leadership of several organizations – the Council on African Affairs, the National Negro Congress, and the American Crusade Against Lynching -- it considered "communist."[17] In October 1946, the Joint Fact-Finding Committee on Un-American Activities in California – chaired by state Senator Jack B. Tenney – called Robeson to testify. Robeson would later face similar questioning from Tenney's counterparts in Congress.[18] As a hint of what was to come, a growing number of lecture and concert halls and public schools refused to allow Robeson to give concerts or deliver speeches on behalf of left-wing groups.

Compounding his problems, Robeson's personal life, including his marriage, was in disarray. When the fictional meeting took place, he had recently ended an affair with White actress Uta Hagen, fearing that his career would be in jeopardy if publicly revealed.

Clancy Hope

One other character appears in the play. Schmidt uses Clancy Hope — a 17-year-old Black bellhop who brings food to the room — as a surrogate for the rank-and-file Black working class. Clancy (the play's only fictional character) is awestruck by the men in the room, asking each for an autograph. He looks at Robeson: "You're a Communist, ain't you?" Robeson: "That seems to be the consensus." Clancy: "My brother Cleveland, he's nineteen. He tells me you're a Communist. Cleveland says you're the finest man alive." Clancy's view of Robeson illustrates why Rickey invited him to the meeting and why he fears Robeson's influence.

The Carlton YMCA Meeting

The meeting depicted in the play is "almost certainly fictitious," Schmidt wrote in his original program notes. In notes for the 1992 production,

Schmidt clarified: "This meeting never took place." It is unclear if Schmidt was aware that Rickey *did* have a meeting with Black leaders. It wasn't a small gathering in a hotel room but a large assemblage at the Carlton branch of the YMCA in Brooklyn.

At Rickey's request, YMCA executive Herbert T. Miller invited 30 Black leaders from Brooklyn to meet Rickey on the evening of February 5, 1947. The audience included lawyers, ministers, realtors, doctors and dentists, teachers, architects, morticians, business people, municipal employees, and other civic leaders. The only White people in the room were Rickey, NYU sociology professor Dan Dodson (who was helping Rickey with his integration plan),[19] Edward Lazansky (a state Supreme Court judge), and Arthur Mann (a baseball writer and Dodger publicist).

The group expected to hear Rickey announce he was promoting Robinson to the Dodgers. Instead, he gave a long, paternalistic, and patronizing exhortation. He bluntly said that "if Jackie Robinson does come up to the Dodgers as a major leaguer, the biggest threat to his success — the one enemy most likely to ruin that success — is the Negro people themselves."

He warned the group that "on the day that Robinson enters the big leagues — *if* he does — every one of you will go out and form parades and welcoming committees. You'll strut. You'll wear badges. You'll hold Jackson Robinson Days...and Jackie Robinson Nights. You'll get drunk. You'll fight. You'll be arrested. You'll wine and dine the player until he is fat and futile. You'll symbolize his importance into a national comedy...and an ultimate tragedy — yes tragedy!"[20] Rickey concluded by outlining what needed to be done to prevent such behavior from "spoiling Jackie's chances."[21]

As Mann reported, the shocked group initially considered Rickey's remarks "a sharp slap against every Negro face in the room." But, by the end of Rickey's talk, "the room broke into deafening applause."[22] Despite Rickey's condescending attitude, the audience embraced his idea and formed a committee to carry out his plan. Their "Don't Spoil Jackie's Chances" campaign included churches, civic groups, and fraternal organizations in Brooklyn and Harlem. It urged Jackie's supporters to exercise restraint, such as "If you're drunk, don't go to the ball game" and "Leave your liquor outside the ballpark."[23]

There was no report of the meeting in either the mainstream or the Black newspapers.[24]

A Battle of Ideas and Personalities

The fictional meeting in Schmidt's play between these disparate personalities is highly contentious. Robeson has a wider agenda beyond giving Robinson a chance to break baseball's color line.

The play is a debate over different approaches to deal with racial injustice, through the lens of baseball. In this, the four Black figures echo a long-standing tension within the Black community, most prominently displayed in the debate between W.E.B. Du Bois and Booker T. Washington during the late nineteenth and early twentieth century. They sharply disagreed about strategies for achieving racial and class justice, the role of Black leaders, and what the Black elite owed to the Black masses.

Robeson, the left wing radical, insists that collective action is more effective than the one-person-at-a-time up-by-the-bootstraps approach. Louis and Bill Robinson share some of Robeson's views, but they are reluctant to undermine Jackie Robinson's chances to become a baseball and racial pioneer. Jackie Robinson recognizes that if Robeson gets his way, he will lose his opportunity to join the Dodgers that season. Put in that awkward situation, Robinson ends up reluctantly defending an individualist approach to racial advancement.

Rickey's paternalistic and patronizing attitude at the real YMCA meeting is reflected in his conversation with the four Black figures in the play. Rickey is used to being treated with deference. All of Rickey's employees – ballplayers, managers, coaches, and office staff, White and Black – referred to him, in person and in the third person, as "Mr. Rickey." Jackie Robinson would call him that even after Rickey died. Yet Rickey's condescension is mixed with some concern for Robinson as an individual or as an asset, depending on how one interprets his comments.

At the start of the play, Rickey instructs Robinson about the behavior he expects, similar to how Joe Louis's managers sought to control his behavior and image. In addition to avoiding any verbal or physical confrontations with players, Rickey tells Robinson that he should attend church, sign autographs, avoid going to nightclubs, return directly home after games, avoid being photographed with White women, and "no politics." Although the Dodgers opening day game is less than a week away – April 15 – Robinson still doesn't know if he'll be sent back to Montreal or play with the Dodgers. But then Rickey opens his briefcase, retrieves a Dodgers jersey, and tosses it to

Robinson. "You're moving up to the varsity," he tells him. "Congratulations, son. From this day forward, it's Rickey and Robinson."

Rickey tells Robinson that he wants the three visitors to believe that their opinions matter. He's especially concerned about Robeson, telling Robinson that "The opposition he could generate if he's not on our side — demonstrations, picket lines, dissension among the Negro ranks — could make life miserable for the both of us. So leave Robeson to me. If you lose your head and charge the mound on him, I'll take the jersey back."

When the three other men enter the room, they greet each other, and Robinson, warmly. Louis and Bill Robinson both know Rickey, but still call him "Mr. Rickey." They are stunned when they hear Robeson greet him as "Branch." It is the first sign that Robeson won't easily acquiesce to Rickey. Schmidt depicts Robeson as proud, idealistic, and arrogant, unwilling to bend his principles. Although he initially focuses his criticism on Rickey, he challenges Jackie Robinson, Bill Robinson, and Louis for being too accommodating toward Rickey, which he views as a symptom of the larger problem of powerful White figures controlling Black lives. He chides Bill Robinson for being "subservient" and says that he made his money "actin' the fool, playin' the happy, grinnin' darkie, then lost it all playing craps." He tells Joe Louis, "You've let other people do your thinking for so long, you can't think for yourself."

In the play, Robeson views Rickey primarily as a profit-seeking businessman. Most Negro League players did not have formal contracts, agreeing to play for a specific amount by a handshake. Players switched teams from year to year. Rickey took advantage of this situation, failing to adequately compensate Negro League teams whose rosters he raided to populate the Dodgers and minor-league rosters. He didn't pay the Kansas City Monarchs anything when he signed Robinson to a contract. Negro League owners were angry about Rickey – and later other major-league owners – poaching their talent. But wary of appearing opposed to racial integration, they muted their protests about the raids on their players.

Robeson tells Rickey, "With your stable of Negroes, the Brooklyn Dodgers will dominate baseball. But my concern is the fate of Bill's team. What will become of his team? What will become of the Black Yankees?" This is the crux of Robeson's argument: Whatever

Rickey's intentions — as a businessman and/or racial reformer — his plan would lead to the demise of the Negro Leagues and the livelihoods of its players and others who worked for the teams. "As they should be," Rickey says. "Five years from now, if I have any say in the matter, the Negro Leagues will be dead and gone, and so will Negro bathrooms and Negro drinking fountains and Negro hotels."

Robeson proposes instead that a Negro League all-star team, owned and run by Black Americans, be chosen to join the major leagues. Black players who aren't picked can sign with another major-league team. "Finally, Negro League owners – like Bill – must be justly compensated for each and every ballplayer they lose and for the certain extinction of their league." Rickey calls Robeson's plan "Head-in-the-clouds, ignorant, arrogant, impractical idealism."

Jackie Robinson interjects that Robeson's proposal is "a waste of my time."

"I understand your opposition, Jack," Robeson responds. "You're afraid you're not good enough to make that elite Negro team."

Robinson predicts that he'll be the Rookie of the Year and then the Most Valuable Player, but Robeson says that there are at least 25 Negro League players who could do better. He named several athletes, including Monte Irvin, who most colleagues believed was the best player in the Negro Leagues at the time. [25] Robinson is clearly offended by that remark, having heard others, including Negro League players and owners, make similar comments. Rickey disputes Robeson's baseball knowledge about these players, explaining why Robinson is the best choice.

But Robeson is making a larger point. He chides Rickey for wanting to be the "savior of the Negro race," but only on his terms. "If it's a World Series you want," Robeson says, "then take all the Negroes. I guarantee you'll win the World Series. Why only one? There are hundreds who deserve this chance." Frustrated by the others' unwillingness to challenge Rickey, Robeson loses his patience, looks directly at Robinson, and says, "And you just sit there in the corner with your mouth shut. Branch Rickey's water boy."

This gets a fierce reaction from Jackie Robinson. "What gives you the sonuvatchin' right to lecture me?" say Robinson. "I'm not some United Auto Worker out on strike, or your comrade over in Russia, or one of the Broadway faithful who's gonna stand up and cheer every time you open your mouth and sing your words of wisdom." Robinson defends Bill Robinson and Louis as heroic Black men, but Robeson arrogantly dismisses that claim.

Robeson tells Louis and Bill Robinson that "We're on different sides now! You are broke and beaten and pathetic because you let other people run your lives, but I never will."

"I didn't sell my soul," Robeson continues. "I didn't compromise. And I won't until the day I die and damn everything else. I fought this battle for years. I demanded the integration of baseball while you were still in college, young Jack Robinson. They have never beaten me."

"And you have never beaten them," Robinson answers, finding his voice in response to Robeson's baiting, expressing the fury that made him a successful athlete and activist. "But I will. Mr. Rickey's the one who opened the door, but I'm the one walkin' out the room... See, I know this isn't about spoiling Jackie's chances. It's about Clancy's chances, and my kid's, and his. I'm gonna catch all the shit they have to throw our way, and then I'm going' back into that Colored Only Room and I'll carry every single goddamn person out on my back."

Jackie Robinson, who had admired Robeson despite their political differences, now views him differently and defiantly. He tells Robeson, "I don't want to end up like them. But I sure as hell don't want to end up like you. You fought the battle all right, you just forgot who the enemy was. Dropped a bomb on your own troops."

Rickey leaves the room after young Clancy Hope told him that a representative of the Commissioner's office wanted to meet with him. That was a ruse, orchestrated by Louis. By the end of the play, Louis, Bill Robinson, and Robeson had still not voted on Rickey's plan. When Rickey comes back — after realizing that one or more of his guests had fooled him into leaving — he finds the door locked. None of the others bothers to open it and Rickey is stuck outside. When he threatens Clancy Hope, warning that he'll get him fired from his hotel job, the young bellhop tells Rickey, "You do it and you can go straight to hell."

Robeson leaves the meeting without saying good-bye to the others. Bill Robinson and Joe Louis tell Jackie Robinson that they support his promotion to the Dodgers. As the three are about to leave together, Bill Robinson looks at Clancy and calls him "the

bravest man I ever met. He did what no man ever done. He told Branch Rickey to go to hell." Jackie Robinson asks Clancy to "tell Mr. Rickey I went home. And tell him I'll be in uniform tomorrow."

The 28-year-old Robinson is about to begin his illustrious career in the major leagues. And the 17-year-old Clancy Hope, who has overheard these leading Black figures debate how to respond to White racism, has found his voice, learning from Robeson to speak up against a powerful white figure. We don't know what happens to Clancy, but we can imagine that he'd somehow be involved in the next two decades of civil rights activism.

Aftermath

Most Black Americans welcomed baseball's integration as they later welcomed the end of separate drinking fountains and segregated buses, parks, and schools. But their enthusiasm was mixed with recognition that opening the major leagues to Black players would sooner or later devastate the Negro Leagues and lead to a loss of jobs for players, stadium workers, and others.

Robinson's predictions about himself came true. In 1947, he was selected as the Rookie of the Year. That year, the Dodgers set road attendance records in every National League park except Cincinnati's Crosley Field. Two years later, he won the National League's Most Valuable Player Award. An outstanding base runner, with a .311 lifetime batting average, he led the Dodgers to six pennants and was elected to the Hall of Fame in 1962.

The tension between Robinson and Robeson depicted in the play is reminiscent of a real encounter between the two men. In July 1949, segregationist Congressman John Wood of Georgia, a former Ku Klux Klan member who chaired the House Un-American Activities Committee (HUAC), invited Robinson to address a hearing on "Communist infiltration of minority groups." Specifically, Wood wanted Robinson to attack Robeson for being a disloyal American and Communist agitator who didn't speak for Black people. The media salivated at the opportunity to portray the clash of these larger-than-life titans as a surrogate for the Cold War between capitalism and communism.

Although he didn't agree with Robeson's Communist views, Robinson was reluctant to testify against Robeson. "I didn't want to fall prey to the white man's game and allow myself to be pitted against another black man," he later wrote. "I knew that Robeson was striking out against racial inequality in the way that seemed best to him."[26]

On July 18, as expected, Robinson criticized Robeson, but it was far from the harsh attack that Wood and his HUAC colleagues had hoped for. Instead, Robinson challenged America's racial hypocrisy and made an impassioned demand for integration. Robinson said that Robeson "has a right to his personal views, and if he wants to sound silly when he expresses them in public, that is his business and not mine. He's still a famous ex-athlete and a great singer and actor."[27] Robinson insisted that Blacks were loyal Americans who would "do their best to help their country stay out of war. If unsuccessful, they'd do their best to help their country win the war — against Russia or any other enemy that threatened us."[28]

Robinson's appearance was a major news story, but the press focused on his criticism of Robeson and virtually ignored his condemnation of racism. It was part of a wider campaign to isolate Robeson, who was denounced by the media, politicians, and conservative and liberal groups alike as being a traitor and Soviet shill. Radio stations banned his recordings. Concert halls and colleges cancelled his performances.

In 1950, the State Department revoked Robeson's passport so he couldn't perform abroad, where he was still popular. His annual income plummeted from over $150,000 to less than $3,000. His name and photo were even stricken from the college All-America football teams. His voice was marginalized during the 1960s civil rights movement. He died a lonely and broken man on January 23, 1976, at age 77.

In his 1972 book, Robinson apologized to Robeson, writing that he wished he had rejected HUAC's invitation to testify against him. "I have grown wiser and closer to the painful truths about America's destructiveness, and I do have an increased respect for Paul Robeson, who, over the span of that 20 years sacrificed himself, his career and the wealth and comfort he once enjoyed because, I believe, he was sincerely trying to help his people."[29]

In 1950, Walter O'Malley gained control of the Dodgers, purchased Rickey's shares, and pushed him out as Dodger president. The following season, Rickey became the Pittsburgh Pirates' general manager, stepping down after the 1955 season. His plan to start a third league, the Continental League, never

got off the ground. He died on December 9, 1965, 11 days before his 84th birthday. He was elected to the Baseball Hall of Fame in 1967.

During his life, Bill Robinson was a benefactor to many charities and frequently donated money to complete strangers facing hard times. He lost much of his fortune at the racetrack. By the time of the play's fictional meeting, he was virtually penniless, a result of his "love of luxury, his extreme generosity, and his undiminished penchant for gambling."[30] At the end of the 1947 season, the Dodgers invited him to attend a Jackie Robinson Day celebration where he presented Robinson and Rachel with keys to a new car. Bojangles told assembled reporters, "I never thought I'd be around to honor a Ty Cobb in Technicolor."[31] He died penniless on November 25, 1949, of heart failure. Harlem schools were closed for a half-day so that children could attend or listen to the funeral over the radio.

Louis kept fighting long after his boxing skills had eroded. He announced his retirement on March 1, 1949. After the IRS told him that, with interest and penalties, he owed the government over $500,000, he kept fighting until 1951, when Rocky Marciano knocked him out. To make money, the desperate Louis became a professional wrestler, appeared on TV quiz shows, took a job greeting tourists at Caesars Palace hotel in Las Vegas, and refereed wrestling matches until 1972. Friends and admirers helped Louis pay off some of his debts.

Louis died of cardiac arrest on April 12, 1981. In 1982, Louis was posthumously given the Congressional Gold Medal, the highest award Congress bestows on civilians. People often said that Louis was "a credit to his race." *New York Post* sportswriter Jimmy Cannon responded: "Yes, Joe Louis is a credit to his race — the human race." In 1954, Jackie said: "I certainly feel that the path for me and others to the big leagues was made easier by the performance and conduct of Joe Louis both in and out of the ring. All of us should give Joe a pat on the back for creating a favorable atmosphere."[32] On another occasion, Robinson observed, "I'm sure if it wasn't for Joe Louis the color line in baseball would not have been broken for another 10 years."[33]

The predictions Robeson made in *Mr. Rickey Calls a Meeting* were also accurate. In 1947 about 311 players filled the rosters of the 12 Negro League teams.[34] By the end of the 1953 season, only 35 former Negro League players had reached the major-league level.[35]

The demise of the Negro Leagues destroyed the careers of many Black ballplayers.[36] Without the same fanfare that greeted Robinson, some former Negro League players signed contracts and served as pioneers, integrating major- and minor-league teams, which was particularly rough in many Southern cities and towns.[37] Many of them languished in the minors for years without ever advancing to the majors.

The quality of Negro League play suffered, as did attendance. In his syndicated column on May 29, 1947, Dan Parker noted that while record crowds attended the New York Giants game at Polo Grounds to watch Robinson, a Negro League game across the river at Yankee Stadium attracted a small crowd.[38] In 1948, the Negro National League – including Bill Robinson's New York Black Yankees – folded. The Negro American League collapsed around 1960. By 1966, the Indianapolis Clowns were the only former Negro League team still playing, primarily by staging exhibition games against local teams, peppering the games with humorous antics, similar to the Harlem Globetrotters basketball team. The Clowns called it quits in the 1980s.

By 1959, Black ballplayers comprised 10 percent of major league players, reaching 20 percent by the mid-1960s. Black ballplayers who pioneered integration in the 1950s learned that simply making it to the majors didn't mean an end to the racial discrimination and segregation they would continue to face in baseball and in the wider society, including the segregation of spring training facilities and the fact that in many cities Black ballplayers couldn't stay in the same hotels, eat in the same restaurants, or take the same taxis as their white teammates.

Jackie Robinson's legacy is not simply that he was the first African American to play in the major leagues in the 20th century. He viewed himself as much an activist as an athlete. He recognized that his opportunity to break baseball's color line was the result of a protest movement and he repaid that debt many times over through his own participation in the struggle for civil rights. The recent upsurge of activism around racial justice among professional athletes, including baseball players, is part of that legacy.[39]

Robinson believed that as an American citizen, and as a Black man in a racist society, he had an obligation to use his fame to challenge the social and political status quo. Years before Colin Kaepernick was born, Robinson wrote: "I cannot stand and sing the anthem. I cannot salute the flag; I know that I am a black man in a white world."[40]

Notes

1 Robinson played his first game as a Dodger a week later, on April 15, 1947.

2 New York's Black elite was a relatively small world of overlapping social circles. Bill Robinson and Robeson lived in the same housing complex – the 511-unit Dunbar Apartments in Harlem, built in 1926, which was also home at different times to W.E.B. Du Bois, poet Countee Cullen, bandleader Fletcher Henderson, union leader A. Philip Randolph and explorer Matthew Henson. Jim Haskins and N.R. Mitgang, *Mr. Bojangles: The Biography of Bill Robinson* (New York, Linus Multimedia, 2014), 191. See also Matthew Gordon Lasner, "Housing To Remember: The Paul Laurence Dunbar Apartments," Gotham Center for New York City History, March 28, 2017 https://www.gothamcenter. org/blog/housing-to-remember-the-paul-laurence-dunbar- In the 1930s, Louis and Robeson both lived in another Harlem apartment building at 555 Edgecombe Avenue. See Paul Hond, "Bittersweet," *Columbia Magazine*, Winter 2016-2017. https:// magazine.columbia.edu/article/bittersweet and "DIY Walking Tour: Historic Harlem Homes," *The Curious Uptowner*, n.d. https://www. thecuriousuptowner.com/post/diy-walking-tour-historic-harlem-homes. In 1941, Robeson recorded a song about Louis, "King Joe," with lyrics by Richard Wright and music by Count Basie. See David Margolick, "Only One Athlete Has Ever Inspired This Many Songs," *New York Times*, February 25, 2001. *https://www.nytimes.com/2001/02/25/arts/music-only-one-athlete-has-ever-inspired-this-many-songs.html*

3 The LA Theatre Works performance is available in CD format. https://www.audiobooks.com/audiobook/mr-rickey-calls-a-meeting/210100

4 Despite these difficult circumstances, Robinson led the International League with a .349 batting average and 113 runs, finished second with 40 stolen bases, and led the team to a 100-54 season and a triumph in the minor league World Series.

5 Allen St. John, "There Was Another Side to the Color Line: Green," *Los Angeles Times*, March 30, 1997. For Rickey's motives, see Lee Lowenfish, *Branch Rickey: Baseball's Ferocious Gentleman* (Lincoln: University of Nebraska Press, 2007).

6 Jules Tygiel, *Baseball's Great Experiment: Jackie Robinson and His Legacy* (New York: Oxford University Press, 1983, 52

7 John McMurray, "Branch Rickey Revolutionized Baseball In More Ways Than One," *Investors Business Daily*, April 12, 2017. https://www. investors.com/news/management/leaders-and-success/branch-rickey-revolutionized-baseball-in-more-ways-than-one/; Allen St. John, "There Was Another Side to the Color Line: Green," *Los Angeles Times*, March 30, 1997.

8 Thomas Barthel, *Baseball's Peerless Semipros: The Brooklyn Bushwicks of Dexter Park* (Harworth, New Jersey: St. Johann Press, 2009).

9 Mark Naison, *Communists in Harlem During the Depression* (Champaign: University of Illinois Press, 2004); and Mark Solomon, *The Cry Was Unity: Communists and African Americans, 1917-36* (Jackson: University Press of Mississippi, 1998).

10 Peter Dreier, "Before Jackie Robinson: Baseball's Civil Rights Movement," in Bill Nowlin and Glen Sparks, editors, *Jackie: Perspectives on 42*, Society for American Baseball Research, 2021, 27-37. https://sabr. org/research/article/before-jackie-robinson-baseballs-civil-rights-movement/ On Rickey's concern about communists, see Dan Dodson, "The Integration of Negroes in Baseball." *Journal of Educational Sociology*, Vol. 28, No. 2 (October 1954), 73-82. On the protest movement to integrate baseball, see Tygiel, *Baseball's Great Experiment*; Chris Lamb, *Conspiracy of Silence: Sportswriters and the Long Campaign to Desegregate Baseball* (Lincoln: University of Nebraska Press, 2012); Irwin Silber, *Press Box Red: The Story of Lester Rodney, the Communist Who Helped Break the Color Line in American Sports* (Philadelphia: Temple University Press, 2003); Kelly Rusinack, "Baseball on the Radical Agenda: The Daily Worker and Sunday Worker Journalistic Campaign to Desegregate Major League Baseball, 1933-1947," in Joseph Dorinson and Joram Warmund, editors, *Jackie Robinson: Race, Sports,*

and the American Dream (Armonk, New York: M.E. Sharpe, 1998); David K. Wiggins, "Wendell Smith, The Pittsburgh Courier-Journal and the Campaign to Include Blacks in Organized Baseball 1933-1945," *Journal of Sport History*, Vol. 10, No. 2 (Summer 1983): 5-29; Henry Fetter, "The Party Line and the Color Line: The American Communist Party, the 'Daily Worker,' and Jackie Robinson," *Journal of Sport History*, Vol. 28, No. 3 (Fall 2001): 375-402; Lowenfish, *Branch Rickey*, and Arnold Rampersad, *Jackie Robinson* (New York: Ballantine Books, 1997).

11 Sammons' comment is from a PBS documentary, *The Fight*, about Louis and Schmeling, cited in Ned Martel, "Schmeling and Louis, Body and Soul," *New York Times*, October 18, 2004. https://www.nytimes. com/2004/10/18/arts/television-review-schmeling-and-louis-body-and-soul.html

12 Quoted in Ira Berkow, *Counterpunch: Ali, Tyson, the Brown Bomber, and Other Stories of the Boxing Ring* (Chicago: Triumph Books, 2014), 38.

13 Ray Robinson, "When Bojangles Came to the Yankees' Defense," *New York Times*, August 22, 2009. https://www.nytimes. com/2009/08/23/sports/baseball/23bojangles.html

14 Neil Lanctot, *Negro League Baseball: The Rise and Ruin of a Black Institution* (Philadelphia: University of Pennsylvania Press, 2004), 276; Lamb, *Conspiracy of Silence*, 275.

15 The following year, after four African Americans were lynched in Georgia, Robeson led a delegation that urged President Harry Truman to support legislation to end lynching, admonishing the president that "the Negroes will defend themselves" if threatened by mob violence. Truman told Robeson that, in the middle of a war, the time was not right to pass such divisive legislation. Robeson disagreed and founded the American Crusade Against Lynching, co-chaired by scientist Albert Einstein, to pressure Truman and Congress, but their efforts were unsuccessful.

16 Martin Duberman, *Paul Robeson* (New York: The New Press, 1995), 282-283; Wendell Smith, "Publishers Place Case of Negro Players Before Big League Owners: Judge Landis Says No Official Race Ban Exists in Majors," *Pittsburgh Courier*, December 11, 1943: 1.

17 Duberman, *Paul Robeson*, 296-335.

18 Duberman, *Paul Robeson*, 307-309.

19 See Dodson, "The Integration of Negroes in Baseball."

20 Arthur Mann, *The Jackie Robinson Story* (New York: Grosset & Dunlap, 1963), 160-65. This meeting is also mentioned in Milton Gross, "The Emancipation of Jackie Robinson," *Sport*, October 1951, and A.S. (Doc) Young, "Jackie Opens the Door," *Ebony*, December 1968. References to the YMCA meeting in subsequent books and articles rely on Mann's first-person account and those by Gross and Young.

21 Mann, *The Jackie Robinson Story*, 164.

22 Mann, *The Jackie Robinson Story*, 162.

23 Mann, *The Jackie Robinson Story*, 164-65.

24 Dodson, "The Integration of Negroes in Baseball."

25 According to Roy Campanella, "Monte was the best all-round player I have ever seen. As great as he was in 1951, he was twice that good 10 years earlier in the Negro Leagues." Many Negro League owners and players as well as Black sportswriters shared Campanella's opinion. Irvin also had other qualifications, including a college education (Lincoln College) and military service, that Rickey was looking for. He was the same age as Robinson, although he had suffered a knee injury from which he never fully recovered. When he came up to the majors in 1949, Irvin acknowledged that "this should have happened to me 10 years ago. I'm not even half the ballplayer I was then." Larry Hogan, "Monte Irvin," SABR bio project https://sabr.org/bioproj/person/monte-irvin. Irvin told Joe Posnanski that Dodger scout Clyde Sukeforth made him an offer to become the first Black player in the majors, but he declined the offer because he didn't think he was ready for that pioneering role. Joe Posnanski, *The Baseball 100* (New York: Simon & Schuster, 2021), 203. He explained to Peter Golenbock that his three years of service in World War 2 had been too hard on him. "I hadn't played at all. That war had changed me." Peter Golenbock, *In the Country of Brooklyn* (New York: William

Morrow, 2008), 148. He told Jeff Idelson that being in a segregated Army unit during the war "affected me both mentally and physically." He said that "Jackie was the right person." Jeff Idelson, "An Interview with Monte Irvin," Baseball Hall of Fame, n.d. https://baseballhall.org/discover-more/stories/baseball-history/interview-with-monte-irvin-2006

26   Jackie Robinson with Alfred Duckett, *I Never Had It Made* (New York: HarperCollins, 1995; original published in 1972), 85-86.

27   Transcript of Robinson's testimony: https://babel.hathitrust.org/cgi/pt?id=uc1.31210019443231&view=1up&seq=37.

28   Transcript of Robinson's testimony.

29   Peter Dreier, "Half a Century Before Colin Kaepernick, Jackie Robinson Said, 'I Cannot Stand and Sing the Anthem,'" *The Nation*, July 18, 2019. https://www.thenation.com/article/huac-jackie-robinson-paul-robeson/

30   Haskins and Mitgang, *Mr. Bojangles*, 216.

31   "Brooklyn Honors Jackie Robinson," *Paterson* (New Jersey) *Morning Call*, September 24, 1947.

32   "Jackie Acclaims Joe Louis at Howard Fete," *Afro-American*, February 13, 1954.

33   Quoted in Randy Roberts, "Joe Louis: 'You Should Have Seen Him Then,'" in Gerald Early, ed., *The Cambridge Companion to Boxing* (New York: Cambridge University Press, 2019), 184.

34   Calculated from annual rosters in Dick Lark and Larry Lester, editors, *The Negro Leagues Book* (Cleveland, Ohio: Society for American Baseball Research, 1994).

35   Calculated from data and examples in Larry Moffi and Jonathan Kronstadt, *Crossing the Line: Black Major Leaguers, 1947-1959* (Iowa City: University of Iowa Press, 1994); Rick Swaine, *The Integration of Major League Baseball: A Team by Team History* (Jefferson, North Carolina: Mc-

Farland & Company, 2009); and Steve Jacobson, *Carrying Jackie's Torch: The Players Who Integrated Baseball – and America* (Chicago: Lawrence Hill Books, 2007).

36   August Wilson's play *Fences* reflects the frustration and anger of Negro League players whose careers ended after the integration of the major leagues. See Peter Dreier, "Denzel Washington Brings August Wilson's 'Fences' To the Screen," *American Prospect*, January 6, 2017 https://prospect.org/culture/denzel-washington-brings-august-wilson-s-fences-screen

37   Bruce Adelson, *Brushing Back Jim Crow: The Integration of Minor-League Baseball in the American South* (Charlottesville, Virginia: University of Virginia Press, 1999); Amy Essington, *The Integration of the Pacific Coast League: Race and Baseball on the West Coast* (Lincoln: University of Nebraska Press, 2018).

38   Dan Parker, "Robinson Attracts Negro Fans," *Camden Courier-Post*, May 29, 1947.

39   Peter Dreier and Dave Zirin, "Making Black Lives Matter On and Off the Diamond," *The Nation*, September 30, 2020 https://www.thenation.com/article/activism/blm-mlb-logo-baseball/; Peter Dreier, "Will Major League Baseball Confront Its Racist Past?" *Dissent*, July 22, 2020 https://www.dissentmagazine.org/online_articles/will-the-mlb-confront-its-racist-history; Peter Dreier, "Athletes' Racial Justice Protest Last Week Made History. But It Wasn't the First Wildcat Strike in Pro Sports," *Talking Points Memo*, September 3, 2020

https://talkingpointsmemo.com/cafe/athletes-racial-justice-protest-history-wasnt-first-wildcat-strike-pro-sports; Dave Zirin, *The Kaepernick Effect: :Taking a Knee, Changing the World* (New York: The New Press, 2021)

40   Jackie Robinson, *I Never Had It Made* (New York: Harper Collins, 1995) (originally published in 1972), xxiv.

Brother on the Wall
Spike Lee's *Jackie Robinson*

By Joshua Neuman

In an Instagram post on March 29, 2020, Spike Lee announced that he would be sharing the 155-page fifth draft of a script for a Jackie Robinson biopic, which he wrote in 1996. The project, he wrote, was an "epic dream" of his that was never realized. The post came at the beginning of a global pandemic and worldwide shutdown and with baseball spring training canceled and the regular season delayed, the never-been-seen script was a window into baseball's past as well as a proxy for its present. As such, it was widely covered by the media with more than a few observers using the occasion to mention that Lee was set to become the first Black president of the Cannes Film Festival,[1] an implicit comparison between Robinson's efforts as a trailblazer and those of Lee.

It wasn't the first time the comparison had been made. Henry Louis Gates, Jr. once described Lee as "the Jackie Robinson of the film community."[2] Both Robinson and Lee have been celebrated as trailblazers, but also criticized for being too militant by mainstream Whites and as sellouts by some Black critics. As a result, making Robinson his subject in a film would be a way for Lee not merely to interrogate the representation of an African-American icon, but also to think about his own meaning as a Black filmmaker.

The script was not the first time that Lee pays homage to Robinson. There have been several over the course of his work—many referencing one another. *School Daze* (1988), the follow-up to his debut film, begins with a photo montage depicting the African-American struggle in the United States going all the way back to the slave ships. A Jackie Robinson still is featured first in a sequence of iconic Black athletes including Willie Mays, Muhammad Ali, and Joe Louis. It's worthy of note because a series of photos lies at the heart of the drama of a film that Lee would release the following year, *Do the Right*

Thing (1989). Those photos belong to the "Wall of Fame" inside Sal's Famous Pizzeria in the Bedford-Stuyvesant neighborhood of Brooklyn, but they are of Italian-Americans rather than African-Americans—this despite the fact that the vast majority of the establishment's patrons are Black. Tension builds between the Italian-American owners of the pizzeria and the Black patrons in the community, a tension that eventually explodes into death and destruction.

Do the Right Thing's main character, Mookie (played by Lee) works as a delivery boy for Sal's Famous Pizzeria and as such, serves as a mediator of sorts between his White employers and the pizzeria's Black patrons. When we meet him, he is wearing a white Brooklyn Dodgers home jersey with Jackie Robinson's name and number 42 on the back. The jersey simultaneously marks Mookie as being on his home turf in Brooklyn, as well as referencing Robinson's own home turf. Robinson and his wife Rachel stayed in a rented room at 526 MacDonough Street in Bedford-Stuyvesant during his trailblazing 1947 season.

Mookie's Robinson jersey stands in opposition to the first of several Italian-American icons on the wall that director Lee reveals in a montage, Joe DiMaggio. According to W.J.T. Mitchell, the Wall of Fame functions as a kind of "exclusion from the public sphere" for the Black patrons, a reminder that in this space they are not equal citizens.[3] Meanwhile, Mookie in his Robinson jersey foreshadows the tension that Lee would have Robinson embody in his screenplay: a symbol for racial tolerance on the surface, but with feelings of rage lurking just below the surface—rage that, when triggered, can easily overflow into violence. There were other, less consequential Robinson references in Spike Lee films, especially around the time he was working on his script for *Jackie Robinson*, including *Malcolm X* (1992), *Crooklyn* (1994), and *Girl 6* (1996).

None of those references captured the imagination of the public the way his Instagram video did in 2020, announcing that he would be making his script available to the public. In the video, Lee sits in front of a poster from 1950's *The Jackie Robinson Story*—an apt backdrop, because his story immediately situates itself against that film. The fifth draft of *Jackie Robinson* (1996) kicks off in the Robinsons' living room in Stamford, Connecticut in 1972. Robinson, 53 and going blind, opts to go to bed instead of sitting with Rachel for a television screening of the 1950 film. "That story should be burned," he says, heading upstairs and leaving Rachel alone to watch by herself.[4] By focusing on Rachel's experience of the old movie in the absence of her husband, Lee establishes two things: that his depiction of Robinson's life will at least in part be seen through Rachel's eyes; and that it will self-consciously critique the icon's other cultural representations, particularly the first and, at that time, last major motion picture that had been made about Robinson—the 1950 film, starring Robinson as himself.

Rachel chose Lee to spearhead the biopic in October of 1994 despite widespread belief at the time that she would bestow documentarian Ken Burns with the opportunity.[5] "I still feel that a black man can understand another black man and all the nuances of his life better than anyone else can," she said at the time.[6] But Rachel and her hand-picked filmmaker had different priorities in rendering Robinson's icon. Rachel long fought the idea that he was an angry man—and to be sure, there is a tendency to portray Black men who are assertive and aggressive as dangerous and angry—but there has been a countervailing tendency to neuter Robinson of his anger—to make his story safe for White audiences and to make Robinson nonthreatening, which was Lee's concern.

His script seems intent on upending an image of the hero, put forth in the 1950 biopic, as overly timid. When the bus of his barnstorming Negro League team stops at a rest stop somewhere in the South in *The Jackie Robinson Story*, Robinson is tasked with going in and getting sandwiches. Sheepishly, he walks in and is rebuffed by the man behind the counter. Robinson hems and haws until a White chef offers to make the players beef and ham and egg sandwiches. Robinson is his most courageous when he deigns to ask, "How about some fried potatoes on the side, chef?" Lee totally turns the episode on its head

having Robinson's Negro League manager, Frank Duncan, politely inquiring. When he is rebuffed, Lee's Robinson insists that the team refuse to fuel up their bus at the establishment, a gesture that Lee tells us has earned a new "respect for the rookie college boy."[7]

Robinson's timidity in *The Jackie Robinson Story* is likely the byproduct of its attempt to cast Rickey, its White hero, in the most courageous light. When a petition begins to circulate among some of the Dodgers, opposing Robinson joining the club, the 1950 film focuses on the anger it rouses in Rickey. "You call yourselves Americans?" he admonishes the signers of the petition. When a local ordinance forbids an integrated Dodgers/Royals exhibition during spring training, an oddly contrite Robinson says to Rickey "I'm the cause of the trouble, Mr. Rickey. Maybe you'd like to call it off?" Rickey rebukes him, "Not on your life, boy! We started this together and we'll finish it together!" In contrast, when Lee's Robinson (up against not only bureaucracy but real hate) is confronted by a segregation-enforcing sheriff who literally shows up in a cloud of dust that Robinson kicks up sliding into home plate—he follows his manager's orders to get off the field, but still manages to get in the last word: "Ok, Skipper, tell him that ah'ma gittin'."[8]

That Lee emphasizes Robinson's aggression doesn't prevent him from also showing his vulnerabilities. He goes to great length to chronicle Robinson's travails in the International League with the Montreal Royals: his stress-induced nausea, exhaustion, and efforts simply to have bat meet ball. *The Jackie Robinson Story* focuses on the challenges imposed upon Rickey. He has to fend off International League President Frank Shaughnessy's last-ditch effort to pressure Rickey into re-thinking his great experiment. As for Robinson, he confesses to Rachel to being a "little nervous, maybe," but given what Shaughnessy has told Rickey about the calamities that are about to befall the league, Robinson seems less courageous than naïve.

Even when Montreal heads (presumably) to Louisville in *The Jackie Robinson Story*, it's unclear how the boos cascading from the stands affect Robinson. When a trio of White racists calling themselves "the welcoming committee" confront him outside the Royals locker room, it is Rickey (not even present!) who is center stage as we hear his words "you can't fight back" echoing in Robinson's mind—just long enough until his (White) Royals teammates can arrive and diffuse the situation. Back on the field, the film transitions to a montage of racist fans and opposing players and coaches hurling epithets at him. Some White fans taunt him with a black cat who he invites into the dugout and cuddles. He's called a "shine" and a "sambo" and mocked by an opposing coach chomping on a giant piece of watermelon, but the film cross-cuts into dissolves not just to Robinson, but to his (formerly?) racist manager Clay Hopper, being won over to Robinson's cause.

In Lee's script, the watermelon incident (not mentioned in his memoir) happens in the majors when the Dodgers meet the Phillies in Ebbets Field in 1947. In a scene since immortalized in Brian Helgeland's *42*, Lee has Philadelphia Phillies manager Ben Chapman lay into Robinson with the most hateful, racist torments of the entire screenplay. As Robinson walks to the plate, the Phillies players hold up watermelons as Chapman hollers "Hey n_____, hey, n_____, you want a cold slice of watermelon?"[9] The over-the-top, almost caricatured racism of the insults hurled at Robinson feels like the quick-cutting montage of racist slurs in *Do the Right Thing* and both have a similar effect: simultaneously demonstrating their absurdity and their cruelty.[10]

Just as it's hard to separate *Do the Right Thing* from Lee's Robinson screenplay when thinking about the writer/director's use of racist slurs, it is difficult not to imagine his image of Robinson holding a baseball bat and not think about *Do the Right Thing*'s Sal brandishing a bat as a weapon. In Lee's 1989 film, the bat was an overt reference to the murder of Michael Griffith, who in 1986, was beaten with a baseball bat by a group of White youths outside a pizza parlor in Howard Beach in Queens and then chased onto a highway where he was fatally struck by a car.

Perhaps more subtle is a visual cue he slips into his Jackie Robinson script when the Dodgers lose the 1947 World Series to the New York Yankees—the image of Joe DiMaggio, whose icon was the first Lee revealed in his "Wall of Fame" montage in *Do the Right Thing*. Going back to W.J.T. Mitchell's notion that the display inside Sal's Pizzeria functioned as a kind of "exclusion from the public sphere" for its Black patrons, the image of DiMaggio (first in the montage and in the center of the Wall of Fame) makes it resonate even more bitterly when it is revealed in *Jackie Robinson* at the precise moment when the Dodgers are denied a world championship. In this sense, DiMaggio's image isn't just a symbol of Dodger

defeat, but an incitement of sorts—that in New York City, the integrated Dodgers are still not the equals of the lilywhite Yankees.[11] The image of DiMaggio is the perfect pivot point in the script for Robinson's evolution in Lee's story. Not long after he has Branch Rickey visit Robinson in his hotel room to tell he no longer needs to turn the other cheek, that it's time to "fight back."[12]

In a scene in Lee's script based on a moment in *I Never Had It Made*, Robinson confesses that the abuse out of the Phillies dugout drove him to think, "To hell with the image of the patient black freak I was supposed to create. I could throw down my bat, stride over to the Phillies dugout, grab one of those white sons of bitches and smash his teeth in with my despised black fist."[13] Lee's Robinson doesn't throw down his bat, but rather, charges into the Philadelphia dugout with his Louisville Slugger. He smashes the Phillies players who Lee depicts, screaming in pain. Then, he has Robinson smash Chapman in the mouth, leaving the Philadelphia manager "out cold, bloody and down for the count."[14] When Lee cuts back to Robinson stepping back into the batter's box, his violent fantasy having ended, we have a heightened understanding of the strain he is under, and are less willing to take his peacefulness for granted, or to dare to think of it as "timidity."

Part of what that meant for Lee was exercising the license to paint a complex picture of Robinson. The Robinson of *The Jackie Robinson Story* is Rickey's obedient, suffering servant being sent to be crucified. We are given no window into his inner turmoil—that, as he tells us in his memoir, "I couldn't sleep and often couldn't eat. Rachel was worried, and we sought the advice of a doctor who was afraid I was going to have a nervous breakdown."[15] In Lee's script, Rachel worries as the Phillies shout racist expletives because "she knows her husband could easily snap."[16]

Lee's Robinson is all too human and as such possesses faults. At times, he really is timid. He is afraid to ask Branch Rickey for a raise[17] and to stand up for himself with Dodgers owner Walter O'Malley.[18] Other times, he's bull-headed. He pushes a fatigued Don Newcombe back to the mound in the ninth inning of the deciding playoff game against the Giants in 1951, causing the Dodgers 4-0 lead to be split in half.[19] Bullheadedness is also framed as the reason he can't bring himself into backing John F. Kennedy for president after he claims Kennedy can't "look him in the eye."[20] Lee's Robinson goes so far as to acknowledge his prideful mistake. Lee has him share via voiceover: "I do not consider my decision to back Richard Nixon over John F. Kennedy for the Presidency in 1960 one of my finer ones."[21]

Most of all, Lee suggests that Robinson's biggest flaw was his impatience. When Jackie, Jr. is 11, Robinson grows impatient with his son's lack of baseball aptitude. He scolds him when he swings and misses at an underhand pitch, "How can you miss that?"[22] And his zealous crusade for integration and incremental change (no matter how small) sometimes seems shortsighted, as does his insistence at staying at the Chase Hotel in St. Louis even though management still refuses to allow Blacks to enter its dining room, night club, or swimming pool. "Why give them white folks my money when I can't get the same privileges as the next man?," asks Roy Campanella. "We're patronizing black businesses," adds Don Newcombe.[23]

Spike Lee, in his Robinson jersey, on the set of *Do the Right Thing*. photo courtesy of Alamy

Though Robinson's impatience also seems to be an occasional virtue. In a line cribbed straight from *I Never Had It Made*, he has Robinson say of his decision to steal home in Game One of the 1955 World Series: "I took off. I really didn't care whether I made it or not. I was just tired of waiting." And just as his zealous impatience produced a momentum shift in the World Series, so too does it produce an unexpected outcome at the Chase. Newcombe ends up joining Robinson at the hotel and the two even gain entry to the hotel dining room.[24]

Lee's biopic also presents more complex views of racism than previous films about Robinson. Dodgers teammate Hugh Casey flippantly tells Robinson that when he was down in Georgia having bad luck at poker, he'd rub "the teat of the biggest, blackest n___ woman I could find." In Lee's description of the action, the screenwriter pauses to editorialize, "AHHH SHIT!!!!!" though Robinson, the character, doesn't find any humor in the slipup. He tells Wendell Smith: "Do you have any idea what it took on my part not to kill that cracker?"[25] But Lee cleverly distinguishes Casey's casual racism from the willful

and sadistic strain belonging to Ben Chapman. It is not the obvious White allies (Pee Wee Reese or Ralph Branca) who Lee has rush to Robinson's defense when Enos Slaughter spikes him in St. Louis, but Casey who only moments earlier had uttered a racist epithet.[26] The effect is not to diminish the significance of Casey's bigotry, but to show a more complicated (and perhaps more modern) version of racism at work—one not necessarily reducible to willful, discriminatory hatred.

Lee's characterization of Leo Durocher also explores this idea. Lee introduces him as a character during spring training prior to the 1947 season when the infamous petition is circulating, and the Dodgers manager is irate. He scolds his players, "I don't care if the guy is yellow or black or if he has stripes like a fuckin' zebra, I'm the manager and I say he plays."[27] But Durocher's egalitarian spirit is nowhere to be found when supporting Robinson is no longer in his interest. We meet him again in 1951 during the Dodgers' three-game series with the New York Giants who he is now managing. Pulling aside Black players Willie Mays, Monte Irvin, and Ray Noble in the Giant's clubhouse, he warns his players that "if the game gets close into the late innings I may be shouting n_____ and watermelon at the guys on other side like Robinson."[28]

Lee never secured financing for his Jackie Robinson script, claiming that he had wanted Denzel Washington to play the role of Robinson but that the then-42-year-old actor thought he was too old. The truth is a little more complicated. When Lee wrote the script, his power in the industry was waning. After a disappointing $48 million at the box office for *Malcolm X* (1992), ticket sales for his films followed a general downward trend. *Crooklyn* (1994) made only $14 million against a $14 million budget. *Clockers* (1995) generated $13 million domestic gross from a $25 million budget, and *Girl 6*, released the same year that Lee finished the fifth draft of his Robinson screenplay, earned a paltry $4.9 million against a $12 million budget. Without Denzel Washington in the starring role, few were willing to provide the $40 million budget Lee wanted for production.[29]

It's a shame because, even more so than Malcolm X, Lee seems comfortable channeling Robinson's voice. He explores the unspoken class tensions between Robinson and his Kansas City Monarch teammates. Satchel Paige tells Robinson to go back to "U.C. of the L.A." for "some mo' schoolin'"[30] and calls him "college boy."[31] When Lee's Wendell Smith calls up Robinson to ask him to venture to Boston for the tryout with the Red Sox in 1945 he tells him, "We need players of your background and ability."[32] When Robinson meets Sam Jethroe and Marvin Williams neither of them speak with the Black dialect in which Lee had the Negro Leaguers speak. Nor does John Wright, the African-American pitcher who joined Robinson at spring training in Daytona Beach, Florida prior to his season with Montreal. When Branch Rickey Jr. steps to the microphone at the press conference announcing Robinson's signing by the Montreal Royals he characterizes Robinson as "a fine type of young man, intelligent, and college bred..."[33] When Paige hears the news he bemoans that "I should have been the one" and that "it's just because Jackie has an education [that he was chosen]."[34]

The idea that Robinson was or wasn't fit to represent the Black people because of his middle-class status is an idea that Lee was particularly in touch with. During the leadup to *Malcolm X*, a rally was held in Harlem in an attempt to urge Lee not to "mess up Malcolm's life." According to the poet Amiri Baraka who had a hand in leading the protest, "We will not let Malcolm X's life be trashed to make middle-class Negroes sleep easier."[35]

It should perhaps come as little surprise that Lee shows Robinson being booed in Harlem by a crowd of "afros, dashikis and raised clinched fists."[36] Robinson's passion for incrementalism which inspired him to endure taunts, attacks, and injustices is precisely what gets called into question. Lee's Robinson defends Nelson Rockefeller's efforts to build a Harlem State Building, "Maybe this isn't the best thing in the world, but it's something" as a new generation of activists accuse him of being a "sellout" and an "Uncle Tom."[37]

Balancing out (or perhaps cancelling out) the critique of Robinson as "sellout" is the idea that he was too controversial, too ideological, too strident— paradoxical claims that have also been leveled at Lee. In the script, Robinson uses the *New York Daily News* columnist Dick Young to articulate a view sometimes referred to today as "shut up and dribble." He contrasts Robinson's frosty relationship with the media with that of his teammate, Roy Campanella. "A lot of newspapermen are saying that Campy's the kind of guy they can like but that your aggressiveness, you're wearing your race on your sleeve, makes enemies," he informs Robinson.[38]

The Jackie Robinson Story (1950) ends with Robinson approaching Rickey in the dugout after the Dodgers have won the pennant and asking whether he should accept an invitation to Washington to speak to the American people about Democracy and, in Rickey's words, "about a threat to peace that's on everybody's mind." After testifying that "Democracy works for those who are willing to fight for it," the camera dissolves to a shot of the Statue of Liberty and the score swells into rendition of "America the Beautiful." The White narrator then proclaims: "Yes, this is the Jackie Robinson story, but it is not his story alone, not his victory alone. It is one that each of us shares..."

Spike Lee's Robinson script ends with Robinson proclaiming that he cannot stand and sing the American anthem or salute the flag knowing that he is a Black man in a White world. The script not only re-situates Robinson as the hero of his own story, renders him a complex three-dimensional person, and paints a picture of a great experiment that was tense, combustible and far from a sure thing. It also gives a greater sense of what his experience means to the Black community.

Until the Dodgers pennant-winning game in 1947 that is the climax of *The Jackie Robinson Story*, Rachel is the only African-American represented in the stands. (And even in that pennant-winning game, the lone additions to Rachel are Robinson's brother Mack, mother Mallie, and a random Black couple who are there for the payoff on a joke about a formerly racist fan being won over by Robinson.) Lee, meanwhile, goes to great length to show the impact that Robinson is having on the Black community—the hundreds of cops enforcing racial quotas at the gates of the stadiums in which he plays, turning away large numbers of Black fans who understand that Rickey's "great experiment" is theirs as much as it is his.

Lee never got to make his Robinson film, but he was able to make a three-minute short film for Budweiser called *Impact,* celebrating Robinson's 100th birthday in 2019. Cutting between a bar filled with Black patrons listening to his first major-league at-bat on the radio and a contemporary naturalization ceremony in which immigrants (including a woman in a Robinson jersey) are taking an oath of allegiance to the country, and narrated by Robinson's daughter Sharon, the film ends with a montage of 11 contemporary activists who presumably had been touched by his "everlasting impact."[39]

Not to minimize the courage it took for Budweiser to connect Robinson's legacy with immigration at the height of then-President Donald Trump's attack against those coming to the U.S. to seek a better life, but there is a certain irony to Spike Lee so thoroughly universalizing Robinson's story after struggling for years to make a film that once and for all captured a particular experience that would be grounded in blackness. "Like a ball hit just right," Sharon Robinson narrates, "he sent us on an irreversible trajectory, reminding us all that not only baseball but that life itself is a game of impact." In the midst of a montage of Robinson artifacts, there is a brief shot of Lee costumed as Mookie on the streets of Bed Stuy: staring straight at us, arms crossed. At first it feels like he's there to stand in judgment of its own inclusion, but he's also there in tacit recognition that Robinson's "impact" today, at least in part, emerges from contemporary conversations about his meaning. Though Spike Lee never got to make his Robinson biopic, he is still very much part of those conversations.

Notes

1. Ryan Lattanzio, "Spike Lee Shares Script for Unmade Jackie Robinson Passion Project – Read Now," IndieWire.com, March 29, 2020. https://www.indiewire.com/2020/03/spike-lee-jackie-robinson-script-1202221317/, Accessed December 20, 2021.

2. Spike Lee as told to Kaleem Aftab, *That's My Story and I'm Sticking to It* (New York: WW Norton & Company, 2005), 174.

3. W.J.T. Mitchell, "The Violence of Public Art: *Do the Right Thing*," *Critical Inquiry*, Vol. 16, no. 4 (1990): 894.

4. Lee, 3.

5. William C. Rhoden, "Jackie Robinson, Warrior Hero, Through Spike Lee's Lens," *New York Times*, October 30, 1994. Lens,https://www.nytimes.com/1994/10/30/sports/sports-of-the-times-jackie-robinson-warrior-hero-through-spike-lee-s-lens.html Accessed December 20, 2021.

6. Rhoden, "Jackie Robinson, Warrior Hero, Through Spike Lee's Lens."

7. Lee, 23.

8. Lee, 51.

9. Lee, 73.

10. *Do the Right Thing* movie clip, https://youtu.be/gLYTObRhcSY

11. Spike Lee, *Jackie Robinson*, unpublished manuscript, 1986: 85.

12. Lee, 86.

13. Jackie Robinson as told to Alfred Duckett, *I Never Had it Made* (New York: HarperCollins, 1995), 59.

14. Lee, 74.

15. Robinson, 49.

16. Lee, 73.

17. Lee, 90.

18. Lee, 103.

19. Lee, 98.

20. Lee, 130.

21. Lee, 129.

22. Lee, 117.

23. Lee, 110.

24. Lee, 112.

25. Lee, 79.

26. Lee, 83.

27. Lee, 66-67.

28. Lee, 95.

29. Lee as told to Aftab, 211.

30. Lee, 16-17.

31. Lee, 18.

32. Lee, 19.

33. Lee, 36.

34. Lee, 36.

35. Evelyn Nieves, "Malcolm X: Firestorm Over A Film Script," *New York Times*, August 9, 1991: B1. https://www.nytimes.com/1991/08/09/nyregion/malcolm-x-firestorm-over-a-film-script.html Accessed December 20,2021.

36. Lee, 136.

37. Lee, 136.

38. Lee, 106.

39. Budweiser ad clip, https://youtu.be/KBvNSznpg0s?t=146

Robert B. Parker's *Double Play*

By Benjamin Sabin

Bent for Blood at Ebbets Field

Do you remember when a gun for hire almost shot Jackie Robinson at Ebbets Field from behind the dugout on the first-base line? Of course, you do. How could you forget a moment like that? Everybody was there: Dixie Walker, Ralph Branca, Clyde Sukeforth, Eddie Stanky, Pee Wee Reese, and Spider Jorgensen. They all saw it. Hilda Chester and her cowbell along with the Dodger Sym-Phony saw it, too. They saw the man in the short-sleeve Hawaiian shirt pull a pistol from his lunch bag and point it at Jackie Robinson.

If you're having a hard time remembering, let me refresh your memory. After the shooter aimed his pistol, but before he got a round-off, he was shot twice, possibly three times, by unknown gunmen.[1] He slumped over dead on the first-base dugout and Jackie continued to play baseball unharmed. The guardian angel shooters were never caught, but nobody really looked that hard for them. The real bad guy was dead and they were the unsung heroes.

Still having a difficult time placing the aforementioned actions? One reason might be because none of it ever happened. Although, given the climate of our country at the time of Robinson's major-league baseball career, and the well-documented history of death threats against him, this kind of violence is not that far-fetched. But no, in reality, there was no man in a Hawaiian shirt bent on assassinating Jackie Robinson only to be foiled in the final seconds. This was all from the mind of author Robert B. Parker and contained within the pages of his exciting novel, *Double Play*.

Getting to know Mr. Parker

When one thinks of Robert B. Parker, if they know anything about him, they don't typically think baseball writer. You're not going to find his image next to W.P. Kinsella's, or his smiling mug sandwiched between Roger Angell and Bill James. You are much more likely to find Parker's list of related searches populated by Elmore Leonard, Dean Koontz, and Raymond Chandler. He was a writer of fast-paced fiction, mostly of the mystery/detective genre, who also had a deep love of baseball, which is evident in the pages of *Double Play*.

Parker was born on September 17, 1932, in Springfield, Massachusetts. He attended Colby College in Maine where he earned a bachelor's degree. Following his graduation, he served in the U.S. Army and fought in the Korean War. Shortly after the completion of his service, he was married to Joan Hall. They were married for 53 years, until his death, and had two sons, named David and Daniel.[2]

After the Parkers were married in 1956, it was time to get down to the business of starting and supporting a family. While Parker's dream was to be a writer, he needed a steady income. So he joined corporate America as an editor and technical writer working in advertising and insurance. Robert quickly tired of the corporate life and decided to head back to college and pursue a teaching career that would also permit some writing time on the side. He graduated from Boston University with a Ph.D. and began teaching at Northeastern University, where he put his writing plan into action.[3] In 1973 his first novel, *The Godwulf Manuscript*, was published.

The Godwulf Manuscript was the first of his Spenser novels; he eventually wrote over 30 books in the series. It was the Spenser novels that put Parker's name on the map, bringing him wealth and critical acclaim. He went on to release two other best-selling series and many other stand-alone novels, all of which saw great success, including the western *Appaloosa*, which was made into a movie starring Ed Harris and Viggo Mortensen. In total, Parker wrote nearly 70 books before his death on January 8, 2010.[4] He suffered a heart attack and was found at his desk. He had been working on a novel when he passed.

Double Play

Robert Parker was well into a successful writing career when *Double Play*, one of three of Parker's novels published in 2004, was released. *Double Play* was a break from the norm for Parker and a nice change of pace for readers who had tired of the previous 30 Spenser novels.

The critical response to *Double Play* was overwhelmingly favorable. *Publisher's Weekly* went so far as to state that "Parker...has never written so spare and tight a book; this should be required reading for all aspiring storytellers."[5] The Kirkus book review took it a step further saying that "the talk is electric, the pacing breakneck, the cast colorful and empathic. After a couple of so-so efforts, Parker flat out nails it here."[6] It is safe to say that Parker critically saved his career with *Double Play* by writing a "deeply felt and intimately told memory tale."[7]

The plot of *Double Play* follows a typical, sometimes referred to as "Parkeresque," novel. The chapters are three to four pages long with short paragraphs and a simplistic, blunt, Hemingway-like writing style. The central character of the book is Joseph Burke, an ex-Marine who took "five .25 caliber slugs"[8] to the chest at Guadalcanal, which sent him to a hospital and put him out of commission for nearly a year. While laid up, Burke's wife left him, leaving behind a deeply scarred man. But, being the supremely trained killing machine that he is, Burke is not only physically tough, but also mentally, and he develops a protective exterior to guard his psychological wounds. He finds that the best medicine is to not care about anything.

But, even those who don't care need money to survive, so Burke looks for a job doing what he knows best, which is being a tough guy. Initially, he tries his hand at boxing, following the advice of a fellow Marine that he served with, but sees little success other than a black eye and a headache. He then becomes an enforcer in the underworld followed by a bodyguard for a spoiled heiress (who he falls for). This path eventually leads him to Branch Rickey who needs someone to protect his new rookie. The rookie is, of course, Jackie Robinson.

Shortly after their meeting, and Rickey's hiring of Burke as Robinson's bodyguard, Jackie and Burke run into some trouble at a restaurant owned by a low-

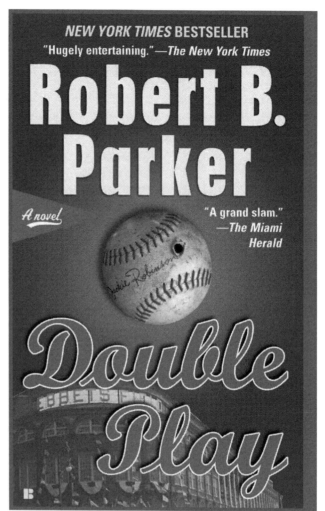

image courtesy of Penguin Random House

level mobster. They are grabbing a bite to eat after a doubleheader against the Giants and the mobster, Mr. Paglia, offers a bottle of champagne to Robinson. Robinson respectfully declines the bottle, but in the process offends Mr. Paglia. It is this confrontation that ultimately sets up much of the action in the story and the dramatic attempted assassination of Robinson at the close of the book. And while the physical drama of the story keeps the reader turning the pages, it is numerous emotional storylines that are the real meat behind *Double Play*.

There are a few different arcs taking place in *Double Play*. The first is that of Burke. We learn about his backstory from how he met his wife, his injury, his descent into being an emotional recluse, and his eventual salvation in the arms of the aforementioned spoiled heiress. The second storyline is that of "Bobby." The storyline of Bobby is completely separate from the rest of the book. The Bobby chapters, of which there are 10, are printed in italics and obviously reflect the experiences of a 16-year-old Parker (whose first name is Robert or Bobby). During the Bobby chapters, Parker discusses his love of baseball, his concern over racial tensions, and seeing Jackie play at Ebbets Field while "sitting among Negroes, between two heavy black women."[9] The Bobby chapters are a way for Parker to tell his story and reflect on why he felt the deep need to write a book about Robinson in his voice.

The third storyline is Jackie Robinson. Robinson doesn't "physically" enter the book until chapter 17 when he is introduced to his intended bodyguard, Joseph Burke, by Branch Rickey. "Robinson came in wearing a gray suit and a black knit tie...[and] moved as if he were working off a steel spring."[10] Burke and Robinson don't necessarily hit it off, but they don't dislike one another either. There is a guarded quality about their first interaction that remains for some time. Initially, it is obvious that protecting Robinson is just a job for Burke, but as he gets to know Robinson that changes. Throughout their time on the road, eating meals, and staying together in Black hotels, Burke experiences the day-to-day racism that Robinson must endure. It is through these experiences that Burke develops an understanding of the Black experience.

We also follow the historical Robinson who is surrounded by numerous Dodger greats, both players and personalities. But most important is Robinson's character and the moral center that it provides in the novel. His temperament gives the reader a barometer to which all others are judged including Robinson's bodyguard, Burke.

Ultimately Robinson and Burke learn to trust each other and make it through a jungle filled with racism and violence, culminating in the shootout at Ebbets Field with the Hawaiian-shirted gunman. Following the squelched assassination attempt, Burke realizes, because of his time with Robinson, that he does care about living. His protective exterior is broken down and he allows himself a chance at love.

And while Burke has experienced the sweetness of redemption, Robinson has all the while been a normal guy just trying his best to make his way in the world and at the same time changing the course of history and opening the door of civil rights.

Parker, Jackie and What They Mean

Parker grew up an out-of-place Dodgers fan in New England. He was born during the Great Depression and was 9 when the Japanese bombed Pearl Harbor.

Until the advent of World War II, he grew up during FDR's New Deal, which helped the country out of the Great Depression. When World War II engulfed the nation and the world in a violent struggle between good and evil everything changed for Parker. His idyllic, prosperous childhood was gone in an instant. It is through *Double Play,* and more specifically the Bobby chapters, that Parker expresses his sorrow for days past. By reliving, through Bobby, his final nice summer days before the war in 1941, he sets the elegiac tone for the book.

While the Bobby chapters are contemplative and dreamlike, the rest of the book is written with a sense of urgency, almost like Parker was trying to bring back what was lost from before the war and his New Deal childhood. It is through Robinson, Parker's hero following World War II, that Parker tries to recapture, or save, what has been lost. If Parker can rescue his postwar hero, Jackie Robinson, in the pages of *Double Play* maybe he can preserve a piece of his prewar childhood.

While Parker attempts to recapture what was once lost through Jackie Robinson, he also puts Robinson in great peril throughout the book. Robinson is hunted both physically and mentally throughout *Double Play*. Both Robinson's fictional story and the real-life events that he experienced are a microscopic reflection of what African American people have experienced in this country since they were forced to come here in chains. And while the physical chains are gone, the immaterial chains are just as strong, or stronger, than they were in 1619 or 1947. Robinson was hunted in real life, and the pages of *Double Play*, as African Americans are still hunted to this day on the streets of their own country. It is a somber thing to say, but sometimes it seems that not much has changed since Jackie Robinson took the field 75 years ago.

Notes

1   Robert B. Parker, *Double Play* (New York: Berkley Books, New York, 2004(, 239.

2   https://www.bookreporter.com/authors/robert-b-parker

3   https://robertbparker.net/author

4   https://robertbparker.net/author

5   https://www.publishersweekly.com/978-0-399-15188-0

6   https://www.kirkusreviews.com/book-reviews/robert-b-parker/double-play/

7   https://www.nytimes.com/2004/05/23/books/crime-594946.html

8   Parker, *Double Play*, 1

9   Parker, *Double Play*, 273.

10   Parker, *Double Play*, 98.

"I Want to Take Your Picture!"
Reconsidering *Soul of the Game* & the "Future" of Jackie Robinson

By Raymond Doswell, Ed.D.

Soul of the Game premiered on April 20, 1996, on Home Box Office (HBO) cable network. The docudrama interpreted the challenges and triumphs surrounding the integration of major-league baseball through the lives of three key figures from the Negro baseball leagues; LeRoy "Satchel" Paige (portrayed by Delroy Lindo), Josh Gibson (Mykelti Williamson), and Jackie Robinson (Blair Underwood).[1]

Soul of the Game sits within a series of dramatic film attempts to capture the experience of African-American baseball history. Since the premiere of *The Jackie Robinson Story* (1950), new authors and creators arrive to offer a refreshed perspective on the story. *The Bingo Long Traveling All-Stars and Motor Kings* (1976) for theatrical release; *Don't Look Back: The Story of LeRoy Satchel Paige* (1981), *Soul of the Game* (1996), and *Finding Buck McHenry* (2000) all made for television release. These efforts were interspersed with new books and documentaries, most notably the popular *Baseball: A Film by Ken Burns* (1994), and many special events that highlighted a national resurgence in Negro Leagues history.

In reconsidering *Soul of the Game* 25+ years after its debut, it can be argued that the film ushers in a more complete interpretation of Robinson. Baseball historians, former players, and many fans feel they know this story because of Robinson's status as a hero for baseball and civil rights. However, the persona presented in this film was revelatory to the broader public at the time. Despite some problematic licensing and storytelling, the film falls appropriately in line with other films detailing the arc of Robinson's life, between *The Court-Martial of Jackie Robinson* (1990) and *42* (2013), about his spring training and first season with the Brooklyn Dodgers.

Delivering any Jackie Robinson story well and accurately weighs heavily on producers and actors, as the films become a hoped-for validation of his pioneering career and teaching tool for new generations of young fans. Moreover, for observers of Negro Leagues history, opportunities to highlight an often glossed over aspect of Robinson's baseball experience, his one season with the Kansas City Monarchs, was enthusiastically welcomed. Robinson's experience as a Negro Leagues infielder is dealt with in *The Jackie Robinson Story*, but *Soul of the Game* placed that experience at the center of the treatment, thus bringing new perspective to the Robinson legend.

Soul of the Game has been thoroughly critiqued and reviewed, praised for very strong portrayals by the actors, and lamented for historical departures and licenses taken by the filmmakers for the sake of drama and entertainment. The film strived to have authenticity, shooting in historic ballparks in Alabama and Indiana, as well as sets in St. Louis, Missouri. However, some highlighted stories are arranged out of sequence with the real history, such as the opening scene of baseball in the Dominican Republic (which would have been years earlier in 1937). Some events were fabricated, such as the situation of Paige and Robinson springing Gibson from a mental hospital to play in a high-stakes Negro Leagues vs. major leagues All-Star game in front of scouts at Griffith Stadium.[2] Small details like incorrect uniform numbers and several other issues annoy some observers. Among the strongest charges was the fact that, historically, Gibson, Paige, and Robinson, although contemporaries and opponents, most likely did not interact as depicted in the film. Depending on perspective, these issues are at worst negligence or at best minor things to nitpick for an otherwise entertaining product.[3]

Creating a documentary treatment was not the filmmaker's goal. However, the license taken, and choices made with the facts, limit the film to a character study of each historic figure. So, did the filmmakers get that right? Are we presented an accurate and compelling interpretation of the great baseball players dealing with monumental change? Examining the many aspects of those questions goes beyond the scope of this essay, but the portrayal of Jackie Robinson does earn our attention.

Exploring the development of the film and choices made by the creators reveals how Robinson's pioneering life establishes future public perceptions of him. Underwood's performance is more informed by material available on Robinson's past and passions leading up to 1945. Among the many things that emerge on film is a sharper focus on Robinson as an intellectual, fiery competitor, and social crusader, and not just a passive participant in the grand schemes of Dodgers General Manager Branch Rickey. History reveals Robinson endured a long grueling season in Black baseball with great success and much media attention for his athletic abilities. We also learn that he stood in stark contrast to his peers, clashing in ideals and motivations for his life. In this film, he symbolizes the future, representing the eminent and abrupt change brought by integration in postwar America, as well as a model for the future of Black athletes.

A Season of Change

Baseball fans know the historic year 1947 as the occasion of Robinson's first major-league season, but they know fewer details of Robinson's ascendance from the Negro Leagues. The setting for *Soul of the Game* is the pivotal year 1945. The real history shows a 26-year-old Robinson looking to pursue opportunities to earn money for his family. He experienced a tumultuous final year in the U.S. Army, and now aspired to marry his fiancée Rachel Isum. Robinson is a known sports celebrity, having made headlines in collegiate football, basketball, and track. However, he arrives at the February spring training in Texas for the Kansas City Monarchs rusty on baseball skills and out of conditioning.

The Monarchs, like many teams in baseball, were depleted of talent due to World War II, but whipped themselves into shape for a May 6 regular season opening. There was even an early spring tryout invitation of Black players for major league baseball's Boston Red Sox, that included Robinson. It was arranged through pressure on the team from the Black press, but it yielded no job offers for the participants.

The Monarchs were on the road constantly, and Robinson earned high praise and media attention for his efforts. Satchel Paige formally joined their travels in late May and made eight known league appearances with the Monarchs between pitching-for-hire/gate attraction opportunities around the country. Team tours included southern and east coast swings, facing teams like the Homestead Grays and slugger Josh Gibson. Robinson generally batted third in the lineup and was rewarded with selection to the East/West All-Star Classic in Chicago. The most complete data shows Robinson appearing in 34 out of 75 league games, with a .375 batting average, four HRs, and 27 RBIs.

Stars of *Soul of the Game*, Mykelti Williamson (l.), Blair Underwood (c.), and Delroy Lindo (r.) at an event honoring the film at the Negro Leagues Baseball Museum. photo courtesy of NLBM

Paige, at age 38, had three wins against three losses, one complete game, 3.55 ERA, 41 strikeouts, and surrendered 10 walks over 38 innings.[4]

The grinding season was winding down with no postseason for the Monarchs. They finished second in the Negro American League to the Cleveland Buckeyes, who swept Gibson's Grays in the Negro World Series. Gibson maintained his solid seasonal play, hitting for a .372 average over 43 recorded regular-season league games, but could muster only two hits and two walks in the championship series.[5]

Robinson had come to a troublesome crossroads of frustration with segregated baseball and a need to make a living. He was summoned to speak with the Brooklyn GM Rickey and offered a minor-league opportunity with the team. The Dodgers had embarked on a clandestine effort to recruit Black players under the ruse of developing a separate Black major league. Robinson's acceptance marked the break that helped his immediate situation and set him on an unimaginable historic path.

Baseball in Black and White

In fall 1995, HBO announced Lindo, Williamson, and Underwood would begin October filming of *Baseball In Black and White*.[6] At about the same time, there were other potential treatments on Black baseball history in the Hollywood pipeline, including separate announced projects in early 1995 by directors John Singleton and Spike Lee. With the hot progressive directors getting all the media attention, there must have been some pressure on HBO to bring their project forward. Ultimately, the logjam of films was avoided as HBO was first to get a script into production. The other projects have yet to be produced.[7]

All these film endeavors rode a wave of culturally broad, increased interest in Black baseball history. Historian Dan Nathan described it as a "steady historical revival" since the 1970s, featuring new research, new exhibitions, player appearances, baseball apparel, and commercial opportunities. "Collectively, these and other cultural texts suggest that more white people may be aware of, knowledgeable about, and interested in the Negro leagues today than when the leagues actually existed."[8]

Soul of the Game was directed by Kevin Rodney Sullivan based on a script by David Himmelstein. After reviewing several potential treatments, Sullivan was drawn to Himmelstein's creative choices. "It found the right time frame for the story because [1945] was the year Jackie was a rookie [for the Kansas City Monarchs]. It brought those three men into the same arena at the most crucial moment and really got us into the race to be first."[9]

"It's an extraordinary story of extraordinary characters at an extraordinary time. The country was going through a huge flux," Himmelstein told the *Washington Post*. In taking license with the factual accuracies of the story, he added that the goal "was to be true to the spirit of the major players. Every time you try to compress a man's life, let alone three lives, into two hours, there's going to be distortion."[10] Himmelstein reflected on his choices 25 years later:

> Sometimes you have to bend the facts in service of the human drama. When I was writing *Soul of the Game* I portrayed Josh Gibson, Satchel Paige and Jackie Robinson as being a lot friendlier than they actually were to each other when they were playing in the Negro Leagues right after World War II. People who were experts immediately pointed that out. But your primary duty is to the story, using it as a springboard to illuminate greater truths. And that same dynamic and push-pull is there.[11]

At some point, the name of the film was changed from *Baseball In Black & White*, to *Soul of the Game*. It is unclear when or why it changed, but the new title became permanent by early 1996.

Blair and Uncle Eli

Excited to play a leading role in the film was actor Blair Underwood. By 1995, the 30-year-old Underwood had a decade of noteworthy television acting credits. The former athlete seemed well suited for the role, both in interest and pedigree. "Football was primarily my game," he told the *Washington Post*. "My father was a four-letter man, not unlike Jackie Robinson. But my great uncle, Eli Underwood, played with the Detroit Stars and barnstormed with the Pittsburgh Crawfords and the Homestead Grays. I've always heard about the Negro Leagues from him."[12]

Underwood family roots are traced to the 1850s in Perry County, Alabama. Blair's grandfather was Ernest Underwood (born around 1902). Ernest's brother Eli (born around 1906) and their three other siblings were raised by father Robert and mother

Isabelle, who were farm laborers. Within a decade of Eli's birth, the family moved north, and Robert worked in the steel mills of Steubenville, Ohio. Eli would later work in the mill, but soon picked up baseball opportunities for Black barnstorming and league teams.

In the 1930s, Eli Underwood pitched and played outfield with the Buffalo Giants based in Steubenville and the Cuban Giants of Grand Rapids, Michigan, which morphed into the Cincinnati Cuban Giants in 1935. Later, he joined the reformed Detroit Stars, part of a new Negro American League, in 1937. One Underwood family legend recounts that Eli, known for having large feet, had Satchel Paige stealing his shoes in a prank. "But Satch gave them back the next day. My great uncle has big feet, but his shoes weren't big enough for Satch," Blair recalled. After baseball, Eli served in the United States Navy.[13]

Eli's older brother Ernest also worked in the Ohio steel mill but later became a police officer. With wife Beatrice they had four sons, including Frank, who became an Army Colonel. Military life took Frank Underwood and family to many national and international locations. Their son Blair was born in 1964 at Tacoma, Washington.

Psychological Makeup

Blair Underwood enthusiastically embraced the challenge of playing Robinson but knew he had work ahead of him to get it right. "I was excited when this came along. There haven't been many stories like it. There was *The Bingo Long Traveling All-Stars & Motor Kings*, but that was more fictitious," he noted.[14] From his family, Underwood had deep perspective on the Black working class, Black migration, baseball history, and military life; all important components to understanding Jackie Robinson. He still wanted to learn more to play the role effectively:

> I knew about Robinson's natural talents and the taunts and insults he faced from racist fans, but I didn't know anything about his psychological makeup. . . I didn't know that this man had a hell of a temper and had to learn how to control it. In my mind, he was someone who pacifically turned the other cheek. Nothing could be further from the truth.[15]

Underwood gleaned even more insights from a noteworthy eyewitness to history, veteran actress Ruby Dee. Dee was Black cinematic royalty. With husband Ossie Davis, the actress had blazed a historic trail of theater, television, and film appearances. She enjoyed one of the most synergistic career arcs in history. Dee starred as young "Rachel Robinson," Jackie Robinson's wife, in the 1950 film *The Jackie Robinson Story*. Then 40 years later, played Robinson's mother Mallie opposite Andre Braugher as "Lt. Jackie Robinson" in the 1990 television film *The Court-Martial of Jackie Robinson*. In addition, Dee and Davis were great friends with the Robinsons for many years, supporting numerous civil rights initiatives together. Underwood recalled:

> She found it hard to believe the image that was presented was the man she worked with. He was decent and hardworking, but also a man with a temper that he had to learn to control. I did not know that. I remember hearing he had to deal with a lot of mess from people, but the fact is he did not always want to turn the other cheek. [16]

Jackie Robinson as an angry Black man is a revelatory nuance that Underwood brings to audiences. Himmelstein's script highlighted this perspective, adding to the drama of the story in many scenes. Many other reflections on Robinson were available to the film creators to inform this perspective.

"And he *would* fight!"

Among available material in the mid-1990s exploring Robinson's life was his autobiography *I Never Had It Made*. In collaboration with Alfred Duckett, Robinson completed the work shortly before he passed away in the early 1970s. In it, Robinson explains his disdain for life in the Negro Leagues and the many pressures weighing on him before his meeting with Branch Rickey. As he explains, the prospect of making $400 a month when he was recruited to the Monarchs was a "financial bonanza" after being discharged from the Army. However, it turned out to be "a pretty miserable way to make a buck."[17]

> When I look back on what I had to go through in black baseball, I can only marvel at the many black players who stuck it out for years in the Jim Crow leagues because they had nowhere else to go. . . These teams were poorly financed, and their management and

promotions left much to be desired. Travel schedules were unbelievably hectic. . . This fatiguing travel wouldn't have been so bad if we could have had decent meals.[18]

It was an extremely stressful time for Robinson. He felt "unhappy and trapped" as he questioned his future.[19]

The book *Baseball's Great Experiment: Jackie Robinson and His Legacy* by historian Jules Tygiel appeared in 1983. Tygiel's seminal work captured important aspects of the Robinson story and beyond. Attention was paid to Robinson's disdain for prejudice he faced in his youth, the military, and during his time in the Negro Leagues. Tygiel interviewed many of Robinson's contemporaries, who years later also confirmed Robinson's temper, competitiveness, and social isolation:

> The Robinson personality had been created by these experiences. His fierce competitive passions combined with the scars imbedded by America's racism to produce a proud yet tempestuous individual. . . His driving desire for excellence and his keen sense of injustice created an explosive urge.[20]

According to Tygiel, this reputation preceded Robinson, but was noted as an unfair critique initially by Branch Rickey because Robinson was known to stand up to White authority. However, Tygiel surmised that Robinson "was the most aggressive of men, White or Black," and that his "coiled tension, increased by [his] constant and justifiable suspicion of racism, led to eruptions of rage and defiance."[21]

Moreover, Robinson was a devout Methodist, a non-drinker, and non-smoker. Biographer Arnold Rampersad described it as a "priggish" attitude towards morals and mores.[22] Much of his attitude clashed ideologically with teammates and stirred-up commotions. Tygiel and Rampersad (writing in 1997) both record accounts from former Negro Leagues players as examples.

Blair Underwood picked up on his unique nature in his studies of Robinson:

> He was kind of an outsider in the Negro Leagues. . . When Branch Rickey approached him about moving to the Dodgers, he had to keep it a secret awhile. But it wasn't that difficult to keep a secret among the players because he was never totally in that inner circle. So that just speaks to his alienation.[23]

The Court-Martial of Jackie Robinson appeared on TNT Television in October 1990. As noted earlier, Ruby Dee and Andre Braugher star in a story that was little known to many, including Braugher. For authenticity, Braugher spoke to his own family members about military life, leaned on reading *I Never Had It Made*, and got first-person advice from Rachel Robinson, who advised the project and visited the set during filming.

A final resource available for *Soul* filmmakers to review was *Baseball: A Film by Ken Burns* which debuted on Public Broadcasting Service (PBS) in fall 1994. "Inning 6, The National Pastime" dealt almost exclusively with Robinson's journey from the Negro Leagues to the Brooklyn Dodgers. In the film, viewers meet Sammy Haynes, a catcher, teammate, and roommate of Robinson with the Monarchs in 1945. Haynes was an eight-year veteran of the Negro Leagues and in his third and final season with the Monarchs when Robinson joined the team. Haynes recalled stories of a rookie who humbly and willfully sat in the stairwell of the crowded team bus on a road trip. He also acknowledged concern for Robinson's ability to handle the abuse to come after deciding to join the Dodgers:

> The one thing we (players) weren't sure of was if Jackie could hold his temper. . . He knew how to fight, and he *would* fight! If Jack could hold down that temper, he could do it. He knew he had the whole black race, so to speak, on his shoulders. So, he just said 'I can take it, I can handle it. I will take it for the rest of the country and the guys,' and that's why he took all that mess.[24]

"I'm playing my position, Mr. Paige!"

In *Soul of the Game*, Robinson's isolation, hostility, and tenacity are presented right away in the introduction of the character. In one of the film's signature moments, Underwood's first words of dialogue have Robinson in defiance of Satchel Paige. During a game versus the Homestead Grays, Paige walks in off the street, late for the game start, to relieve Hilton Smith with runners on base. He immediately throws a double play ball to ease the threat. Then, Paige famously "calls in the outfielders" to leave the field when Josh Gibson comes to bat. Historically, this gag bit had become a signature fan favorite antic employed by Paige. The crowd erupts in approval, but shortstop Robinson is not amused. As Gibson stands in the batter's box, Paige, annoyed, turns to Robinson, who has not left the field:

Paige: What are you doing?

Robinson: I'm playing my position, Mr. Paige!

Paige: (*chuckles*) Boy, you don't even know yo' position. Let me help ya out. Yo' position on this team, is right over there (*pointing to the Monarchs bench*).

Robinson: (*angrily*) You're not pitching, you're putting on a bullshit show. . .

Paige: Wait a sec, hold up there, junior! This my game. This is my game and my show! And you best learn how to act in my show!

Team manager Frank Duncan (Brent Jennings) runs out to retrieve Robinson. With the crowd now jeering him for defying Paige, he storms off the field and confronts Monarchs team owner J.L. Wilkinson (R. Lee Ermey) in the dugout:

Robinson: I signed onto this organization to play baseball. This is not baseball! You got clowns out there doing some kind of song and dance; how do you expect me to do my job. . .

Wilkinson: (*interrupts*) Hey, don't you tell me what's baseball! That clown out there is paying your wages. (*dismissively*) Do you think all these people came here to today to watch Jackie Robinson?

Gibson: (*mumbles to the catcher*) Lawd, they gettin' younger and stupider.

It is interesting to note that, in an early draft of the script *Baseball in Black and White*, this scene features the initial exchange of Paige and Robinson much friendlier, before it descends into the chaos to follow. By condensing the scene, an interesting editorial choice is made to have Underwood's Robinson make his first impression towards Paige more defiant rather than reverential. The earlier version, which was not used, reveals Paige, still ever the showman, initiating veteran advice for Robinson to ease the rookie's tension:

Paige: You new?

(*Robinson nods.*)

Paige: Know who I am?

(*Robinson nods.*)

Paige: 'Course you do. A blind man can see you're one smart fella. How much Wilkie payin' you?

Robinson: Three hundred

Paige: That a week or a month?

Robinson: Month.

Paige: Guess you ain't so smart. . .But don't you feel bad; Wilkie's so tight he wouldn't pay 5 cents to see Jesus Christ ridin' a bicycle!

(*Jackie smiles, won over by Satch's easy charm.*)

Paige: Gonna be throwin' low and slow. Know what that means?

Robinson: A lot of grounders.

Paige: That's right darlin'. Now can you go pick 'em?

(*Jackie nods*)

Paige: Good. . .'cause Satch don't like standing out in the fresh air any more 'n he have to.[25]

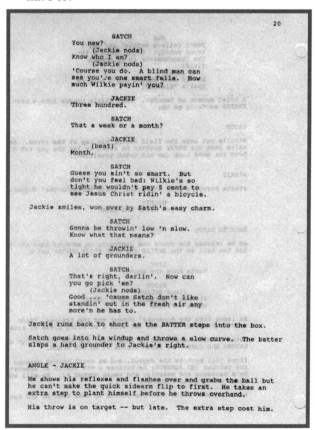

A page from the script of *Soul of the Game*.
image courtesy of the Negro Leagues Baseball Museum

After a couple of fielding miscues and close defensive plays by Robinson, Paige tries to calm the frazzled Robinson:

> SATCH Rubs the ball and looks over at Jackie as the fans JEER.
>
> **Paige**: Don't worry 'bout that. Just take your phone off the hook an' do it![26]

Little has been chronicled about the relationship of Paige and Robinson in real time. Publicly, they showed great admiration for one another, especially when the announcement came near the end of 1945 that Robinson was chosen by the Dodgers for a contract. However, Paige biographer Larry Tye suggested more of a schism existed privately. Paige certainly expressed great disappointment to family and close friends that he was passed over for Robinson. He seemed to hold no personal grudges, but was confused that, with all he had done in baseball, a rookie on his primary team would be the choice. Conversely, Tye describes fellow baseball barrier-breaking player Larry Doby and Robinson as "dourer" men than Paige. He quotes Doby saying Robinson "detested" Paige:

> Satch was competition for Jack. Satch was funny, he was an outstanding athlete, and he was black. He had three things going. Jack and I wouldn't tell jokes. We weren't humorists. We tried to show that we were intelligent, and that's not what most white people expected from blacks. Satch gave whites what they wanted from blacks—joy.[27]

The character set to personify and respond to internal team tensions brought by Robinson is Jesse Williams (Joseph Latimore). In the film, Williams is initially supplanted at shortstop upon Robinson's arrival, but Paige later asks manager Duncan to move him to second base because he showed a lack of arm strength. That news came after fisticuffs between Robinson and Williams. Latimore plays Williams as a bitter thorn on Robinson's psyche, picking at his seemingly fragile temper like a scab. He is resentful of Robinson's perceived pretensions, and it boils over when he reads a newspaper story praising Robinson. This scene in the Monarchs locker room has Williams taunting Robinson loudly in front of the team:

> **Williams**: I think Wilkie finally went out and got himself a good ol' white boy! Oh yeah, he looks black enough y'all! Show don't sound like it. Maybe like some fancy house n___. . .

The insult was a dare and got the expected effect of lighting Robinson's fuse in retaliation. Williams taunting seems to represent some comeuppance for Robinson's perceived snobbishness while adding a bit of rookie hazing.

The real-life Jesse Williams, by most accounts, may not have been such an instigator. Jesse "Bill" Williams from Texas was a respected premier infielder in the Negro Leagues. He joined the Monarchs in 1939, was a two-time Negro Leagues All-Star, and a key member of the 1942 championship team. Although he had a stellar 1944 season at shortstop, he was switched to second base to help make room for Robinson on the team. The move was seen as positive, but 1945 was Williams' last full year in the Negro Leagues. Robinson and other Black players advanced to the major leagues while Williams toiled in Mexico and on barnstorming teams for another decade. If he shared any resentment of Robinson, it does not appear reflected in any interviews or published material.[28]

A New Generation

Pivotal points of the film turn on discussions of Robinson's time in the military. The news article that stirred envy in the Williams character was an interview conducted the previous day by the local news reporter and photographer (Bruce Beatty) after Robinson's defiant response to Paige on the field. After the embarrassing incident, Robinson came to bat, legged out a double with blazing speed, then scored on a botched throw to third after he stole the base. In the locker room after the game, the reporter is initially regaled by Paige with folksy witticisms before turning questions to Robinson:

> **Reporter**: Hey um, Robinson? Satch says your problem is you got a bad temper.
> *(Robinson glares at the reporter while getting dressed, then tries to ignore him.)*
> **Reporter**: Hey, are you the Jackie Robinson that played half-back at UCLA?
> *(Robinson nobs, sheepishly, yes.)*
> **Reporter**: Damn, I knew it, just by the way you were running those bases! I heard you just got out of the army.
> **Robinson**: That's right.
> **Reporter**: So, what did you do?
> **Robinson**: *(standing)* Platoon leader, 761st Tank Battalion, Fort Hood.
> **Reporter**: You a Sergeant?

Robinson: Lieutenant.

Reporter: An officer? Man, in that kind of position, what you were doing must seem a lot different from this?

Robinson: Well, I don't know, but there are some areas where the skills are similar.

Reporter: Like what?

Robinson: *(with quiet confidence, but loud enough for everyone to hear)* Like the discipline of managing your time. Setting goals. Taking personal responsibility for seeing them through. Ya' know, things like that.

Reporter: *(impressed)* I want to take your picture!

It's an important scene, meant to showcase Robinson's confidence and intelligence. Moreover, it is meant to signal future change. The reporter realizes and appreciates he is witnessing someone of impact, unlike any athlete he has known. This scene survives the many script edits the film would undertake, and Himmelstein's notes in the early draft of *Baseball In Black and White* highlight the significance he hoped for with the exchange:

CLOSEUP- SATCH: For the first time, he begins to realize that if the 'New Age' ever does come, he may be left behind. It is painfully obvious that Jackie is from a new generation, and he, while still vibrant and successful, is inarguably from the old. 'POP' – his face is illuminated in the reflected light of the big flash as the reporter snaps Jackie's picture.[29]

In the film, Robinson's military record and courage do impress his teammates and is used to grant him a measure of *bona fides* or credibility. J.L. Wilkinson relates the story of Robinson's military court-martial to imply why Williams and others should back off on hazing Robinson. Before heading out of town on a road trip:

Monarch player: Hey, did Robinson get traded?

Wilkinson: He and Satch got loaned to Harrisburg. They'll catch up to us in New York.

Williams: Good! Don't want him on our bus no-ways.

(Wilkinson chuckles)

Williams: What's so funny?

Wilkinson: Well, Robinson and buses.

Williams: Yeah, what about it?

Wilkinson: Well, when he was in the service, some driver told him to get to the back of the bus. He set the guy straight and got himself court-martialed.

He beat it, too.

IN TEXAS.

Let's go guys. *(Pointing towards the bus).*

Monarch players who were listening nod, impressed by the story.

Williams: *(a bit awed by the story reacts quietly)* Good for him.

Determined Yet Confused

Most film reviews and critiques of *Soul of the Game* exalt Delroy Lindo's performance as Satchel Paige the driving force of the production, and rightfully so. All the actors received high marks, but comments on Underwood's Robinson were more muted. However, in his review of the film, Phil Gallo of *Variety Magazine* adequately summarizes the film and Robinson's portrayal:

The riveting depth of the telefilm's p.o.v. is embellished by the stellar acting, which dissipates any concern for the blurring of fact and fiction. . .. Underwood plays Robinson as determined yet confused, cautious in his acceptance of the role Rickey assigns him. Robinson's collected nature is emphasized over his athleticism, contrasting with the veterans' determination to cross baseball's color line.[30]

Director Kevin Rodney Sullivan hoped that *Soul of the Game* could show viewers that the Negro Leagues, "was a great thing all to itself," and that it "celebrates what was there and not just what they (players and fans) didn't have."[31] That sentiment comes through early in the film, but the core of the story was to capture the moment when feelings change towards aspirations of something new – the major leagues. Jackie Robinson is the agent of change. Despite the objections of some observers and criticism of its overall approach in telling the history, *Soul of the Game* did succeed in bringing audiences closer to the historical Jackie Robinson in full. His complexity, passion and competitive fire become clearer through the years after 1996 and bring us nearer to knowing who this consequential man truly was.

Notes

1   In December 2020, Major League Baseball announced that seven of the Negro Leagues would be defined as major leagues. This was not the reality experienced by Jackie Robinson and others. Acknowledging that reality, this article will reflect the distinction prior to the recent (and welcome) recognition.

2   Retrosheet.org notes several Negro Leagues vs major-league exhibition games in October of 1945, including a five-game series played on consecutive Sundays featuring players led by Biz Mackey for the Negro Leaguers and Charlie Dressen for the "major leaguers." Although the games featured future Black major-league players, such as Monte Irvin and Don Newcombe, neither Paige, Gibson, nor Robinson participated. https://www.retrosheet.org/NegroLeagues/1945IR.html. See also William Brashler, *Josh Gibson: A Life in the Negro Leagues* (Chicago, Ivan R. Dee Publishing, 1978), 133. Brashler references that Gibson would be hospitalized and released on weekends to play, accompanied by hospital attendants, which is like the scenario depicted in the film.

3   A complete and thorough autopsy of *Soul of the Game* can be found at the "Underdog Podcast," https://underdogpodcasts.com/soul-of-the-game ; see also contemporary reviews and analysis, David Bianculli, "*Soul of the Game* Hits a Triple," *New York Daily News*, April 19, 1996; Hal Boedeker, "The Acting is a Hit, but HBO's 'Soul of the Game' Delivers More Myths than Facts About Three Legends of the Negro Leagues," *Orlando Sentinel*, April 20, 1996; Paul Petrovic, "'Give 'Em the Razzle Dazzle': The Negro Leagues in *The Bingo Long Traveling All-Stars and Motor Kings* and *Soul of the Game*," *Black Ball* Journal, Volume 3, no. 1, Spring 2010, 61-75; Lisa Doris Alexander, "'But They Don't Want to Play with The White Players, Right?': Depictions of Segregation and Negro League Baseball in Contemporary Popular Film," *Black Ball* Journal, Volume 5, no. 2, Fall 2012, 19-34.

4   Jesse Howe, "1945: Jackie Robinson's Year with the Kanas City Monarchs," *Flatland* Newsletter web site, https://www.flatlandkc.org/people-places/1945-jackie-robinsons-year-kc-monarchs/ ; Aaron Stilley, "Jackie with the Monarchs: Reliving the 1945 Kansas City Monarchs Season," blog http://jwtm1945.blogspot.com/; www.Seamheads.com Negro Leagues Database.

5   www.Seamheads.com Negro Leagues Database.

6   "HBO's Coming Attractions," *Los Angeles Times*, September 25, 1995.

7   Although the film was never produced, in March 2020, Spike Lee released a completed version of his Jackie Robinson script, free for the public to review on his social media platforms. A live virtual table reading was conducted by the Los Angeles based arts group The Talent Connect on April 15, 2020.

8   Daniel A. Nathan, "Bearing Witness to Black Baseball: Buck O'Neil, the Negro Leagues, and the Politics of the Past," *Journal of American Studies*, volume 35, no. 3, 2001, 453-469.

9   Susan King, "The Hard Run to First," *Los Angeles Times Magazine*, April 14, 1996: 5.

10   Michael E. Hill, "HBO'S Film Touches Heart of the Matter," *Washington Post*, April 14, 1996.

11   Drew Himmelstein, "A Talk with My Dad, screenwriter of 'My Name Is Sara,' his first Jewish film," *Jewish News of Northern California*, February 4, 2021.

12   Hill, *Washington Post*

13   Hill, *Washington Post*; family research from www.Ancestry.com U.S. Census records; Eli Underwood baseball research courtesy of historian Gary Ashwill and www.Seamheads.com Negro Leagues Database.

14   Hill, *Washington Post*.

15   Eirik Knutzen, "*Soul of the Game* Recalls Pivotal Point in Baseball History," Copley News Service and the *News-Pilot*, San Pedro, California, April 16, 1996.

16   King, *Los Angeles Times Magazine*.

17   Jackie Robinson, *I Never Had It Made: The Autobiography of Jackie Robinson* (New Jersey, The Ecco Press, 1995), 23.

18   Robinson, 22-23.

19   Robinson, 23

20   Jules Tygiel, *Baseball's Great Experiment: Jackie Robinson and His Legacy*, Expanded Edition (New York, Oxford University Press, 1997), 62.

21   Tygiel, 63.

22   Arnold Rampersad, *Jackie Robinson: A Biography* (New York, Alfred A. Knopf, 1997), 118.

23   King, *Los Angeles Times*.

24   *Baseball: A Film by Ken Burns*, "Inning 6: The National Pastime, 1940-1950," Florentine Films, 1994.

25   David Himmelstein, "Baseball In Black and White, First Draft Revisions, June 1995," HBO Films, 20. Script is from the collection of the Negro Leagues Baseball Museum

26   Himmelstein, 21.

27   Larry Tye, *Satchel: The Life and Times of an American Legend* (New York, Random House, 2009), 200.

28   Tim Hagerty, "Jesse Williams," SABR BioProject, https://sabr.org/bioproj/person/jesse-williams/ .

29   Himmelstein, 28.

30   Phil Gallo, "Soul of the Game," *Variety* Magazine, April 18, 1996.

31   King, *Los Angeles Times Magazine*.

Telling Jackie's Story through Children's Literature

By Leslie Heaphy

Jackie laughed. "Baseball isn't all about home runs," he said. "It's a team sport. You have to trust the other players as much as you trust yourself."[1]

When Jackie Robinson debuted for the Brooklyn Dodgers in April of 1947 many of his new teammates were not happy he was on their team. Robinson would have to work hard to change their attitudes, to show them he belonged. That story of triumph over adversity is one of the many themes to be found in writings about Robinson and his life. Historians, journalists, writers, and fans have studied Robinson's whole life. In addition, there are many books written for children and young adults using Jackie's life story as the central focus and as inspiration to teach children important life lessons. A thorough examination of children's literature reveals key themes and approaches, as well as highlights important strengths Jackie displayed in order to accomplish all that he did in his life. The questions to be explored and answered by examining the literature are: how is Jackie Robinson's story presented to children of different ages? What lessons are taught? Why is he a hero to so many?

The children's literature on Robinson is extensive, dating back to the 1970s, with new books coming out all the time. There are books for every age, from graphic novels to picture books, both fiction and non-fiction. Included among the published works are a series of books by Robinson's daughter Sharon Robinson. Sharon has written stories about specific events in her father's life and has also used his accomplishments as inspiration for other children's stories. Because of her connection to Jackie, her stories deserve their own examination and will be dealt with in another chapter.

Books about Jackie Robinson teach children about topics ranging from segregation to civil rights to family life, bullying, the military, and baseball. Common themes that emerge discuss courage, responsibility, bravery, hope, inspiration, and other positive messages which make these books important. Jackie Robinson once said, "A life is not important except in the impact it has on other lives." These books continue to extend Jackie's impact to future generations.

One of the first children's books published about Robinson came out in 1971, just a year before Robert Peterson's groundbreaking work about Negro League baseball, *Only the Ball was White*. Kenneth Rudeen wrote *Jackie Robinson* (1971) to tell young children about the challenges and struggles Robinson faced as the first Black ballplayer to enter what was then known as the major leagues. He focuses on the strength and courage it took for Robinson to be able to play at the level he did, especially since he was not welcomed. Rudeen incorrectly identifies Robinson as the first Black player in the majors, since his book was written before researchers had uncovered the stories of Moses Fleetwood Walker and his brother who played in the nineteenth century.

A second early children's book, *Thank You Jackie Robinson* by Barbara Cohen, was published in 1974, just two years after his death. Cohen's book is a fictional story about the friendship between a young boy, Sam, and a cook named Davy. That friendship is tested when Davy gets sick, and Sam hopes that getting the great Jackie Robinson's autograph will help Davy get well. The story focuses on the friendship that blossoms between Sam, a young Jewish boy, and Davy, a Black cook, who comes to serve as a role model for Sam who lost his own father. They are drawn together by their love of the Dodgers and especially their new ball player Jackie Robinson.

The book tells a story of friendship, courage, and inspiration in the face of loneliness and societal barriers. Robinson is their hero because he stood strong in the face of all the challenges thrown at him because of his skin color. Their friendship grows despite the differences in race and religion just as Robinson perseveres and triumphs despite his race.

Another book published in the 1970s, *The Value of Courage,* by Spencer Johnson brings out some of the same themes. The key difference is that Johnson provides a biography of Robinson's life without any fictional characters. Johnson recounts Robinson's baseball career to show the importance of bravery and hard work. Robinson had to work hard to overcome prejudice and break down barriers placed in his way because of his race. He also displayed tremendous courage when he joined the Brooklyn Dodgers and broke the color barrier. He stood alone in facing fans, players, and managers who taunted him and wanted to hurt him. Johnson's biography is designed to help elementary and middle school children see what can be accomplished when you have a dream.

During the 1980s a few books began to introduce young readers to the larger story of Black baseball. Margaret Davidson's biography tells young people that White and Black athletes have not always played baseball together. In *The Story of Jackie Robinson: The Bravest Man in Baseball*, Davidson tells young readers what it took to be able to play baseball before 1947 as a Black man in America. She focuses on the idea that Robinson had to break the rules of society in order to play baseball like any White ballplayer. Author Jim O'Connor broadens the knowledge of young readers by placing Jackie Robinson's career in the larger context of Black baseball in *Jackie Robinson, The Story of All Black Baseball*. O'Connor has six chapters in his book and only two are devoted to Robinson. O'Connor covers the problems Robinson faced but also his accomplishments from breaking the color barrier to being named Rookie of the Year and helping the Dodgers win the World Series. Young readers also learn about the existence of all-Black baseball teams and some of the stars who never got the chance to play in the major leagues because of their skin color. O'Connor tells the story with an appropriate level of language for second and third graders, and also includes a number of black and white photos from the time period to help students get a full understanding of who these players were.

Many of these early themes and approaches continued in the 1990s when an increasing number of books were published as more attention was brought to the Negro Leagues after the Ken Burns *Baseball* television documentary series was released. The years 1992 and 1997 were also the 45th and 50th anniversary of Robinson's debut with the Dodgers, bringing new attention to Robinson's legacy and importance. Two new books kicked off the decade with their publication in 1990. Carol Greene and Steve Dobson published *Jackie Robinson: Baseball's First Black Major Leaguer* and Barry Denenberg came out with *Stealing Home: The Story of Jackie Robinson*. Greene and Dobson focus on how Robinson helped to shape American history when he was signed by Branch Rickey. The book provides a chronology of life events from his childhood until his death in 1972. The story does not provide any analysis, just a narrative of accomplishments with lots of photographs. O'Connor's earlier work gives young readers a more in-depth look at Black baseball. Denenberg provides a biography for slightly older children, focusing on not just Robinson's courage but also his role as a pioneer.

Edward Ferrell picks up on the theme of inspiration in *Young Jackie Robinson: Baseball Hero*. What Robinson was able to accomplish on the baseball field helped produce much larger changes in society. His achievements made Robinson not only a hero to look up to but also to aspire to emulate. His life provided a lesson in what others could do in the face of everyday challenges. Peter Golenbock continued the emphasis on change but broadened the focus beyond Robinson in *Teammates*. Golenbock provides a well-illustrated story of the power of friendship. When Golenbock's Robinson walks out alone onto the baseball diamond, one can feel his sadness, but then Pee Wee Reese steps up and makes Robinson feel welcome. From a perspective other than Robinson's, Reese takes a stand when he extends the hand of friendship, teaching children the difference one person can make.

Manfred Weldhorn brings the focus back to Robinson's abilities on the field in *Jackie Robinson* (1993). Weldhorn tells middle school readers a more in-depth story about Robinson's on-field play. Weldhorn provides the stories to help children see what is possible when you are not afraid to go after your dreams. Robinson overcame all the obstacles in his way by using his athletic abilities to prove he belonged. David Adler brings this story down to the youngest readers in *A Picture Book of Jackie Robinson*.

In a short but well-illustrated biography Adler shows children how one person can help change the world. Adler also provides a timeline of key dates and a bit of information about other important figures in the desegregation of baseball at the conclusion of the book.

Following the 50th anniversary celebrations a new spate of books was published. Among them were three children's books published in 1998-99 that added to the different approaches used to tell Robinson's story. Herb Dunn wrote *Jackie Robinson: Young Sports Trailblazer* to tell middle school readers the story of this great ballplayer. Dunn's book is part of a larger series on the childhood of famous Americans such as Abigail Adams, Thurgood Marshall, and George Washington. The book is filled with colorful illustrations by Meryl Henderson, who is actually the author as well, writing under the pseudonym of Dunn. Robinson is presented as a trailblazer even before he entered the majors. She tells of how he went to integrated schools, served in the military, and played for the Kansas City Monarchs in the Negro Leagues. Derek Dingle wrote *First in the Field: Baseball Hero Jackie Robinson* for early readers to learn about someone who paved the way for those that followed. Unlike many other Robinson biographies, Dingle focuses primarily on Robinson's early years and less on his civil rights career after baseball. The final book published in 1999 was Dan Gutman's *Jackie and Me*. This is a fictional story about a youngster named Joe Stoshack who can travel in time. Joe wants to interview his hero Jackie Robinson and so he uses his baseball card to take him back to 1947. Here Joe not only meets Robinson but also finds himself initially unable to return to his own time. It is Robinson who helps him find his way.

As the number of children's books about Jackie Robinson increased a great deal starting in the 2000s, the question to ask is what else was there to tell? What new approaches or stories can these books provide? We find both new stories but also new approaches such as graphic novels and graphic flash format novels. Each author saw in Robinson's life story lessons to be taught and learned. For example, *Dodger Dreams* (2010) by Brandon Terrell was written as a graphic flash format novel which is designed to help the story move more quickly for today's young reader who is used to the beauty and speed of computer graphics. The format combines graphic novel style pages with more typical book pages to give readers the best of both. Terrell uses this format to talk about the importance of strength of character but also addresses bullying and standing up for what is right. Robinson did that every time he stepped on the diamond but also in his daily life. In the story Max Owens receives 1955 World Series tickets from his grandfather so he can see his idol play in person. Though the Dodgers lose the game Max gets to see Robinson steal home plate while also experiencing segregated seating in the stands. After the game Max gets to help another young fan who is being bullied and gets to meet Robinson in person. Robinson reminds Max the importance of doing what is right. To help young readers get more from the story, Terrell also includes a timeline and discussion questions.

A number of fictional stories have been published in the last 20 years that use Robinson's career as the centerpiece to teach students a variety of important lessons, including Bette Bao Lord's, *In the Year of the Boar and Jackie Robinson* (2019). Middle school readers are introduced to Shirley Temple Wong who arrives in the United States from China. She speaks little English and has trouble fitting in until she discovers Jackie Robinson and baseball in 1947. Wong joins her classmates playing stickball and listens to the Dodgers on the radio. Robinson's story provides hope to Wong and other immigrant children that America could become a home for them too. Lord uses the idea of baseball as America's National Pastime to show how Robinson's ball playing changed America for the better.

In *Just Like Jackie* (2018), Lindsay Stoddard provides a story about family, acceptance, bullying, and so much more. The story centers around Robinson Hart and her grandfather as a family of two. Her grandfather raised her on stories of baseball and life. Robbie finds herself having to fight to protect her family as her grandfather battles with memory loss. Like the real Robinson, Robbie struggles to gain acceptance for her non-traditional family and fights to overcome the obstacles of keeping them together. Written for middle schoolers, the book provides wonderful lessons about family, acceptance, illness, and bullying – all while using Jackie Robinson's story as a backdrop to learn from.

Another type of fictional story can be found in *A Big Day for Baseball* (2019), written by Mary Pope Osborne. This book is part of the Magic Tree House series which uses both fiction and non-fiction stories to teach about history, science, mystery, and more. Osborne introduces young readers to Jack and Annie, two youngsters who want to be great ballplayers but have not learned to play much yet. Their librarian Morgan gives them magic baseball caps that transport the children back to 1947. Jack and Annie are surprised to find themselves as batboys and not players when they arrive. The first barrier the children face is realizing that girls cannot be batboys in 1947 so Annie tells everyone she is Andy. The children have arrived on Opening Day in 1947, a big day indeed for baseball as the Dodgers take on the Boston Braves with Robinson making his debut. Jack and Annie find themselves learning many lessons at Ebbets Field—lessons about hard work, trust, and even the rules, not just of the game, but of life. Since this book is a part of the Magic Tree House Series, educators and parents will find a wide range of additional materials available to help teach the book and the many lessons that can be learned from Robinson's struggles and triumphs.

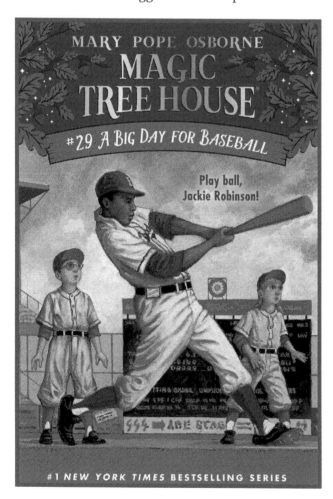

illustrated by Sal Murdocca. image courtesy of Penguin Random House

Moise Michel uses the technique of time travel in the book *Kwame and his Great Adventure* (2017). Kwame invents a watch that can take him back in time. Kwame goes back to meet his hero Jackie Robinson. Kwame wanted to play baseball but he did not make the team because others told him he was not good enough. Robinson teaches Kwame about following his dreams no matter what others might tell him.

Using Robinson's minor-league stint with the Montreal Royals as the backdrop, Nancy Russell tells the story of young Matt Parker and his hero Jackie Robinson in *So Long, Jackie Robinson* (2007). Matt's family moves to Montreal and he has to leave behind everything and everyone he knows. He ends up in a city where everyone is a hockey fan and they all speak French. Things begin to change for the better when Matt gets a job selling concessions at the Royals ballpark. He gets to see Jackie Robinson play every day. Montreal turns out to be exactly where he wanted to be in 1946. The unique contribution this book makes is simply the focus on Robinson's minor-league career which is usually left out of most children's books.

Another story not usually covered is Robinson's military career. Sudipta Bardhan-Quallen tackles this part of Robinson's life in *The United States v. Jackie Robinson* (2018). Everyone knows Robinson faced prejudice on the diamond but this story shows readers he faced those same issues every day while he served in the military during World War II. Though written for new readers, this book does not shy away from the topic of segregation but tackles it head on. Robinson faces all those who would stand against him with strength and grace.

Tania Grossinger provides another new approach to Robinson's story by telling it through the eyes of a young girl. In *Jackie and Me: A Very Special Friendship* (2017), Tania's family operate the famous Grossinger's Hotel in the Catskill Mountains of upstate New York. Tania feels that she does not really fit in with the guests or with her stepfamily. Then she meets one of the guests, Jackie Robinson, who plays ping pong with her. The game helps bring her out of her shell and starts to improve her self-confidence. After that game Tania and Robinson continue to write letters until his death in 1972. Through the eyes of Tania readers learn about Robinson the man and the struggles he faced, and how he learned to cope and stand strong. While Grossinger shines a light on a more personal story, Mary Beth Lorbiecki focuses her attention on the field in *Jackie's Bat* (2006). Lorbiecki tells Robinson's story through encounters with a White batboy who does not treat him the way his White teammates do. Written for early readers both books are a great way to introduce young children to differences that exist in the world and how to not only try to cope with them but to find ways to change how we deal with differences. Acceptance is a huge part of the message of both these books.

In 2010 author Myron Uhlberg captures the excitement of the 1947 season in *Dad, Jackie, and Me*. A young boy listens to the Brooklyn Dodgers every day on the radio, signing the highlights to his father who is deaf. The boy dreams of one day seeing Robinson play in person but does not believe that will happen. Then one day his father brings home tickets to a Dodgers-New York Giants game. Dad tells his son he wants to see Robinson play. The two storylines can be seen to overlap as Robinson and the father both struggle to fit in and find their place.

Continuing the story line of not fitting in and working to overcome barriers is Cathy Goldberg Fishman's *When Jackie and Hank Met* (2012). Fishman bases her story around the first meeting between Hank Greenberg and Jackie Robinson in May 1947. The two ball players collide at first base and rather than give in to the urging of the fans to fight one another, they both go on to become players others could look up to. Each man had to overcome obstacles in order to achieve their dreams. For Robinson it was his skin color and for Greenberg it was his religion. Young readers can watch how these two men did not give in to hatred but instead worked to change people's minds, to find their own place in the world. The book is beautifully illustrated and also includes a biography of each player with a timeline and additional resources for those wanting to learn more.

What's Your Story, Jackie Robinson? (2015), by Emma Carlson Berne, introduces young readers to interviewing skills. The story is told as an interview between a cub reporter and Robinson. Each question gives Robinson a chance to tell the young readers about his career and the obstacles he had to overcome. Robinson says, "But I showed them that prejudice hurts sports teams. Teams are stronger when everyone plays together."[2] The message is clear, we need to find ways to play together and ultimately live together. Each question is interspersed with a written response and photographs of Robinson's family and his playing days with the Kansas City Monarchs and the Brooklyn Dodgers. The interview approach teaches young students about how to ask questions to learn from others.

Among the many other non-fiction children's books written about Robinson there are a few that are part of larger book series that have a specific approach or message. One example is *Character Counts! Young Jackie Robinson* (2014) by Edward Farrell. Farrell has written about Robinson's story of struggle and triumph as part of a program that focuses on the Six Pillars of Character. Farrell chose to focus on the pillar of responsibility in telling Robinson's story. We each have a responsibility to work to make the world a better place. Another book that fits this pattern of being part of a series is Brad Meltzer's *I am Jackie Robinson* (2015). This book is the fifth in a series focusing on how ordinary people can change the world. Robinson's bravery is highlighted to show kids how to dare to dream big and then go for those dreams no matter what.

Jackie Robinson's life is a story of hard work, perseverance, and courage. He challenged prejudice and segregation every day and pushed boundaries to make America a place where all could find a home. Writers and illustrators have found his achievements on and off the field to be a great way to introduce young readers to difficult topics, and also as a way to inspire hope and a sense of responsibility in each of us. Whether their books are biographies or fictional stories, each author mentioned, and many others in the bibliography that follows, found a hero in Robinson and have shared his life as lessons for all of us to learn, no matter our age.

List of Books

Abraham, Philip. *Jackie Robinson* (Danbury, Connecticut: Children's Press, 2003) (grades k-3)

Adler, David A. *A Picture Book of Jackie Robinson* (New York City: Holiday House, 1994) (grades pre-k-k)

Amoroso, Cynthia. *Jackie Robinson* (Mankato, Minnesota: The Child's World Inc., 2014) (grades k-2)

Bardham-Quallen, Sudipta. *The United States v. Jackie Robinson* (New York City: Balzer and Bray, 2018) (grades k-3)

Berne, Emma Carlson. *What's Your Story, Jackie Robinson?* (Mankato, Minnesota: Lerner Publications, 2015 (grades k-3)

Berrios III, Frank John. *My Little Golden Book about Jackie Robinson.* (Racine, Wisconsin: Golden Books, 2018) (grades pre-k-1)

Burleigh, Robert. *Stealing Home: Jackie Robinson against all Odds* (New York City: Simon and Schuster, 2007) (grades k-2).

Christopher, Matt. *Jackie Robinson: Legends in Sports* (New York City: Little, Brown Books for Young Readers, 2006) (grades 3-5)

Cohen, Barbara. *Thank You, Jackie Robinson* (New York City: HarperCollins, 1997) (gr. 3-7)

Davidson, Margaret. *The Story of Jackie Robinson, the Bravest Man in the World* (New York City: Yearling Books, 1971) (grades 3-7)

De Marco, Tony. *Jackie Robinson, Journey to Freedom* (Mankato, Minnesota: The Child's World, Inc., 2014) (grades 3-5)

Denenberg, Barry. *Stealing Home: The Story of Jackie Robinson* (New York City: Scholastic Paperbacks, 1990) (grades 4-7)

Dingle, Derek. *First in the Field: Baseball Hero Jackie Robinson* (New York City: Scholastic Inc., 1999) (grades k-3)

Dunn, Herb. *Young Sports Trailblazer* (New York City: Simon and Schuster Children's Publishing, 1999) (grades 3-6)

Farrell, Edward. *Character Counts! Young Jackie Robinson, Baseball Hero* (New York City: Scholastic Publishing, 1992-2014) (grades pre-k-k)

Fishman, Cathy Goldberg. *When Jackie and Hank Met* (Seattle, Washington: Two Lions, 2012) (grades k-2)

Golenbeck, Peter. *Teammates* (Boston, Massachusetts: HMH Books for Young Readers, 1992)(grades k-2)

Grabowski, John. *Jackie Robinson* (Baseball Legends) (New York City: Chelsea House Publishers, 1990) (grades 4-6)

Gregory, Josh. *Jackie Robinson* (New York City: Scholastic Library Publishing, 2015) (grades 3-6)

Greene, Carol and Steve Dobson. *Jackie Robinson: Baseball's First Black Major Leaguer* (New York City: Scholastic Library Publishing, 1990) (grades k-3)

Grossinger, Tania. *Jackie and Me: A Very Special Friendship* (New York City: Sky Pony Press, 2017) (grades pre-k-k)

Gutman, Dan. *Jackie and Me* (New York: Harper Collins, 1999) (grades pre-k- 5)

Haldy, Emma. *Jackie Robinson (My Itty-bitty Bio)* (Ann Arbor, Michigan: Cherry Lake Publishing, 2016) (grades k-1)

Hansen, Grace. *Jackie Robinson: Baseball Legend* (New York City: Little, Brown Books for Young Readers, 2017) (grades k-2)

Herman, Gail. *Who was Jackie Robinson?* (New York City: Penguin Workshop Publisher, 2010) (grades 3-7)

Johnson, Spencer. *Value of Courage* (Oxfordshire, England: Oak Tree Publishers, Inc., 1977) (grades k-6)

Kaiser, Lisbeth. *Who was Jackie Robinson?* (New York City: Penguin Workshop Publisher, 2021) (grades pre-k-k)

Krensky, Stephen. *Play Ball, Jackie !* (Lansing, Michigan: Millbrook Printing, 2011) (grades 2-3)

Lord, Betty Bao. *In the Year of the Boar and Jackie Robinson* (New York City: Harper Collins, 2010), (grades 3-5)

Meltzer, Brad. *I Am Jackie Robinson* (New York City: Dial Books, 2015) (grades k-2)

Michel, Moise. *Kwame and his Great Adventures: Kwame meets Jackie Robinson* (Conneaut Lake, Pennsylvania: Page Publishing Inc., 2017) (grades 1-3)

O'Connor, Jim. *Jackie Robinson and the Story of All-Black Baseball* (New York City: Random House Books for Young Readers, 1989) (grades 2-4).

Osborne, Mary Pope. *A Big Day for Baseball* (New York City: Random House Books, 2019) (grades 2-4)

Patrick, Denise Lewis. *Jackie Robinson: Strong Inside and Out* (New York City: Harper Collins, 2005) (grades 2-4)

Prince, April Jones. *Jackie Robinson: He Led the Way* (New York City: Penguin Young Readers, 2007) (grades 1-3)

Russell, Nancy. *So Long, Jackie Robinson* (Santa Fe, New Mexico: Leaf Storm Press, 2007) (grades 4-6)

Scaletta, Kurtis. *Trailblazers: Jackie Robinson: Breaking Barriers in Baseball* (New York City: Random House Books for Young Readers, 2019) (grades 3-7)

Schaeffer, Lola. *Jackie Robinson* (Mankato, Minnestota: Capstone, 2002) (grades pre-k-2)

Sexton, Colleen. *Jackie Robinson: A Life of Determination* (Hopkins, Minnesota: Bellwether Media, 2007) (grades 3-5)

Simmons, Matt. *Jackie Robinson Breaking the Color Line in Baseball* (New York City: Crabtree Publishing Company, 2014) (grades 4-6)

Smolka, Bo. *Jackie Robinson Breaks the Color Barrier* (Fort Wayne, Indiana: Sportzone Publishing, 2015) (grades 3-5)

Stoddard, Lindsay. *Just Like Jackie* (New York City: Harper Collins, 2018) (grades 3-6)

Terrell, Brandon. *Dodger Dreams: The Courage of Jackie Robinson* (Bloomington, Minnesota: Stone Arch Books, 2009) (grades 3-6)

Thorpe, Andrea. *The Story of Jackie Robinson* (Emeryville, California: Rockridge Press, 2021) (grades 1-5)

Uhlburg, Myron. *Dad, Jackie, and Me* (Atlanta, Georgia: Peachtree Publishing, 2010) (grades 1-2)

Walker, Sally M. *Jackie Robinson* (Minneapolis, Minnesota: Lerner Publishing Group, 2002) (grades 2-5)

Weldhorn, Manfred. *Jackie Robinson* (New York: Simon and Schuster Children's Publishing,1993) (grades 4-7)

Notes

1 Brandon Terrell, *Dodger Dreams* (Bloomington, Minnesota: Stone Arch Books, 2010), 43.

2 Emma Carlson Berne, *What's Your Story, Jackie Robinson?* (Mankato, Minnesota: Lerner Publications, 2015), 4.

Jackie, the Supporting Character

By Nick Malian

For many, Jack Roosevelt Robinson is the most important and recognizable figure in the history of Organized Baseball. He is a cultural icon who revolutionized American sports when he took first base on April 15, 1947. But despite the impact that Robinson has had on sport and society, popular culture largely remembers him for that singular act of breaking the color barrier. He is, what Michael G. Long calls, "unjustly stuck in 1947," instead of evaluated for the whole person that he was.[1]

At his very essence Robinson was flawed and complicated. He rightfully challenged authority and was relentless in his pursuit as a civil rights activist. He spent his entire life fighting for first-class citizenship for Black Americans and other disenfranchised people. His commitment to activism transcends his major-league career, yet his accomplishments on the field are what he is most remembered.

Society largely ignores the difficult and uncomfortable qualities of our heroes and icons. Hollywood bears much of the responsibility for controlling that narrative. As this volume makes clear, there are no shortage of movies, television shows, and plays with the Jackie Robinson character, fictional and non-fictional alike. As a main character, stories told of Jackie Robinson often focus on the same events in his life, and rarely do they explore the nuance that defined him. Interestingly, however, Robinson is often not the main character in the fictional worlds in which he appears. In minor roles, the Robinson character serves as an important literary aid, either driving the plot, revealing qualities about the main characters, or setting the tone for the story.

The Jackie Robinson character appears in minor roles in several movies and television shows that span decades. The allure of having a "Jackie Robinson

character" is that it brings tremendous value to the story because of his legacy. The problem is that his character is portrayed as largely one-dimensional and is usually a trope for racism, prejudice, tolerance, and heroism. More often than not, his character is a misrepresentation of the "real" Robinson either by physical appearance, or demeanor which may have deleterious effects on his legacy. Yet despite the many inaccuracies in his portrayal and liberties taken to create his character, Jackie Robinson still serves as an important symbolic figure in a minor role.

As a minor character Jackie Robinson recently appeared in the first episode of HBO's *Lovecraft Country*, titled, "Sundown," which first aired in September 2020. *Lovecraft Country* was adapted from the novel of the same name written by Matt Ruff, about a Black American man, Atticus, traveling across the Jim Crow United States in search of his father. The novel is based on the characters, imagery, and themes from influential author H.P. Lovecraft who was considered the father of cosmic horror and science-fiction. His canon featured grotesque, and fantastical creatures with immense power over humans. Lovecraft was also an unapologetic racist. Ruff took the monsters that Lovecraft created and authored a story using a Black man as a protagonist, in protest of Lovecraft.

Creator and show-runner of *Lovecraft Country*, Misha Green, adapted the novel for television to "reclaim all of those storytelling styles for characters who've typically died at the beginning of those stories."[2] Green noted that Robinson was an ideal choice for a character because Atticus loved baseball, but given the protest angle for the story, Robinson's pedigree makes him the most suitable athlete hero. Robinson's character appears twice in "Sundown," first as part of the powerful narration of *The Jackie Robinson Story* and second in person to save Atticus.

The character plays a key role to establish themes of racism, discrimination, and triumph over evil.

The opening scene of "Sundown" begins with Atticus fighting through the cosmic trenches of a Korean war battlefield. Overlaid is the narration from *The Jackie Robinson Story*, "This is a story about a boy and his dream but more than that. It's a story of an American boy and a dream that is truly American." The narration continues, with sinister, Jim Crow voices, "Where are you going, Black boy? Black boy, we're the welcoming committee." The narration serves two purposes. One, to tell the viewer that they are watching a dream, and two it sets the tone for *Lovecraft* as a series about the racism and discrimination in the United States.

Robinson's second appearance is in the flesh to save Atticus from a giant, grotesquely tentacled monster, Cthulthu, Lovecraft's most famous creature. As the towering Cthulthu bears down on Atticus, the beast is suddenly sliced in half and collapses to the ground. Behind it, Robinson appears in his Brooklyn Dodgers uniform, covered in slime, shouldering his bat, *a job well done*. As Robinson struts towards Atticus, he says, with a grin, "I got you, kid." Then, almost immediately, the monster respawns larger than before, and lunges towards Robinson. Robinson, ever ready to confront a challenge, stands-in to re-attack at which time Atticus wakes up from his dream.

Misha Green posits that *The Jackie Robinson Story* would have been released around the same time that *Lovecraft Country* is set, meaning that Atticus would have likely seen the movie and been thinking about Robinson, his hero.[3] However, the decision to have Atticus dream of Robinson may be part of the larger context of Robinson's influence on and devotion to American youth. Robinson lived in the hearts and minds of young Black men throughout the 1940s and 1950s. He was their incomparable hero. So, it come as no surprise that Atticus summoned Robinson to save him. Given that the real-life Robinson devoted his time and money to support American youth, it was fitting to have him come to Atticus' aid.

There is no question that Robinson's notoriety came from "breaking the baseball color barrier" in 1947, and he should be remembered for this. The problem, though, is with every portrayal of his character that focuses on that act, his larger legacy erodes the nuance that made Robinson the person that he was, and his efforts as a civil rights activist are at risk of being diluted or forgotten entirely. To that extent, Robinson's minor character role was an important symbolic figure in *Lovecraft Country* not for saving Tic's life in his dream, but for his relentless effort battling Cthulthu, demonstrating his perseverance, grit, and courage for when the deck is stacked against him; in the same manner he fought for first-class citizenship in the United States.

Cold Case is a CBS police procedural drama where homicide detectives re-investigate unsolved crimes. Episode four, season three, titled, "Colors," centers around the mysterious death of a promising young Negro League baseball player, Clyde Taylor.[4] Taylor's dead body was discovered following an exhibition game between the Negro League and major-league baseball all-stars in which Taylor hit the game-winning home run. Robinson's minor character role was important to Taylor, as he acted like a big brother to the star, a common theme for fictional Robinson. His character appeared in three scenes and was portrayed as a shell of the man he was, yet he was a symbolic figure.

In Robinson's first appearance Taylor is up to bat, with the game on the line, looking nervous. Robinson encouragingly remarks to a pessimistic teammate, Moody Brown, that Taylor "is gonna be just fine, he's got a ton of guts." No doubt a nod to Branch Rickey, but out of context. In his second scene, Robinson very calmly diffuses an altercation between Taylor and Moody by merely walking up to the two and asking, "Hey, what's going on?" In his third and final appearance, Robinson suggests to his teammates as they prepare for the game that Taylor will be "the first Black player to play in the major leagues."

Robinson is the most famous and recognizable Black baseball player that ever lived. It is no surprise that a "Jackie Robinson" character had a role in an episode about a Black baseball player in the 1940s. To a CBS audience that is historically older, White adults, Robinson's character brought familiarity to the themes of racism and discrimination as well as historical context to the viewer.[5] The use of his character in this manner also reveals more about how society remembers Robinson and reinforces how society wants to continue to remember him.

Howard Bryant noted that "Robinson lives in the chamber of American sainthood, what he symbolized was far more important than the details of his life."[6] "Colors," continued that narrative by portraying an exceptionally clean, safe, and non-threatening character, one which the predominantly White audience could relate to and like. There was no sense of urgency or competitiveness in his character; he seemed subdued and overly cordial. He did not resemble the man who was pained by pervasive discrimination in every aspect of his life.

It was also interesting to see Robinson's character outwardly supportive and protective of his teammates because of what is known about Robinson's real-life experience in and thoughts about the Negro Leagues. Robinson was famously outspoken about his brief time as a Kansas City Monarch, lamenting that "it turned out to be a miserable way to make a buck."[7] He did not approve of his teammates carousing with women. He did not smoke or drink, making him somewhat of a pariah, and during the 1945 season he attempted to leave the Monarchs on multiple occasions. If that was not enough expression of his displeasure, in 1948, he penned a scathing indictment about the Negro Leagues in *Ebony* magazine titled, "What's Wrong with the Negro Leagues."[8] This portrayal of Robinson was a missed opportunity to provide an edge to an otherwise tame hour of television.

The Robinson character also plays an important, symbolic role when it is unseen. The character contributes more to the plot and determines the main actor's decisions and evokes their emotions. Two television specials, *A Home Run for Love* and *Brooklyn Bridge*, use the Robinson character as the central figure of their plots, despite the man himself never making an appearance.

A Home Run for Love used the Robinson character primarily as a learning opportunity for children. The movie was adapted from the children's novel, *Thank You, Jackie Robinson*, and produced as part of the *ABC Afterschool Special* series, airing in 1972.[9] *Afterschool Special* was an anthology of one-hour long installments that tackled difficult issues facing children, teenagers, and young adults. It spanned 25 years and 143 episodes ranging from topics of underage drinking, teenage angst, sexual health, and abuse. The stories were authentic and relatable, with non-fairy tale endings as an opportunity to teach children about the hardships in life.

A Home Run for Love is about the journey of an unlikely friendship between a young White boy and an older Black man in the 1940s. Sammy Greene is a typical boy, curious, occasionally defiant and consumed with Brooklyn Dodgers baseball. Sammy's mother owns a local inn where he works the front desk and buses tables in the dining room. His father

recently passed away. Davey Henderson is the newly hired Black cook who takes a special interest in Sammy. Their relationship blossoms when they discover each other's love of the Brooklyn Dodgers and Jackie Robinson.

The ABC specials take complex and difficult themes and distill them down for children and youths to comprehend. Robinson's character is important because it is used to teach children about prejudice, tolerance, and loss through the eyes of a child. Robinson's role was small, only appearing for a few lines midway through the movie, but the friendship that Sammy and Davey forged was a direct result of Robinson playing in the major leagues. And even though Robinson is a minor character, his legacy outweighs any role that he plays. He is symbolic because he represents the fight for tolerance and acceptance in America. It is not until Sammy attends his first Dodgers game that he learns a valuable lesson about the hardships that Jackie Robinson and other Black Americans faced.

Davey and his family take Sammy to his first Dodgers game. Oblivious to the disapproving stares from White spectators, Sammy is reveling in the afternoon. However, his enjoyment grinds to halt when he witnesses a player "spike" Robinson as he slid into second base. The crowd is in hysterics. Sammy, distraught, disbelieving, and searching for answers, asks Davey, "Did you see that? They spiked him deliberately and nobody did anything." Davey then explains to Sammy, "that's just part of what the first Negro in major-league ball has to put up with." Sammy was speechless and looked like he was trying to make sense of Davey's comment. For a young viewer, this was a powerful scene because it was an honest commentary on the life of Jackie Robinson.

Robinson's character in *Home Run* garners a call to action. For all his efforts to fight racial injustice at the systemic level, Robinson also encouraged people to act against prejudice at the individual level. "So I think the first step for each of us...is to stop thinking in terms of what we heard...and instead make certain that we judge other people as individuals."[10] Children observe two realities when watching the movie: first, they learn that it was wrong that Robinson was spiked without recourse, and two, he was attacked because he was Black. *Home Run* shows children to stand up for their beliefs and speak up when something is wrong, the way Robinson did.

Brooklyn Bridge was a CBS sitcom about the life of

a teenage boy, Alan Silver, growing up in the 1950s, whose life revolved around his family, friends, and the Brooklyn Dodgers. It aired for two seasons and 33 episodes between 1991-93. *Bridge* was short-lived due to its small audience, yet it has received much acclaim on the entertainment websites, Rotten Tomatoes and IMDB. *Bridge* is far from "prestige TV," but its stories are wholesome, and the characters are charming.

Robinson's character is at the center of the plot for season one, episode 11, "Where Have You Gone, Jackie Robinson?" In this episode, Alan and his family cope with disastrous news: an extra-marital affair in the family and Jackie Robinson being traded to the New York Giants. Both are devastating to this close-knit Jewish family, but the Robinson ordeal was felt worse. Alan's younger brother, Nathaniel, refers to the Robinson trade as a "family emergency." Upon hearing the news of the trade, Cousin Bernard sobs hysterically, Uncle Willy, the adulterer, blames himself stating, "me moving to Long Island means nobody is safe, anyone can leave Brooklyn." Phyllis Silver, Alan's mother copes by reciting Robinson's rookie year stat line, and biographical information to the family. And Nathaniel refers to Robinson as "more than a baseball player, he's like a friend." Their collective responses may appear dramatic and embellished even for television, but the real-life relationship between Robinson and Jewish people reveals the impact that Robinson had on their community which was felt by the Silver family.

In the United States in the 1940s and 1950s Jewish people identified with Robinson through their shared experiences of bigotry and persecution.[11] Robinson was their hero as they believed that if he could successfully integrate what was then defined as major-league baseball, Jewish people could be welcomed in America.[12] Robinson's fame and admiration among Jewish people was further fueled by their love of the Dodgers as, at that time, a third of the Brooklyn population was Jewish.[13] Rachel Robinson even noticed that they were making more Jewish friends when they lived in Brooklyn, "We made friends. For whatever reason, many happened to be Jewish...they were interested people who wanted to know us, just as we wanted to know them."[14] In all likelihood, the Robinsons began making friends with Jewish people as they were more ready to accept the Robinsons than any other Whites.[15]

It was not only Jewish Brooklynites that admired and supported Robinson. In his 1948 autobiography,

Jackie Robinson, My Own Story, Robinson recounts his first interaction with Jewish baseball legend Hank Greenberg. Following a collision between the two players at first base, Greenberg offered Robinson the following words of advice, "Don't pay any attention to these guys who are trying to make it hard for you. Stick in there, you're doing fine." This meant the world to Robinson because he believed that Greenberg truly understood his struggle.[16]

As his career progressed, Robinson leveraged his celebrity to address social injustice. His relationships with Jewish people strengthened through his dealings with the Anti-Defamation League (ADL); Robinson, recognizing the success of the ADL, sought to align their strategies with Black civil rights groups. In 1950, Robinson was awarded the Good Sportsmanship Trophy by the Maccabi Association (a major Jewish athletic group) for his work advancing tolerance and understanding of minority groups in America.[17] There is no doubt that Jackie Robinson would have made an impact on the fictional Silver family as a Brooklyn Dodger. During his tenure, the team won six pennants and the 1955 World Series. However, accolades aside, it would be fair to say that the Silver family would have had a strong connection to Robinson beyond his baseball career which reflected in their emotional response to his trade. This rarely explored aspect of the Robinson legacy, his connection to the Jewish community, is an underreported perspective of the character of Robinson.

Jackie Robinson serves as an important symbolic figure as a minor character because of the weight that his legacy carries. His image is synonymous with heroism and bravery. His character often does not need to speak or be visible for the audience to feel his presence. Right or wrong, his legacy is largely defined by breaking the baseball color barrier and as such his character is used to provide important historical context for stories about race and baseball. Furthermore, his character is often a misrepresentation of the *real* Robinson likely to make the audience comfortable and to seamlessly move the story. As such, Hollywood misses an opportunity to elevate their stories because the best of Robinson was not only his on-field heroics, but his passion for his family, commitment to doing what is right, and his grit in the face of adversity. But in the end, it's Robinson's legacy that is ultimately at stake with each inaccurate portrayal of him as a minor character.

Notes

1   Michael G. Long, ed., *42 Today: Jackie Robinson and His Legacy*, (New York: New York University Press, 2021), 4.

2   Ariana Brockington, "This is What Lovecraft Country Really Means," *Refinery29*, August 16, 2020. https://www.refinery29.com/en-us/2020/08/9959175/what-lovecraft-country-means-hp-racism

3   @MishaGreen, Misha Green. 2021. "The characters were baseball fans in @bymattruff's novel. *The Jackie Robinson Story* came out in 1950, which means Atticus would have seen it. So that naturally evolved into using the voice over from the movie, & having Atticus's biggest hero save him from Cthulhu in his dream." September 22, 2021. 5:41 PM https://twitter.com/MishaGreen/status/1440793384529002506

4   Season three ran from September 2005 to May 2006.

5   Emily VanDerWerf, "CBS is remarkably defensive for being American's most-watched network, *Vox*, May 17, 2017. https://www.vox.com/culture/2017/5/17/15655310/cbs-fall-schedule-2017

6   Howard Bryant, "Righting the wrongs of '42'.," *ESPN.com*, April 24, 2013. https://www.espn.com/mlb/story/_/id/9207998/42-gets-some-jackie-robinson-history-wrong-starts-conversation

7   Jackie Robinson, *I Never Had It Made* (New York: G.P. Putnam's Sons, 1972), 35.

8   Donn Rogosin, *Invisible Men* (Lincoln: University of Nebraska Press, 1983), 178.

9   Barbara Cohen, *Thank You, Jackie Robinson* (New York: Harper Collins, 1997)

10   Michael G. Long, ed., *Beyond Home Plate; Jackie Robinson on Life After Baseball* (Syracuse: Syracuse University Press, 2013), 66

11   Rebecca Alpert, "Jackie Robinson, Jewish Icon," *An Interdisciplinary Journal of Jewish Studies* Vol. 26, No. 2 (2008): 45.

12   Alpert, 47.

13   Ilana Abramovitch & Seán Galvin, eds., *Jews of Brooklyn* Waltham, Massachusetts: Brandeis University Press, 2002), 346.

14   Arnold Rampersad, *Jackie Robinson, A Biography* (New York: Random House Publishing Company, 1997), 221.

15   Rampersad, *Jackie Robinson, A Biography*, 221.

16   Jackie Robinson, *My Own Story* (California: Allegro Editions, 1948), 146-147.

17   Rampersad, *Jackie Robinson, A Biography*, 221

The Books of Sharon Robinson

By Sharon Hamilton

"It takes courage to be a pioneer"[1]

There is a lovely scene in Ken Burns' documentary series *Jackie Robinson* in which Robinson's daughter, Sharon, remembers what it was like for her to spend time with him when she was a child. After Robinson's retirement from baseball in 1957, just before Sharon turned 7, he regularly commuted from the family's home in Stamford, Connecticut to Manhattan, where he had accepted a position as president of personnel with the New York-based coffee business Chock full o'Nuts. "My special time with my dad was going into New York City," Sharon recalled. "So I put on white gloves and I was all dressed up. But it was just dad and I in that car driving along."[2]

Sharon was only 22 when her father died of a heart attack, but what you repeatedly find in the many books she has written about him shows that although they had relatively few years together, the father left an indelible impression on the daughter. His example inspired her own uniquely enriching forms of service to the world, as a writer, consultant, businesswoman, and health care professional. Things were not guaranteed to work out so well. It can be hard to be the child of a celebrity. In the pages of her books, Sharon candidly reveals many of her own personal troubles, and those of siblings.[3]

Compared to many other depictions of Jackie Robinson on the page, Sharon Robinson's important contribution to the wealth of material that has been written about her father consists of stories based on her personal experiences that provide readers with intimate insights into what Jackie Robinson was like as a person off the field, to his family, in the privacy of his home.

The Turquoise Bathrobe

Jackie Robinson occupies a storied position in the pantheon of American heroes. He was a skilled baseball player, a civil rights activist, and a trailblazer. In considering a life lived to such a high pinnacle of achievement, it can be difficult to picture the individual behind the icon. For this reason, while reading Sharon Robinson's books about her father, one finds oneself most touched by the personal details that reveal to us what Robinson was like as a man.

There is a wonderful scene at the beginning of Sharon's autobiographical *Child of the Dream: A Memoir of 1963*, a chapter book for young readers, in which she describes the morning before her 13th birthday. Her father is not at home. He had been hospitalized for a knee operation. Further complications from infection kept him in the hospital. Sharon experiences natural disappointment at not having her father with her for such an important life moment—the transition from being a child to being a teen.

She looks over at her mother and grandmother who are making breakfast and thinks to herself that normally her father would have been standing beside them stirring the grits.[4] Robinson remains in the hospital, cut off from this intimate family scene and his usual position within it. This memory of Robinson at the stove demonstrates who this great hero of American sports was to his child, the role he played for his daughter as part of fondly recalled domestic patterns.

On the day of her birthday, the family goes to see the 43-year-old Robinson at the hospital. When they enter his room, Sharon says "I see Dad sitting in a chair. He is wearing his favorite turquoise bathrobe."[5] In that description the reader is given the gift of intimacy, seeing a titan of baseball as a person, and in a moment of vulnerability as he struggles to recover his health.

Although the scene celebrates a moment of relief for Sharon, since Robinson appears to be doing better, there is a pathos as well. As readers we know what the child did not, that although Robinson would defeat this injury, he had only a handful of years to live. That knowledge renders this vivid glimpse of him in a hospital room wearing his favorite turquoise bathrobe even more poignant. While *Child of the Dream* is a book for young readers, such intimate insights make the book a welcome read for readers of any age who are interested in learning more about Robinson's life in all its fullness.

Wings

Early on in *Jackie Robinson: American Hero*, a biography about her father written as a chapter book for young readers, Sharon includes a breathtaking photograph. The picture shows Robinson as a young man of college age wearing a white University of California at Los Angeles (UCLA) tank top and white shorts. He is in the act of doing something seemingly impossible.

Like a bird of prey, he hovers high in the sky, one muscled arm flung out horizontally beside him, the other thrust powerfully behind. His legs lunge forward, extended above empty air, high above the people shown standing in the background. He drives one bare foot forward with such force it appears on the verge of kicking through the frame. This picture of Jackie in the midst of a flying broad jump is one of the best illustrations in *Jackie Robinson: American Hero*. The reader witnesses him seemingly able to stride through mid-air, like a god. Viewed as a symbol, this picture of Robinson feels like an appropriate image for someone so many see as an emblem of resilience and success.

This photograph draws attention to the extraordinary fullness of Robinson's accomplishments. This is something Sharon carefully does in many of her books. We tend to think of Robinson in his Brooklyn Dodgers uniform with the famous 42 on the back. But Sharon's selection of such photos reminds us that Robinson excelled at a wide range of sports.

As Sharon recounts in *Jackie Robinson: American Hero*, at one time Robinson "set a record for competing in two different sports in two different cities on the same day." In the morning he had been in Pomona, where he set "a new broad-jump record of 25 feet 6½ inches." That afternoon, he played shortstop in Glendale and "helped bring them a championship!"[6] While at UCLA, Sharon reminds us, her father excelled on their football, baseball, basketball, *and* track and field teams.

Sharon never witnessed most of the athletic feats she describes. She was only 6 when Jackie Robinson retired from baseball. As she explains in *Child of the Dream*, she learned about her father's extraordinary athletic prowess mainly from the awed descriptions provided to her by his fans. During one visit to his Chock full o'Nuts office in New York, while her father conducted business upstairs, Sharon recalls sitting at the lunch counter while the servers and patrons told her stories about seeing her father play.

> Once my father and I took the train all the way to Pittsburgh just to see Jackie play. You know that no one since Babe Ruth brought more fans into ballparks."
>
> "Your daddy kept the pitchers guessing while he danced on and off the base. Then, just when the pitcher figured out his rhythm, he'd steal home![7]

These excited retellings about Robinson during his glory days as a ballplayer enlivened Sharon's mental image of what her father had been like on the field. As Robinson re-entered the coffee shop to collect his daughter, she noticed all the laughter and good spirits just talking about him had provoked, the wonder and magic of what his extraordinary athletic gifts had brought into the world: "*He is so important to them*, I would think each time."[8]

Bread upon the waters

In a television interview with the Canadian Broadcasting Corporation in 1963 – the same year in which Sharon Robinson's *Child of the Dream* is set – the interviewer asks Robinson what had most helped him in overcoming the difficulties and deprivations of his childhood and what advice he would give others about how best to meet life's challenges.

Robinson considers for a moment and then says, "My mother insisted when I was a youngster that I get a church background." He explained that he had taught Sunday School classes and while he did not claim to be "the greatest religious person in the world," this upbringing had shaped his perspective. As a result of this upbringing, he said he had developed "a sincere interest in other people." He adds, "I believe, frankly, that a person who casts his bread upon the waters it will come back twofold."[9] This expression arises from the wisdom literature contained in the Bible's Hebrew scriptures, where it appears in this form in the Book of Ecclesiastes: "Cast thy bread upon the waters: for thou shalt find it after many days."[10] As Robinson explains to the interviewer, what this meant for him was that "in helping others I have helped myself."[11]

If Sharon Robinson in her books depicts Jackie Robinson in moments of personal vulnerability and at the height of his athletic achievements, she also captures his generosity of spirit – the ways in which, as he said himself, he wished to enrich the lives of others. One of the books in which Sharon Robinson beautifully captures Robinson's deep spirit of altruism is *Jackie's Nine: Jackie Robinson's Values to Live By.*

Near the beginning of this book, Sharon writes about a visit she and her son Jesse made in 1987 to see the Reverend Jesse Jackson and his family. They were there for Thanksgiving and as they spoke Sharon noted that their conversation led to a discussion about her father. "We talked about why some athletes' fame lives on and others' fades with time." Reverend Jackson thought the difference lay between what it means to be a champion and what it means to be a hero. "A champion" he opined, "wins a World Series or an Olympic event and is hoisted on the shoulders of teammates and fans. A hero carries the people on his shoulders."[12]

Sharon shows how her father carried others on his shoulders by sharing stories about Robinson – supplemented by those of other heroes and *she*roes (as she writes). These various accounts exemplify what Sharon saw as her father's core strengths of character: Courage, Determination, Teamwork, Persistence, Integrity, Citizenship, Justice, Commitment, and Excellence.

Legacy

One of the strengths Sharon Robinson brings to her writing is that she had to grapple with the question of how she would find and share her gifts with others while living in the shadow of one of America's most celebrated individuals. As they were growing up, this fact made life somewhat difficult for Sharon and her two siblings, Jackie Jr. and David. As she recalls in her memoir *Stealing Home*, "As childhood faded, the pressure to achieve escalated. The question was in what area and by what criteria should we measure our own success?"[13]

This idea of how to find and develop your personal abilities animates many of Sharon Robinson's books. She encourages her readers not merely to admire Robinson but to learn from his example. There is a humbleness in this task that Sharon admits to having learned from her parents, but she also exercises this gift in ways unique to herself. In so doing she situates her depictions of her famous father in ways that point to questions we all harbor: "Who am I?" "Why am I here?" "What will be my legacy?"

In *Child of the Dream*, Sharon discusses learning as a child about one of Jackie Robinson's most important legacies beyond baseball: his contributions to the civil rights activism of the 1960s.

One evening while sitting on the sofa at home, Sharon hears George Wallace's 1963 inaugural speech as the newly-elected governor of Alabama on the TV: "*Segregation now, segregation tomorrow, segregation forever!*" She reacts to his speech with understandable fright, leading her mother, Rachel Robinson, to reassure her that there are also people fighting for things to change.[14]

This leads to a discussion about her father's involvement in helping to advance those rights, and about the fact that some of the protests have incurred vicious reprisals, including the jailing of civil rights activists and the bombing of churches. Sharon, worried by this information, asks how there can be an end to the violence. Her mother replies, "One institution at a time. Baseball, the army, public buses—these are all fights that have been won."[15]

Rachel asks her daughter if she remembers the nine students from Little Rock, Arkansas. She does. Sharon remembers that there were nine Black students enrolled in an Arkansas high school. The governor had called in the National Guard to stop them from attending. She remembered that the students had reached out to her father. "I'm so proud they called Dad," she says. "What they did was so important."[16]

Sharon had been only 7 at the time, so her mother is impressed that she remembers. "Those students were inspired by his bravery," her mother explained. "It takes courage to be a pioneer and stand up against injustice. Doesn't matter where it happens, on the baseball field, marching in the street, or entering a school that doesn't want you there."[17]

On another occasion, after her older brother Jackie Jr. has run away from home, Sharon remembers that during that tense, heartrending time for her family she had a significant conversation with her father about institutionalized racism. He recognized that the teenaged Sharon had been shaken by what she had heard George Wallace saying on TV about segregation lasting forever. One night Robinson comes to her bedroom and gently broaches the topic with her. In response to her concerns, he admits that the challenge is real, but that people will protest and that the leaders of the civil rights movement plan to march for freedom. Surprised at his choice of words, Sharon asks, "But aren't Black people already free?" To which he replies, "Guess it depends on how you define freedom."[18]

Testing the Ice

In her memoir *Stealing Home* Sharon provides a story that she realizes provides a perfect metaphor for her father's life-long habit of self-sacrifice. As children, the Robinson siblings loved skating and playing hockey on the lake that was situated on the family property. In the winter after the lake froze, her father would go out on the ice to test its thickness, tapping methodically with his broomstick as he moved farther onto the lake. Sometimes he would hit an air bubble, causing a great noise of cracking. The children feared the ice might break. This image stayed strongly with her and later became the basis for her picture book for young children *Testing the Ice: A True Story about Jackie Robinson.*[19]

Sharon recognized while reflecting on those childhood memories how fraught this activity was with danger. As an adult she realized this activity of carefully checking the ice to ensure its safety was like her father's integration of what was then considered major-league baseball. "No one really knew what would happen"; he had to "feel his way along an uncleared path."[20]

In the books of Sharon Robinson, among all the intimate details of her father that she provides, this is the Jackie Robinson who emerges most strongly on the page: an individual who had the courage to go out in advance of others, at great peril to himself, to make conditions better for those who would follow.

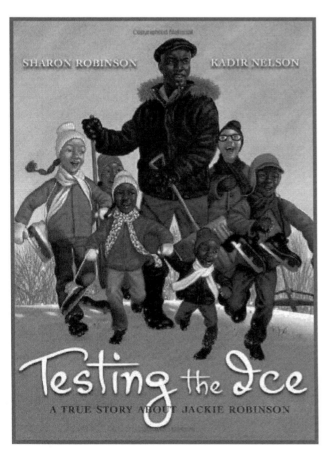

Testing the Ice, illustrated by Kadir Nelson.
image courtesy of Scholastic Publishers

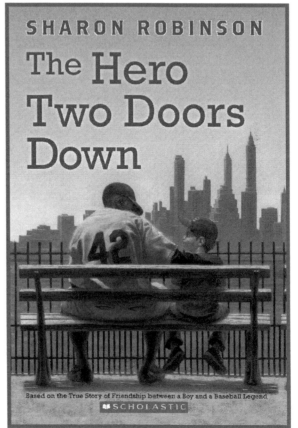

The Hero Two Doors Down illustration by Kadir Nelson & cover design by Elizabeth B. Parisi & Mary Claire Cruz.
image courtesy of Scholastic Publishers

Notes

1 Rachel Robinson in dialogue recalled by Sharon Robinson in Sharon Robinson, *Child of the Dream: A Memoir of 1963* (New York: Scholastic Press, 2019), chap. 7, Kindle.

2 Sharon Robinson, interview, in Ken Burns, Sarah Burns, and David McMahon, *Jackie Robinson*, a two-part, four-hour documentary on Jackie Robinson (2016): https://kenburns.com/films/jackie-robinson/

3 A list of Sharon Robinson's books can be found on her website: http://www.sharonrobinsonink.com/books

4 Sharon Robinson, *Child of the Dream*, chap. 1, Kindle.

5 Robinson, *Child of the Dream*, chap. 6, Kindle.

6 Sharon Robinson, *Jackie Robinson: American Hero* (New York: Scholastic Press, 2013), chap. 2, Kindle.

7 Sharon Robinson, *Child of the Dream*, chap. 11, Kindle.

8 Robinson, *Child of the Dream*, chap. 11, Kindle.

9 Jackie Robinson, interview, "Baseball star Jackie Robinson talks race relations" (1963), Canadian Broadcasting Corporation, Digital Archives, https://www.cbc.ca/player/play/1664440038

10 Ecclesiastes 11: 1. King James Bible.

11 Jackie Robinson, interview, "Baseball star Jackie Robinson talks race relations."

12 Sharon Robinson, *Jackie's Nine: Jackie Robinson's Values to Live By* (New York: Scholastic Press, 2001), Introduction, Kindle.

13 Sharon Robinson, *Stealing Home: An Intimate Family Portrait by the daughter of Jackie Robinson* (New York: HarperCollins, 1996), 92.

14 Robinson, *Child of the Dream*, chap. 7, Kindle.

15 Robinson, *Child of the Dream*, chap. 7, Kindle.

16 Robinson, *Child of the Dream*, chap. 7, Kindle.

17 Robinson, *Child of the Dream*, chap. 7, Kindle.

18 Robinson, *Child of the Dream*, chap. 8, Kindle.

19 Sharon Robinson, *Testing the Ice: A True Story About Jackie Robinson* (New York: Scholastic Press, 2009).

20 Robinson, *Stealing Home*, 45.

42

By Adam C. MacKinnon

The New York City skyline gleams in the background. A gravelly but urgent voice begins talking as the music swells to the climactic line delivered by the legendary Harrison Ford before it drops to the epic Jay-Z anthem "Brooklyn (Go Hard)." Slick action shots of diving catches and epic home runs peppered in between intense scenes of confrontation and triumph, punctuated by the slow-motion cap tip, and BAM! The nation's pastoral pastime gets an epic trailer, all centered on arguably its most important player ever, Jackie Robinson. You didn't have to be a baseball fan to feel the neck hairs begin to move after watching that.

It was 2013 and baseball hadn't just lost its toehold in modern American culture, it had nearly fallen off the cliff altogether. The 2012 World Series recorded the lowest TV ratings (at that time) since the games had begun broadcasting in 1968 and, despite the critical success of 2011's *Moneyball*, a baseball movie hadn't really had a notable cultural impact since *A League of Their Own* in 1992. Lucrative TV contracts had moved baseball off of national networks, fracturing the game's fans into fenced-in compounds and leaving behind generations of younger fans who had turned away from the cable companies that fostered these high-dollar deals. The game needed to reach new, younger fans while telling stories that took place before even their parents were alive. It seemed an opportune time for a baseball movie to bring some flash and style to a game that seemed to be very much lacking it at the moment. Who better to bring those qualities than the man who brought it to the game in real life? Jackie Robinson.

While portrayals of Robinson had appeared on stage (*The First, Play to Win*) and on TV (*The Court Martial of Jackie Robinson, Soul of the Game*), an all-encompassing biopic hadn't made its way to the silver screen since 1950, when Jackie played himself in *The Jackie Robinson Story*. Such a project hadn't really gained a lot of traction until the 1990s, when Spike Lee had floated the idea as a passion project, wanting Denzel Washington (then in his 40s) to play Robinson. According to Lee himself in an Instagram post in 2020, he recalled that Denzel was the one who cited his age as a factor for turning it down, saying "...I wrote a script for Jackie Robinson. I wanted Denzel to play Jackie, but Denzel said he was too old."[1] The film project allegedly evaporated over creative differences, and the idea of a Jackie Robinson biopic seemed to wither on the vine until Robert Redford reportedly took up the concept in 2004. Development of the idea didn't begin until 2011, which had Redford serving as not only the film's producer, but also playing the role of Branch Rickey, until Harrison Ford signed on to play the charismatic Dodgers executive. Brian Helgeland of *LA Confidential* fame signed on to direct, and a young, relatively unknown television actor named Chadwick Boseman was brought in to play Jackie Robinson.

Boseman was a relative newcomer when *42* was released in 2013. A native of South Carolina and graduate of Howard University, Boseman had seen some success on television with his roles in *Lincoln Heights* and *Persons Unknown*, but had yet to make his debut as a leading man in a movie before being selected to take on the part in *42*. Helgeland was impressed with Boseman, though, and later said during a *Washington Post* interview, "He had to play one of the bravest men who ever lived, so I thought that he came in brave was a great indication."[2] It doesn't take long into the movie to see that bravery pay off, as we see him become Jackie Robinson.

When first seeing Boseman in the vintage Dodger white and blue jersey, one can't help but notice the physical differences between him and Robinson. His slender frame and raspy vocals are notably a ways off

Chadwick Boseman portrays Robinson in the Warner Bros/Legendary Entertainment motion picture. image courtesy of Alamy

from Robinson's muscular build and higher-pitched voice, but those physical differences melt away as the movie takes shape. Boseman truly embodies the range and depth of Jackie, giving emotion and life to someone who was told to be silent and stoic. Probably most impressive is how he shows Jackie's sense of humor during the movie, as a sort of coping mechanism for the horrendous abuse he endures. His wry smile makes an appearance multiple times, like when Wendell Smith (the writer assigned to Robinson's personal needs during his time with the Dodgers, here portrayed by André Holland) is frantically driving Robinson out of town in the middle of the night away from the threat of racist tormentors. Smith frantically explains why he's speeding off into the night only to be shocked by Robinson's laughter. He thought Smith was driving him away at such an odd hour because he was cut from the team.

The true standout moment from the film though, is the exchange between Philadelphia Phillies manager Ben Chapman (played chillingly well by otherwise likable actor Alan Tudyk) and Robinson. Chapman spews a seemingly endless fountain of racial slurs and epithets at Robinson, which may cause modern (White) audiences to shift in their seats or avert their eyes, but was unfortunately true to life for that time in history. While on the field, Robinson takes the abuse seemingly unaffected, but after a particularly brutal verbal assault, he grabs a bat and escapes to the tunnel where he releases a guttural shout and smashes the bat to kindling. He collapses in tears, spent from both the penting and release of the anger that consumes him, only to be picked up by Branch Rickey, who appears almost celestially behind him, quietly reminding him of the importance of his task, and nudging him back to the field. It is a powerful moment, where we truly see the cracks in the otherwise impenetrable hide of the story's hero. It is a powerful moment, and lends a more human element to Robinson than his typical image, where he took those fountains of hate in stride and never broke a sweat. It's hard to see how he didn't, given the magnitude not only of the pressure on him to absorb the abuse, but the added pressure of having to perform. While that moment in the film may never have happened in the actual story, it reminds the audience that this incredible person doing this incredible thing is still a person—a human being.

As with a lot of American stories that get the Hollywood treatment, parts are often embellished for dramatic effect, or paper over aspects of the truth that may not be as convenient for moviegoers that one can assume may not be as familiar with the subject matter. After all, watching baseball isn't a prerequisite to buying a ticket to *42*. To help balance the temptations of oversimplifying the story with staying authentic to the life of the man himself, Rachel Robinson, Jackie's widow, was brought on to ensure that it was being told properly. She told Fox Sports Detroit in an interview when the movie was released, "I didn't want them to make him an angry black man or some stereotype, so it was important for me to be there."[3] One could argue that she succeeded on this front, because *42* offers a trait to its lead that is often deliberately omitted from major biopics, in order to retain its hero's "above the fray" status: compassion. We see Jackie doting over his newborn baby son before heading off for a game. We see him playfully flirting with his wife, being attentive, affectionate, even vulnerable with her. These are traits that more often than not are left out of characters in order to make them seem more determined, focused on the task at hand. To see this emotional range is a compliment to the acting of Boseman and writing of Brian Helgeland, but on a higher level, it is a credit to Rachel Robinson and her involvement. To much of White America, the defining trait of Jackie Robinson was his toughness, his ability to endure the punishment to the point where he becomes an almost biblical figure. In this movie, you see a human side to him that could only really be told by someone who saw it in real time, up close and personal.

The release of *42* brought a wide range of critical reactions but ultimately aggregated into a moderate success among the movie-learned. Harrison Ford and Chadwick Boseman in particular received praise for their roles, with one critic noting that, "Harrison Ford said he wanted to disappear into the role of Branch Rickey, and he damn near does."[4] Boseman was also given kudos for relishing his first leading role in a major movie, including "It's not easy to play a stoic, but Boseman anchors the movie, and when he smiles, *42*, already such a warm story of such cold times, gets even brighter."[5] There were some though, who argued that the parts didn't exactly sum up to a great movie, most notably Richard Roeper saying that the movie was "...a mostly unexceptional film about an exceptional man."[6]

One nagging shortfall of the movie isn't necessarily what it *did* do, but the opportunities that were missed in the telling of how Robinson came to be on the Dodgers, and the ripple effects of his arrival. There's a brief mention of some other Negro League players like Satchel Paige in the beginning, with Rickey quipping "I need a player with a future, not a past," before dismissing him as a potential addition to the team, but that element is left to die on the vine. Robinson's embarrassment of a tryout for the Boston Red Sox in 1945 is completely omitted, and the embrace he received from fans in Canada is never even mentioned. Probably the biggest head-scratcher of the movie, though, is that rather than expand on the path that Jackie forged for other Black players, and really emphasize the scope of what his arrival and his handling of it accomplished, it ends honing in on the pennant race of 1947, basically just playing out the rest of the regular season. Those incredibly impactful points and historical landmarks? Relegated to footnotes in a brief epilogue, like a slideshow thrown in at the end of a history lesson. For a film that was clearly designed for the non-baseball enthusiast, it felt like a real swing-and-miss moment.

Regardless of whatever shortcomings, the movie showed up strong at the box office, grossing over $95 million, good enough for second all-time for baseball movies only behind *A League of Their Own* in 1992, which grossed $107.5 million. Of course, the latter had the contemporary star power of Rosie O'Donnell, Gina Davis, Tom Hanks, and Madonna to propel its draw, while *42* had a notable star in Ford, but relative unknowns or character actors in every other corner. One could argue that makes the financial accomplishments of the film even more remarkable, especially when you consider that *42* had obstacles like the internet to deal with. One could attribute its success at the box office to the fact that it broke the mold of previous baseball movies that placed the game at its center and built the stories around it. Instead, Brian Helgeland created an action movie with baseball as its stage. It took a game that many younger viewers thought was too slow and out of touch, and gave it a shot of adrenaline to get younger eyes to the screen and keep them there. It was a baseball movie that conformed to the times it was made, not the times it depicted.

Even if *42* may have fallen short in breaking ground the same way its subject did, the biggest takeaway is that Chadwick Boseman's portrayal of

Jackie Robinson was captivating, complete, and charismatic. The movie allowed us to see Robinson beyond what we learned in our history books and painted a very human picture of a legend, and gave those who may not have known his story something to remember. Much like Robinson himself, the stage may not have been perfect, but Boseman played the part like no one else could.

Notes

1   "Spike Lee shares Unproduced Screenplay for Dream Jackie Robinson Biopic," *Collider*, March 30, 2020. https://collider.com/spike-lee-jackie-robinson-script/

2   Mark Jenkins, "Jackie Robinson film '42' Opens, starring Howard Graduate Chadwick Boseman," *Washington Post*, April 11, 2013. https://www.washingtonpost.com/goingoutguide/jackie-robinson-film-42-opens-starring-howard-graduate-chadwick-boseman/2013/04/11/dbdc8664-9e02-11e2-a941-a19bce7af755_story.html

3   "Rachel Robinson reflects on role in making '42'," *Fox Sports Detroit*, April 15, 2013. https://www.foxsports.com/detroit/story/rachel-robinson-reflects-on-role-in-making-42-041513

4   Jason Fraley, "Jackie Robinson Hailed as Mythic Hero in '42'," wtop.com, April 11, 2013. https://wtop.com/reviews/2013/04/jackie-robinson-hailed-as-mythic-hero-in-42/

5   Mary Pols, "*42*: The Jackie Robinson Biopic is a Solid Hit," entertainment.time.com, April 12, 2013.https://entertainment.time.com/2013/04/12/42-the-jackie-robinson-biopic-is-a-solid-hit/

6   Richard Roeper, "42," rogerebert.com, April 11, 2013, https://www.rogerebert.com/reviews/42-2013

Ken Burns' *Jackie Robinson*

By Pat Ellington Jr.

Ken Burns's film, *Jackie Robinson*, perfectly fits the definition of a documentary by providing a factual record or report. As a Black member of the audience, it was extremely important for me to hear from Black people in cultural context and to see honesty about the racism embedded in America. The film production crew devoted a great deal of attention to detail, seeking out accounts from those who were close to Jackie Robinson both inside and outside of the game of baseball, including some of professional baseball's most reputed writers and historians, politicians, and other cultural figures, all with the blessing of and cooperaton with the Robinson family.

It's easy for one to be skeptical about a White person capturing the life of a man of African descent, a man who intentionally did everything he could both publicly and privately to change the status of Black people as bottom-class citizens around the globe – someone who arguably had a revolutionary impact. Would Burns be able to grasp, or be willing to go far enough to explain, the absurdity of racism and bigotry? Would he be able to capture the fact that Jackie Robinson fought back on and off the field as often as he turned the other cheek? One wondered whether Burns would be willing to tell Jackie Robinson's flat-out truths that contradict the myth that is the American Dream—a myth that at the time the country was founded was created to intentionally be inaccessible to Black people, an era in which at best a Black person was considered to be 3/5ths of a human being.[1]

Ken Burns did all this, and portrayed Robinson in an honest tone that showed who he was at the beginning and the end of the day – a fighter and trailblazer for his people. He didn't hesitate to address some of the myths that were a product of Robinson's extraordinary life. For instance Burns confronted the apocryphal story of Pee Wee Reese putting his arm around Robinson. He interviewed eyewitnesses who provided first-hand accounts, and pointed out the lack of photographs. In their own way, some of these fictional tales attest to the the importance and impact of Robinson. Burns, the documentarian, approached them in an honest way.

The documentary's focus on Jackie's wife Rachel Robinson is key to the quality of the documentary. Positioned right next to the second baseman throughout the majority of his life, it was both imperative and rewarding to feature her perspective. The extremely close relationship that the Robinsons had was evident in her recounting his life, thoughts, dreams, and fears. She saw how restless the mistreatment of Black people in America made her husband, and how he used baseball to fight against it.

Any idea that Jackie Robinson did nothing but turn the other cheek and keep silent about his mistreatment as an individual of African descent is a flagrant myth. He constantly countered certain White players, members of the press, and even heckling fans with his words, his actions, and his continued success on and off the diamond.[2]

There has been a "pacification" of Robinson that was meant to soften his image in hindsight, as his radicalness against racism and third-class citizenship remains challenging for a significant portion of the population. This was not the only major myth about Robinson that was officially debunked during the documentary. At the same time Burns subtly presents an important theme of the documentary— that American society needs myths and obscurations of Jackie Robinson's image, words, and intentions, in addition to his wondrous feats on the diamond, in order for it to accept who he was.

Burns consistently looked at Robinson's struggle to find a place within the movement he helped found, as he got older and had reaped some of the success

Rachel Robinson and Ken Burns discuss Robinson's legacy. photo by Frederick M. Brown/Getty Images

of his efforts. He wove the first-hand accounts into the story brilliantly, using Robinson's relationship with the *New York Post* as a great example. When Robinson first started writing columns at the paper, it was radical and effective. As time passed, and as the Civil Rights Movement became more militant, the flock of blades that were Robinson's articles gradually dulled. He was soon booted from the paper as he went from criticizing conservatives to being labeled as one for his political affiliations.[3]

Burns does an excellent job of revealing Robinson's struggles even further by showing his experiences and connections with other Black people who were trying to dismantle racism in the United States and abroad, and how they heavily mirror *and* contrast his failures negotiating with the establishment on behalf of his people. His relationship with Malik el-Shabazz (a/k/a Malcolm X), and el-Shabazz's rhetoric for militancy and self-defense is a perfect example. Their mutual misunderstandings during the latter part of their relationship are well-known and well-covered,[4] but Burns included the fruitful and productive parts of their relationship as well. El-Shabazz is on record as citing the impact of listening to the second baseman's early career while Malcolm Little was in prison, and credits Robinson's pathbreaking career as a huge inspiration.

Dr. Martin Luther King Jr. was another individual inspired by Jackie Robinson's career when he was a young man and saw how baseball intersected with society. King later collaborated with Robinson and they became close confidants. This friendship helped King see the inherent revolutionism in Black baseball culture. Dr. King went on to foster a similar relationship with Afro-Puerto Rican Roberto Clemente.[5]

Robinson's dismal track record with politicians on both sides of the United States political spectrum was addressed. Burns highlights Robinson's naïveté in trusting the political establishment at face value; he undertook relationships with such a figure as Richard Nixon and the Republican Party in 1960, without leverage or an organization of his own, and crashed and burned. This relationship only looked worse when Barry Goldwater and his "Southern strategy" changed the party dramatically in the 1964 election.

One particularly important portion of the documentary demonstrated how Burns was willing to go above and beyond, and that was the inclusion of Afro-Cuban Hall of Famer Minnie Miñoso, who expressed how Robinson's success inspired him to become the first Afro-Latino to wear a major-league baseball uniform. This emphasized how Robinson fought for and served as an example to the entire

African diaspora. The histories and experiences of the various nationalities and ethnicities that comprise the African diaspora are inextricably linked, and the 150 years of history that people of African descent across the globe have with the game of baseball exemplifies that fact.[6] It is one rarely covered correctly – or even mentioned by many of those deemed to be the sport's pundits. Burns dedicated a segment to explore this topic.

All in all, this documentary accurately portrayed the highlights and shadows of an individual who has had his story distorted and twisted many times over. The lengths to which Burns went, utilizing first- and second-hand accounts from important sources while layering music, photos, and videos between interview clips was masterful. His selection of who to include and what stories they told was as well.

Burns's acknowledgements of Robinson's flaws were not ingenuous or solitary; they are positioned alongside his self-awareness and his dedication to being an inspiration for Black people around the globe. Robinson kept trying to overcome his own shortcomings and make up for his failures. The documentary shows us a man who knew he was not infallible, but who consistently tried to evolve as the revolution needed him to grow. Robinson would never have seen himself as a revolutionary, but as we look back on his contributions 75 years later, one could well argue that his integration of baseball helped prompt a seismic change in American society. Today, he remains one of the most visible examples of Black baseball's inherent revolutionism. Ken Burns has successfully captured that story.

Notes

1   Malik Simba, "The Three-Fifths Clause of the United States Constitution (1787)," blackpast.org, October 3, 2014. https://www.blackpast.org/african-american-history/events-african-american-history/three-fifths-clause-united-states-constitution-1787/, accessed March 16, 2022.

2   Matt Welch, "When Jackie Robinson Fought Back," *Reason*, July 2013, https://reason.com/2013/06/30/when-jackie-robinson-fought-back/, accessed March 16, 2022.

3   Matt Welch. "On Jackie Robinson Day, Let's Remember When He Was Fired From the New York Post For Being Too Republican." *Reason*, April 15, 2015, https://reason.com/2015/04/15/on-jackie-robinson-day-lets-remember-whe/, accessed March 16, 2022.

4   Justin Tinsley, "Jackie Robinson vs. Malcolm X," *Andscape*, May 25, 2016, https://andscape.com/features/jackie-robinson-vs-malcolm-x/, accessed March 16, 2022.

5   José de Jesus Ortiz, "Martin Luther King Jr. and Roberto Clemente Had a Deep Bond," *Our Esquina*, January 17, 2022, https://ouresquina.com/2022/martin-luther-king-jr-and-roberto-clemente-had-deep-bond/, accessed March 16, 2022.

6   Library of Congress, "Drawing the Color Line: 1860s to 1890s." https://www.loc.gov/collections/jackie-robinson-baseball/articles-and-essays/baseball-the-color-line-and-jackie-robinson/1860s-to-1890s/, accessed March 16, 2022.

Stealin' Home

By Steve Butts

Jazz and baseball are two distinctly American forms of entertainment which have close ancestors that originally began in Europe, but were probably not recognizable as either jazz music or the game of baseball (as we know it) until they were each imbued with their own respective uniquely American character. This American character is something intangible that seemingly comes from America's ability to quickly combine, incorporate, and alter older ideas while simultaneously producing newer ones. "Both uniquely American innovations, the history of jazz and baseball are intertwined. The word 'jazz' got its start in baseball; it was the early-20th century baseball term for 'pep, energy' before it became the term for the new frenetic style of music," notes historian Shakeia Taylor.[1]

This "frenetic style of music" and propulsive pastoral game each arguably achieved their cultural high-water marks in New York City almost simultaneously in 1947, when Jackie Robinson integrated major-league baseball with the Brooklyn Dodgers. He immediately brought a decidedly new style of "pep, energy" in his brand of play. This all would seem to be more than just a coincidence, in a rapidly changing world.

Both baseball and jazz share the capabilities of being excellent vehicles for idiosyncratic, individual expression while often reflecting the harmonious, synchronous beauty of collaboration and teamwork. Robinson, with his military experience and extensive sports background, could likely see the delicate balance between the individual and the team. The whole might be greater than the sum of its component parts in some cases, while in others the single best talent prevails over all, because that talent is so decidedly sublime when compared to other competitors. It only made sense that with his awareness, and the aforementioned linkages between the game of baseball and jazz music, that he would also eventually become a fan of that music form.

According to journalist Michael G. Long, "Robinson and his wife were jazz enthusiasts who personally knew some of the famous musicians of their day. With help from their friend Marian Logan, a former jazz singer, the Robinsons soon put together an impressive lineup of jazz artists who agreed to play [a benefit concert on their property in Stamford, Connecticut] for free. Meanwhile, handy neighbors erected a canopied bandstand."[2] This initial event, in 1963, was successful enough that it encouraged the Robinsons to host numerous concerts, with proceeds raised for several charitable causes and civil rights organizations each time. After her husband died in 1972, Rachel hosted the concert annually, with the majority of the proceeds going to the Jackie Robinson Foundation, which grants scholarships to talented minority students. Sharon Robinson (Jackie and Rachel's daughter) now runs the Jackie Robinson Foundation and helps produce the concert.[3]

The Robinsons were resourceful in their philanthropic efforts and were committed to help in any way they could. Still, jazz had a compelling allure when it came to supporting the Civil Rights movement. According to Rachel Robinson, "Jazz is the perfect medium to reflect life and the need people have to improvise and transcend barriers."[4]

Spending much of his young life fighting personal battles that placed him squarely in the middle of the fight for social justice only emboldened and further energized Jackie Robinson to do whatever he could to support those pressing for social change, especially for those in the Civil Rights movement. These concerts and their proceeds initially were intended to help in the defense of several members of the Southern Christian Leadership Conference (Dr. Martin Luther King Jr.'s organization) who had recently been arrested during the Birmingham, Alabama campaign.

In 1962, Martin Luther King, Jr. recognized the importance of Jackie Robinson as an energetic forerunner to the continually emerging civil rights movement. "(He) [Robinson] was a sit-inner before the sit-ins, a freedom rider before the Freedom Rides," King said.[5] The year 1963 brought a further coalescence of the Robinsons' role in the movement.

As civil rights demonstrations escalated at lunch counters and in segregated businesses, Robinson was further compelled to directly show his support for the movement. He said, "Whenever and where in the South the leaders believe I can help, just the tiniest bit, I intend to go."[6]

On August 28, 1963, two months after the first "Afternoon of Jazz," the Robinsons were a part of the March on Washington, where Dr. Martin Luther King, Jr. gave his iconic "I Have a Dream" speech. Years later, when he recalled that day, Robinson wrote: "I have never been so proud to be a Negro. I have never been so proud to be an American."[7]

***

In continuation of the larger historical legacy of the Robinsons' philanthropy, in 2019 a collaborative enterprise began to germinate, one that would celebrate the life and legacy of Jackie Robinson in both baseball and jazz. In December of 2018, Terry Cannon and his wife Mary ran into jazz cornetist/ trumpeter Bobby Bradford at their local bank. Cannon, who had been diagnosed recently with cancer, had an idea.

"Right away, Terry told him about his health situation and asked, 'Bobby, if I survive my upcoming cancer (bile duct) surgery, would you be interested in composing a musical suite on the life of Jackie Robinson?'" according to Mary. "It's going to be his centennial year. There was an immediate answer, 'Yes!' and straight away, Bobby was humming and singing, 'Robinson, Rob-in-son....'"[8]

Cannon was the director of both the Baseball Reliquary and the Institute for Baseball Studies at Whittier College in Whittier, California. Per their mission, the Reliquary is a nonprofit educational organization whose goal is to foster an appreciation of American art and culture through the prism of baseball history, and to explore the national pastime's unparalleled creative possibilities.

"In 2018 the centennial anniversary of Robinson's birth loomed, and Cannon was unsure about what

the city of Pasadena might plan, so he doubled-down on his own brainstorming."[9] Cannon was increasingly feeling the need to step up and do something as a concern grew over a lack of plans.

In keeping with the Baseball Reliquary's mission statement and its director's ability to tell the part of the story that often went untold, Cannon's mind sprang into action. "We had never commissioned a musical project before," said Cannon. "I knew that Jackie and his wife Rachel loved jazz so it hit me that this might be something that would be meaningful."[10]

Cannon had spent many years fostering the arts and music in Pasadena. He wrote about jazz for a local paper and acquired a massive collection of jazz LPs. He had attended lots of musical performances and had previously developed a relationship with Bobby Bradford. He also had started the Pasadena Film Forum (which became the Los Angeles Film Forum) and supported other fine arts.

Cannon's audacious ability to organize and coordinate came from his considerable personal talents and the ability to inspire others to get behind whatever he was doing. As a young man, reading Bill Veeck's *Veeck – as in Wreck* remained a formative and lasting influence.[11] The Detroit-born Cannon's outsider vision of baseball and his attraction to one of the true rebels and rabble-rousers would later offer a prime example of what an inductee to the Reliquary's Shrine of the Eternals might be: an iconoclast with both a sense of humor and a sense of purpose. Veeck was the second major-league baseball owner (and the first in the American League) to integrate after Jackie Robinson, by adding Larry Doby and Satchel Paige.

2019 was a major year for Cannon because the Baseball Reliquary had also commissioned an art triptych commemorating the 100th anniversary of Rube Foster's forming the Negro Leagues at the Paseo YMCA in Kansas City, Missouri, as depicted by Greg Jezewski, a work entitled *The House That Rube Built*. Commissioning *Stealin' Home*, the eventual title of the finished jazz piece, would be another major step for fostering further creativity in the community.

Enter Bobby Bradford. Not only did he have considerable musical and creative talents, he also had valuable life experiences as someone who had also served in the military and grew up in an America that offered far less opportunity for African Americans. He witnessed first-hand and directly felt the changes that Jackie Robinson was bringing about.

"Seventh grade. When black wasn't beautiful.

There was no basketball, no community baseball. But in 1947, when Jackie Robinson joined the Brooklyn Dodgers? We were all cued up for that," remembers Bradford. "He was a rebel. We had our eye on him. All Black America had their eyes on him."[12]

Bradford also had his eyes on a career in jazz that brought him to Los Angeles and eventually Robinson's alma mater, Pasadena City College, as a music educator. Bradford possessed a bit of Robinson's rebellious spirit, being right there at ground zero with sax player Ornette Coleman at the birth of free jazz, which expanded jazz musicians' possibilities for creative freedom without an imposed musical structure. Bobby was one of a select few performers who grasped Ornette Coleman's harmolodic concept that offered even more unfettered freedom of expression to musicians. When I talked with Bradford, we discussed this in the context of a musical group playing like a team, where each performer was like a player.[13]

Cannon's Baseball Reliquary co-conspirator Albert Kilchesty spoke further, "On the face of it, Branch Rickey—the baseball Mahatma—and Sonny

The final performance of *Stealin' Home*, featuring Bobby Bradford (cornet), Chuck Manning (tenor saxophone) and Vinny Golia (bass saxophone). image courtesy of Jon Leonoudakis

Rollins—saxophone colossus—would appear to have nothing in common except for knowing Jackie Robinson, but each blew the same message: Luck is the residue of design. Actually, Rickey said that and Rollins intuitively knew that which is why he spent so many of his dark, wee hours alone, standing on or pacing around the pedestrian walkway of the Williamsburg Bridge, practicing--always practicing, always thinking, always chasing excellence. Each different man understood that without steady, proper preparation for the moment--to react to a crack of the bat, to riff breathtaking improvisational phrases--the outcomes will always disappoint. America's Game, at its highest level, and American Art Music, at its dizziest height."[14]

Cannon's not being particularly didactic about the project was also helpful for Bradford. "So you do know what kind of music I play," Bradford recalled, rolling into a chuckle. "Terry reassured me, 'I don't want something necessarily sweet and romantic,' he told me. 'I want something how you do something.'"[15]

The Baseball Reliquary's proximity to Los Angeles and Robinson's Pasadena home had made Robinson and the Dodgers prominent in many of the Baseball Reliquary's past programs. Two of its relics, the Ebbets Field Cake and Michael Guccione's Jackie Robinson icon painting, can be viewed at the Jackie Robinson Center in Pasadena. When the social services center opened in 1974, it was the first public facility in Southern California to be named after Robinson. Both Rachel and Jackie Robinson have also been inducted into the Baseball Reliquary's "Shrine of the Eternals," or "The People's Hall of Fame," as it was referred to by Shrine-inductee Jim Bouton.

During their first Shrine of the Eternals ceremony in 1999, Terry Cannon read a note of encouragement written decades earlier by Robinson to Dock Ellis, a charter member of the Shrine, encouraging Ellis's continued bravery in standing up for racial equality. Robinson wrote, "I want you to know how much I appreciate your courage and honesty. In my opinion, progress for today's players will only come from this kind of dedication. Try not to be left alone. Try to get more players to understand and you will find great support. You have made a real contribution. I surely hope your great ability continues. That ability will determine the success of your dedication and honesty."[16]

Ellis's induction was deeply moving. By connecting the Shrine of the Eternals directly with the cultural change previously spurred on by Robinson's integration of major-league baseball with Robinson's note of encouragement, it showed that these processes of social change are not frozen in time but are part of a larger continuing and ongoing social justice project. Composing a thematic piece to mark the 100th birthday of Jackie Robinson and the travails that he faced further extended that project.

The jazz septet (Bobby Bradford and Friends) itself has a progressive feel, both in the touches of free jazz soloing and in the densely arranged Mingus-like ensemble sections which drive the music with considerable power and emotional voicing. Bradford's challenging imprint is definitely there.

I talked with Bobby Bradford about composing the songs for the recording and it was an enlightening experience. The 87-year-old submerged himself further into several defining moments of Robinson's life, trying to understand his thoughts and feelings about overcoming the obstacles that were so often placed before him in his personal and professional life as a Black man in America. Bradford had never been commissioned to compose a thematic piece before and he took the challenge very seriously and did considerable research on the life and career of Robinson.

Until the 2019 thematic composition of *Stealin' Home* began, there had only been a select handful of songs written about Jackie Robinson, most famously Buddy Johnson's "Did You See Jackie Robinson Hit That Ball?" There were also lesser-known songs by rock band Everclear and folk performer Ellis Paul, as well as songs entitled "The Jackie Robinson Boogie" and "Jackie Robinson Blues," according to the Library of Congress. Nikki Giovanni has also written a Robinson poem entitled "Stealin' Home."[17]

One thing that I noticed and asked Bradford about was the superficial similarity between *Stealin' Home* and the old gospel standard, "Steal Away," which had a cultural connection to the Underground Railroad during the United States Civil War. Bradford responded that he had given it some superficial consideration but excised the idea when it became clear that it was not fitting into his broader conception of the Robinson piece.[18]

The songs focus on pivotal stages of Robinson's life and reflect his taking the agency of choosing his own path, despite the many obstacles placed before him. The first cut, "Lieutenant Jackie," features a martial, structured beat that becomes looser as time goes on, presumably as Robinson has a true assessment of his surroundings and feels more comfortable about his place within them. The song also deals with Robinson's experience as an Army officer and the events of his court martial.

William Roper's spoken section near the end of that selection highlights the ambivalence of serving one's country yet eventually returning to civilian life as a second-class citizen. Bradford draws from his own personal life experience as a military man in this section, too. He recounted the tale of the time a service member had died and his family requested military buglers to play for the funeral. He and another bugle player (who was White) arrived to play for the funeral and the family immediately protested Bradford's presence because he was an African American.[19]

The next song, "Up From The Minors," represents the confusion and anguish of being the first African-American major leaguer, asked to shoulder considerable enmity with an elevated sense of grace. This is the most free and chaotic composition, with the crying swirl of reeds and Bradford's vocal mimicking trumpet. To Bradford's credit, he deftly balances raucous and unsettling sections with more conventional sections, which seems to restore order and security for the listener. Bradford also had thought about the Robinsons' first spring training, when they were unable to make their entire flight to Florida, after the plane stopped to refuel in New Orleans and they were removed just because they were African American.

"Stealin' Home," the song that gave the album its title, represents Jackie at the peak of his powers, exuding mental confidence and playing with his own special flair. People inspired by Robinson's life often look to this event as a particularly symbolic and defining moment in his career.

While researching for the album, Bradford considered the irony of Robinson finally getting his chance in the major leagues in the song, "0 for 3," only to go 0-for-3 in his first game (with a sacrifice and scoring one run after taking a walk). All of Black America was paying attention and hoping for something dramatic. It was very important and emblematic that Robinson had found a way to contribute, even if he did not have his best game.

Talking with Bradford, we mutually agreed that even if Robinson had gone 3-for-3 that day, there would have likely been several fans critical of his performance as a means of demeaning him.

The album closes with a more somber and reflective tone on "High and Inside," seemingly indicating that Robinson was realizing that even though he might be ending his highly impactful playing career, societal changes were only just beginning.

In all, there were five Jackie Robinson Centennial concerts presenting *Stealin' Home*. Notably, several of the performances were opened by jazz vocalist Byron Motley, who is the son of Negro League umpire Bob Motley. The shows were well attended and favorably received. Greg Jezewski remembered going early to help Cannon with the first concert, which he said Cannon had fully under control (as he generally did). Cannon, a production veteran, still looked and acted like he had butterflies, hoping that the event would be well attended and go on nearly without a hitch.[20]

"The event was an extraordinary celebration of an extraordinary man, made even more meaningful by taking place in Jackie's adopted hometown," said Kathy Robinson-Young, Jackie's niece. Robinson-Young added, "Bobby Bradford's stellar group blew the house away with their musicianship and unique take on Jackie's journey. One piece about Jackie's rise through the minor leagues was an abstract montage of the ugly experiences Jackie faced on his way to Brooklyn. It was unsettling and remarkable. This event is yet another chapter in the brilliance of the Baseball Reliquary, who continue to produce some of the most remarkable events and experiences

celebrating the human side of baseball and its impact on culture."[21]

There is also a burden that must be carried in every social legacy. Bradford and I discussed Robinson's burden. In a previous interview with the *Los Angeles Times*, Bradford mentioned being a youngster and seeing his hero Louis Armstrong perform. He said that Armstrong played craps and put pomade in his hair and acted more naturally around other African Americans. But as soon as a White person entered the room, he put on his "mask."[22]

This "mask" was a way of both protecting himself and meeting expectations for the White folks. Not only that, it was giving them an acceptable caricature of himself. It was the dichotomy of balancing your public and private personas, except in this case, your genuine persona is always muted in deference to the members of another race.

I asked Bradford whether having to carry this "mask" as an African American man could cause mental or physical damage and Bradford responded that he could not "speak with any authority on the physical or mental impact except (in) my own experience. The mask requires a lot of psychic energy at a price."[23]

Cannon's dying only 10 months after the *Stealin' Home* concerts reminds us of that commitment to the ongoing project for social change. Bradford has since retired from teaching and has performed sparingly as the Covid-19 pandemic continues to limit and inhibit live performances nearly everywhere. I asked Bobby Bradford about his thoughts about his partnership with The Baseball Reliquary and the Cannons. He responded that "In times like these of racial, cultural and religious strife, people like Terry and Mary Cannon are reminders that the world is still full of wonderful people."[24]

Author's Note

A full performance of Stealin' Home *can be viewed at: https://www.youtube.com/watch?v=mAlrpnHLwek*

The final performance of *Stealin' Home*, featuring Don Preston (piano), Henry Franklin (bass) and Tina Raymond (drums). image courtesy of Jon Leonoudakis

Notes

1   Shakeia Taylor, "Prospectus Feature: Baseball and Jazz," Baseball Prospectus, February 6, 2019, https://www.baseballprospectus.com/news/article/46970/prospectus-feature-baseball-and-jazz/

2   Michael G. Long, "The Undefeated, Music to his ears: How Jackie Robinson's love of jazz helped civil rights movement," theundefeated.com, April 15, 2020. https://theundefeated.com/features/how-jackie-robinsons-love-of-jazz-helped-civil-rights-movement/

3   Michael G. Long.

4   Michael G. Long.

5   "Robinson, Jackie," *The Martin Luther King, Jr. Encyclopedia,* The Martin Luther King, Jr. Research and Education Institute, Stanford University, https://kinginstitute.stanford.edu/encyclopedia/robinson-jackie

6   Christina Knight, "Five Important Years in Jackie Robinson's Life," *Thirteen,* https://www.thirteen.org/program-content/five-important-years-in-jackie-robinsons-life/

7   Christina Knight.

8   Mary Cannon, "Backstory: Thoughts from Mary Cannon," liner notes for Bobby Bradford's CD, *Stealin' Home,* 2019, 1. The CD has never been commercially released.

9   Lynell George, "Play to Win!" liner notes to Bobby Bradford, *Stealin' Home.*

10   Lynell George.

11   David Karpinski, Baseball Roundtable, https://baseballroundtable.com/the-baseball-reliquary/

12   Lynell George.

13   Bobby Bradford interview with Steve Butts, January 21, 2022.

14   Albert Kilchesty, friends-only Facebook post, May 16, 2020, Accessed February 4, 2022.

15   Lynell George.

16   David Karpinski, Baseball Roundtable, https://baseballroundtable.com/the-baseball-reliquary/

17   "Did You See Jackie Robinson Hit That Ball," United States Library of Congress, https://www.loc.gov/collections/jackie-robinson-baseball/articles-and-essays/baseball-the-color-line-and-jackie-robinson/did-you-see-jackie-robinson-hit-that-ball/

18   Author interview with Bobby Bradford.

19   Author interview with Bobby Bradford.

20   Author interview with Greg Jezewski, January 19, 2022.

21   Terry Cannon, "Celebrating Jackie Robinson in Pasadena," Facebook post, December 16, 2019.

22   RJ Smith, "An L.A. jazz legend pays homage to Jackie Robinson with a pitch from a library assistant," *Los Angeles Times*, September 25, 2019. https://www.latimes.com/entertainment-arts/music/story/2019-09-25/bobby-bradford-jackie-robinson-stealin-home

23   Author interview with Bobby Bradford.

24   Author interview with Bobby Bradford.

Contributor Bios

Adam Berenbak is an archivist with the National Archives Center for Legislative Archives in Washington, DC. He has been a member of SABR for over a decade and his research focuses on the history of baseball in Japan, on which he has published articles in the SABR *Journal* and *Our Game*, curated an exhibition with the Japanese Embassy's Cultural Center in DC, and contributed to a number of articles and books. He has also published several essays on other topics related to baseball history in the SABR *Journal*, *Prologue*, *Zisk*, and an exhibition in conjunction with the Museum of Durham History and the Durham Bulls Athletic Park. His work will also be featured in upcoming SABR books on Jackie Robinson and US Tours of Japan.

Dr. Milbert O. Brown, Jr., is a multi-talented storyteller. During his career, he has captured the historical and cultural tapestry of the Black community using his gifts as an artist, photojournalist, and writer. Currently, Dr. Brown produces independent creative projects as the principal consultant of Brown Images. Brown's interest in the Negro Leagues began in the 1990s when he interviewed and photographed several Negro League players. Earlier in his distinguished journalism career, Brown worked as an editor and photojournalist at the *Boston Globe* and *Chicago Tribune*. At the *Tribune*, Brown shared journalism's highest honor- the Pulitzer Prize in Journalism for Explanatory Reporting as a contributing staff member in 2001. The Indiana native graduated from Morgan State University with a Doctorate in Higher Education Leadership. Brown also earned a Master of Arts degree from Ohio University's School of Visual Communication and a B.S. in Journalism from Ball State University. oeditorbrown@gmail.com

Steve Butts is a long-time book and record store employee who is in his first year as a member of SABR. He is also is a Facebook page administrator for The Baseball Reliquary and Institute for Baseball Studies. He collects custom art cards with a growing personal collection focused upon "The King" Eddie Feigner.

Ralph Carhart is the author of *The Hall Ball: One Fan's Journey to Unite Cooperstown Immortals with a Single Baseball* [McFarland 2020], and the creator of the eponymous artifact that visited with every member of the Hall of Fame, living and deceased. With *Not an Easy Tale to Tell*, Ralph has contributed to six SABR volumes. His latest effort for SABR was the biography of Rachel Robinson, which appeared in 2021's *Jackie: Perspectives on 42*. He is currently writing a history of Brooklyn, dating back to the Lenape Indians, as told through the lens of baseball.

Ray Danner lives in Cleveland Heights, Ohio, where he is a local real estate investor. He can also be found underwater at the Greater Cleveland Aquarium as part of the dive team. He was on the sports beat for "The Cauldron" at Cleveland State University and a contributing writer at "It's Pronounced Lajaway", a member of the ESPN SweetSpot Network. Ray also plays rover on a vintage baseball club, the Whiskey Island Shamrocks. A SABR member since 2012, he is a lifelong Strat-O-Matic fan and enjoys contributing to SABR's Games Project and BioProject.

Bryan Dietzler has been writing about sports for close to 20 years. While he has written about football for the most part, Dietzler has written most recently about the Chicago White Sox and is getting ready to get back into writing more often. He currently lives in North Liberty, Iowa and works in the Educational Technology Industry.

Raymond Doswell, Ed.D. is Vice-President of Curatorial Services for the Negro Leagues Baseball Museum in Kansas City, Missouri. He manages exhibitions, archives, and educational programs. He holds a B.A. (1991) from Monmouth College (IL) with a degree in History and training in education. He taught high school briefly in the St. Louis area before attending graduate school at the University of California-Riverside. He earned an M.A. (1995) in History with emphasis on Historic Resources management. Doswell joined the staff of the Negro Leagues Baseball Museum in Kansas City, MO in 1995 as its first curator. The museum has grown into an important national attraction, welcoming close to 60,000 visitors annually. He earned a doctorate in Educational Leadership (2008) from Kansas State University through work in partnership with the museum to develop educational web sites and programs.

Peter Dreier is the E.P. Clapp Distinguished Professor of Politics at Occidental College. His articles have appeared in the *New York Times, Washington Post, Los Angeles Times, The Nation, American Prospect, Dissent, Huffington Post* and many other publications, including scholarly journals. He has written or edited eight books. Two books co-authored with Robert Elias - *Baseball Rebels: The Players, People and Social Movements That Shook Up the Game and Changed America* and *Major League Rebels: Baseball Battles Over Workers' Rights and American Empire* – were published in April 2022.

Pat Ellington Jr. is a 23-year-old journalist, screenwriter, and novelist from Northeast Ohio.

Sharon Hamilton is the chair of the Society for American Baseball Research's (SABR) Century Research Committee, which celebrates important milestones in baseball history. She served as project manager for the special 100th anniversary SABR Century 1921 project at SABR.org.

Tom Hawthorn is a senior writer for the government of British Columbia. He had a 40-year career as a newspaper and magazine writer in Canada, where he has served on the selection committees of two sports halls of fame. He is a frequent contributor to SABR publications.

Leslie Heaphy is an associate professor of history at Kent State University at Stark. Leslie has written numerous articles, book chapters and books on the Negro Leagues and women's baseball topics as well as the New York Mets. Leslie currently serves as the vice president for SABR and is on the board of directors for the International Women's Baseball Center.

Tom Lee is a recovering Emmy Award-winning broadcast journalist and attorney in Nashville, where he is member-in-charge of the Nashville office of Frost Brown Todd LLC, one of the country's largest law firms. He graduated Order of the Coif from Vanderbilt University School of Law, where he was executive editor of the Vanderbilt Law Review. Tom is a member of the Grantland Rice-Fred Russell Chapter of SABR, where he has presented on Jackie Robinson's political engagement as a mirror for understanding America's shifting political landscape in the 1960s. Like Robinson, Tom is a lifelong United Methodist; he preaches in Tennessee churches as a lay speaker. A frequent contributor to the Bitter Southerner and other publications, this is Tom's first book chapter for SABR.

Luisa Lyons is an actor, musician, and writer. She grew up in Sydney, trained in London, and now lives and plays in the New York City area. Luisa holds an MA in Music Theatre from the Royal Central School of Speech and Drama, and runs www.filmedlivemusicals.com, the most comprehensive online database of stage musicals that have been legally filmed and made public. Visit www.luisalyons.com to learn more. @luisalyons

Adam C. MacKinnon is a lifelong baseball fan and author of *Baseball For Kids: A Young Fan's Guide to the History of the Game*. His writing can also be found in *Baseball Almanac, Call to the Pen*, and his own blog and podcast, *Romantic About Baseball*. He currently lives in Delaware with his wife and daughter.

Nick Malian lives with his wife and daughter in LaSalle, Ontario, Canada, where he was born and raised. Growing up in a border city, he idolized Detroit Tiger greats Cecil Fielder and Alan Trammell. As an impressionable 12-year-old, his allegiance shifted from the Tigers to the New York Yankees following their post-season dominance in 1996. He still attempts the "Derek Jeter jump-throw" (with limited success) at his weekly softball games. Nick is a pharmacist by day and amateur home-chef by night. He enjoys reading anything about baseball and getting lost in science-fiction and fantasy novels. This is his first baseball publication.

Kate Nachman has loved words all her life and began editing as a side-gig in college. She has since edited works of fiction and nonfiction including plays, poetry, novels, short stories, blogs, academic and legal papers, and the occasional website. Kate only learned to love baseball in her forties, thanks to an editing project. Her autographed copy of *The Hall Ball* by Ralph Carhart is one of her treasures and it enjoys a place of honor in her home. A fairly newly minted Mets fan, she has only ever seen Citi Field from the outside and hopes to change that someday.

Joshua Neuman is a writer and producer whose work has appeared in *Slate, Esquire, Vice, Los Angeles Magazine, Victory Journal*, and *Heeb* (which he edited for nearly a decade). He is currently working on a book about former owners of the L.A. Rams, Carroll Rosenbloom and Georgia Frontiere.

Bill Nowlin was born in Boston, two years before Jackie Robinson began playing for the Brooklyn Dodgers but well aware at age 14 that the Red Sox had yet to integrate. Fortunately, Pumpsie Green joined the team later in 1959. A co-founder of Rounder Records and a frequent contributor to SABR publications, Dr. Nowlin still lives within a few miles of Fenway Park and takes in an inordinate number of games each year.

Zac Petrillo has a BA from Hunter College and an MFA from Chapman University's Dodge College of Film and Media Arts. He has created multiple short films and produced shows for Comedy Central and TruTV. In 2016, he was instrumental in the launch of Vice Media's 24/7 cable network, Vice TV. As a member of the Society for American Baseball Research, he focuses his work on post-1980s baseball and the cross-section between the game and the media industry. He is currently the Director of Post Production at A+E Networks and teaches television studies at Marymount Manhattan College.

Carl Riechers retired from United Parcel Service in 2012 after 35 years of service. With more free time, he became a SABR member that same year. Born and raised in the suburbs of St. Louis, he became a big fan of the Cardinals. He and his wife Janet have three children and he is the proud grandpa of two.

Benjamin Sabin is a baseball writer and editor for *Last Word On Sports*, editor-in-chief of *Cheap Seats Press*, and a baseball card artist. He enjoys keeping score at ballgames and prefers sauerkraut on his dogs. He is a proud SABR member since 2017.

SABR Books on the Negro Leagues and Black Baseball

From Rube to Robinson: SABR's Best Articles on Black Baseball

From Rube to Robinson brings together the best Negro League baseball scholarship that the Society of American Baseball Research (SABR) has ever produced, culled from its journals, Biography Project, and award-winning essays. The book includes a star-studded list of scholars and historians, from the late Jerry Malloy and Jules Tygiel, to award winners Larry Lester, Geri Strecker, and Jeremy Beer, and a host of other talented writers. The essays cover topics ranging over nearly a century, from 1866 and the earliest known Black baseball championship, to 1962 and the end of the Negro American League.

Edited by John Graf; Associate Editors Duke Goldman and Larry Lester
$24.95 paperback (ISBN 978-1-970159-41-7)
$9.99 ebook (ISBN 978-1-970159-40-0)
8.5"X11", 220 pages

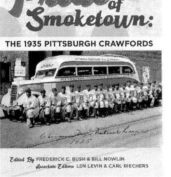

Pride of Smoketown: The 1935 Pittsburgh Crawfords

The 1935 Pittsburgh Crawfords team, one of the dominant teams in Negro League history, is often compared to the legendary 1927 "Murderer's Row" New York Yankees. The squad from "Smoketown"—a nickname that the *Pittsburgh Courier* often applied to the metropolis better-known as "Steel City"—boasted four Hall-of-Fame players in outfielder James "Cool Papa" Bell, first baseman/manager Oscar Charleston, catcher Josh Gibson, and third baseman William "Judy" Johnson. This volume contains exhaustively-researched articles about the players, front office personnel, Greenlee Field, and the exciting games and history of the team that were written and edited by 25 SABR members. The inclusion of historical photos about every subject in the book helps to shine a spotlight on the 1935 Pittsburgh Crawfords, who truly were the Pride of Smoketown.

Edited by Frederick C. Bush and Bill Nowlin
$29.95 paperback (ISBN 978-1-970159-25-7)
$9.99 ebook (ISBN 978-1-970159-24-0)
8.5"X11", 340 pages, over 60 photos

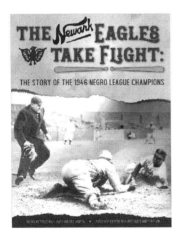

The Newark Eagles Take Flight: The Story of the 1946 Negro League Champions

The Newark Eagles won only one Negro National League pennant during the franchise's 15-year tenure in the Garden State, but the 1946 squad that ran away with the NNL and then triumphed over the Kansas City Monarchs in a seven-game World Series was a team for the ages. The returning WWII veterans composed a veritable "Who's Who in the Negro Leagues" and included Leon Day, Larry Doby, Monte Irvin, and Max Manning, as well as numerous role players. Four of the Eagles' stars—Day, Doby, Irvin, and player/manager Raleigh "Biz" Mackey, as well as co-owner Effa Manley—have been enshrined in the National Baseball Hall of Fame in Cooperstown. In addition to biographies of the players, co-owners, and P.A. announcer, there are also articles about Newark's Ruppert Stadium, Leon Day's Opening Day no-hitter, a sensational midseason game, the season's two East-West All-Star Games, and the 1946 Negro League World Series between the Eagles and the renowned Kansas City Monarchs.

Edited by Frederick C. Bush and Bill Nowlin
$24.95 paperback (ISBN 978-1-970159-07-3)
$9.99 ebook (ISBN 978-1-970159-06-6)
8.5"X11", 228 pages, over 60 photos

Bittersweet Goodbye: The Black Barons, The Grays, and the 1948 Negro League World Series

This book was inspired by the last Negro League World Series ever played and presents biographies of the players on the two contending teams in 1948—the Birmingham Black Barons and the Homestead Grays—as well as the managers, the owners, and articles on the ballparks the teams called home. Also included are articles that recap the season's two East-West All-Star Games, the Negro National League and Negro American League playoff series, and the World Series itself. Additional context is provided in essays about the effects of baseball's integration on the Negro Leagues, the exodus of Negro League players to Canada, and the signing away of top Negro League players, specifically Willie Mays. Many of the players' lives and careers have been presented to a much greater extent than previously possible.

Edited by Frederick C. Bush and Bill Nowlin
$21.95 paperback (ISBN 978-1-943816-55-2)
$9.99 ebook (ISBN 978-1-943816-54-5)
8.5"X11", 442 pages, over 100 photos and images

Made in the USA
Middletown, DE
21 April 2022